Adolescent Suicide

André Haim

Adolescent Suicide

Translated by
A.M. Sheridan Smith

International Universities Press, Inc.
New York

First published in 1970 by Payot, Paris.
© *Payot, Paris 1969.*
© *English translation Tavistock 1974*
Published by International Universities Press, Inc., New York

Library of Congress Catalog Card Number: 73-9250
ISBN: 0-8236-0090-4

Manufactured in Great Britain

Contents

Introduction

Adolescent suicide is an object of fascination and astonishment. Its treatment in a book of this kind is also fraught with very special difficulties. To begin with, it concerns the two notions about which, perhaps, we know least: death, of which man can have no knowledge, and adolescence, the period in our lives when we have the greatest difficulty in understanding our mobile subjectivity.

But there is another obstacle: both death and adolescence arouse fear. And the suicidal adolescent, because he is an adolescent and because he is suicidal, the bearer of desire and of death, arouses the maximum fear. Unconsciously, he arouses feelings associated with an unnatural phenomenon. For everyone, adolescence is synonymous with energy, enrichment, joy, promised satisfactions, invincible hope — that is, with everything that one associates with life. How, then, can one think of death? But adolescence is also, as a result of pubertal maturation, the resumption and resolution of the Oedipus complex, the renunciation of the Oedipal love object and the castration anxiety. It is also a renunciation of childhood pleasures, for which some people retain a nostalgia throughout their lives, a renunciation of childhood dreams at a time when one has to confront the reality of the adult. It is a time of multiple loss, and sometimes of despair, as well as a revival of the most deeply buried motions, the transitory disintegration of impulses, and the emergence of hetero-aggressivity and auto-aggressivity.

The feelings that the suicidal adolescent arouses account for his constant presence in literature, but they also account for the variable scientific interest that he generates. In certain periods he has been ignored, in others he has given rise to speculations advanced as facts, which distort the knowledge that we think we have of the subject. It is true that an approach to the actual experience of the young suicide, and an attempt to elucidate it, often puts one in a highly uncomfortable position, and it would be a distortion of the truth to pass over in silence my own experience. This book took a long time to write, and, although there may have been quite extraneous reasons for this, there are certainly others directly associated with the subject: for this subject arouses resistance that has to be overcome, and which constitutes one of the *données* of the problem — a fact that has helped me to understand why scientific work on this theme has sometimes been rare.

However, for some years now adolescent suicide has been the subject of a relatively large number of works, all desirous to criticize and to revise traditional notions. I have borrowed a great deal of valuable material from the authors of such works.

One must avoid the temptations of intellectual speculation and verbal magic, which in fact are an obstacle to understanding. But an attempt to understand does necessitate the development of ideas and conceptualization. One must constantly strive to strike the right balance, and adolescent suicide requires a particular effort in this direction.

For all the reasons outlined above, my work has consisted not so much in affirming new ideas as in challenging what we think we believe, not in a spirit of systematic rejection, but in order to set aside what has not been confirmed by observation, and to re-examine in a new perspective what has been confirmed. To acknowledge that one does not know is the first stage in any search for knowledge.

So my position is quite intentionally less 'advanced' on certain points than the body of current notions, and this may disappoint some readers. Some may feel that I do not give enough credit to the statistics, others that I do not attach enough importance to the philosophical aspects of suicide, or that I show too much reserve towards this or that theory as to the causes of suicide. But I prefer to leave certain notions in uncertainty, rather than take up positions that are inadequately supported. I will mention three such examples.

There are a great many unknowns where adolescence is

concerned. The ages at which adolescence is supposed to end vary considerably, and the criteria for determining those ages are subject to controversy. For this reason I have extended the scope of my study to the age of twenty-five. This is certainly a purely arbitrary boundary, without any theoretical significance. In any case, it is possible that the suicides of young adults are the culmination of suicidal developments that began between the ages of fifteen and twenty, and have the same significance as adolescent suicides.

Another example concerns terminology. It has often been suggested that we should distinguish between subjects with suicidal ideas and subjects who have made suicide attempts. Although such a distinction is useful from the medico-legal point of view, and from the point of view of the medical or surgical consequences of the attempt, it seems to me to be not only useless but actually an obstacle from the medico-psychological point of view. Two questions arise when one is confronted by an adolescent with suicidal tendencies: what risk is there that he will resort to action, and why has he suicidal tendencies? These questions arise whether or not the adolescent has already made an attempt. Of course, the fact that the subject has already undergone the experience of a suicide attempt may have its own effects. But the nature of those effects is uncertain and difficult to evaluate. The performance of the act may protect the adolescent from the desire or the need to try again, or, on the contrary, it may establish a tendency to act that may make it all the easier to resort to the same form of action.

In any case, it seems to me that the only psychologically useful distinction lies between the adolescent who manipulates the idea of death and suicide, and the adolescent who manifests a tendency to suicide that may pass over into action. Where there is such a risk, I prefer to speak of suicidal adolescents, a term that embraces all gradations in a unitary conception.

A third example concerns the possible distinction between fatal suicide and attempted suicide. Some contemporary works bring interesting arguments to bear in favour of the distinction, but others do the opposite. This distinction does not seem to me to be a desirable one, at least as far as the adolescent is concerned, in the present state of our knowledge. There are too many interfering factors involved in the determination of the act to decide which of them influenced the outcome in favour of death or survival. So I prefer to regard suicide as a whole, to speak only of the suicide act, and to distinguish only between consequences, between suicide deaths and suicide attempts.

The plan of the book is as follows. In the first part I outline the general data at my disposal: the notions of suicide and adolescence, and the statistical information as provided by official and scientific publications.

In the second part I deal with the attitude of adults to adolescent suicide, and the resistance that it gives rise to in them. Although this question may seem peripheral, I consider it to be of the utmost importance. Indeed, it forms the crux of my study; without it, we cannot understand why we have so few accurate statistics at our disposal, and why we know so little of the causes of suicide. It forms an indispensable preliminary stage of any approach to the question, and is therefore one of our fundamental *données*.

In the third part I examine the causes of adolescent suicide. This is the most important question, and the one that I have discussed the most. But, abondoning the traditional conception of a single cause, I use the hypothesis of an association of factors. After studying and discussing the most commonly cited factors — circumstances, sociological factors, psychiatric factors — I devote several chapters to the possible role of adolescence proper in the suicide tendency. This question is obviously of fundamental importance, since, if such a role exists, it would account for the specific quality of adolescent suicide.

Lastly, in the fourth part, I offer a few conclusions, or rather hypotheses for most of them are yet to be verified and are valid only as research propositions, on the nature of adolescent suicide, its significance, its boundaries, its definition, and its therapeutic and preventive implications.

Two further points should be made clear. First, I have purposely refrained from illustrating my text with actual clinical cases. For various reasons, it does not seem to me to be possible to give an adequate account here of the cases with which I have been personally concerned. I hope I shall be forgiven for what some readers may regard as a certain theoretical dryness.

Secondly, this book is about the suicidal adolescent, not the adolescent in general. For methodological reasons I have had to isolate or emphasize whatever concerns death and suicide. But to confine adolescence to these aspects would, of course, be an error. Adolescents must be seen in a richer, more varied context than the one that I have artificially isolated. In actual fact, there are relatively few adolescent suicides, and these constitute only one type of youth. But, even though they are exceptional, the problems that they raise are of concern to us all.

Part One
The notion of suicide

Introduction: The general numerical position

The suicide of the adolescent immediately raises two main questions:
— is it similar in nature to adult suicide?
— can it be regarded in the same light as other adolescent behaviour?

Above all, these questions involve a study of the causes and the significations of the act of the young suicide. But if they are to be correctly evaluated, the whole problem must first be seen in relation to suicide, to adolescence, and also to its numerical importance. This is what I shall attempt to do in this first part.

Suicide and adolescence each has its own definition, its own history, its own boundaries. The contemporary theories that have superseded the traditional ones that sought to describe and to explain suicide and adolescence are worthy of our attention. I shall try to examine these in my first two chapters.

Statistics also play an important role in any study of suicide, and are supposed to constitute an objective means of assessment. They are all inaccurate. However, useful information can be derived from them, not only in estimating the frequency of the suicide act among adolescents, but also in helping us to approach the question of its nature. And their inaccuracy, which is interesting in itself, constitutes a *donnée* that is capable of some development. In line with my wish to see adolescent suicide in its double context, I shall examine successively in Chapter 3 the numerical data of suicide in general, in Chapter 4 those of adolescent suicide, and in Chapter 5 the numerical data according to sex and method used. In Chapter 6 I shall provide a brief account of foreign statistics — a longer account would have required a process of verification that would be difficult to carry out at a distance. I conclude Part 1 with a few reflections on the numerical data.

1·The notion of suicide

The notion of suicide is apparently clear: a human being kills himself by shooting, drowning or poisoning himself with drugs or domestic gas, by throwing himself under a train, or by any other action that complies with the definition of 'self-murder' laid down for us in 1737 by the Abbé Desfontaines. Yet the question becomes more complicated when one consults the various authors that have written on the matter. Did the subject commit this act because he no longer expected to derive any satisfaction from life, or because he feared some acute suffering in the near or distant future; was such a fear merely imaginary or was it well founded in reality; or did he regard himself as unworthy to enjoy life because of some serious offence against honour or the social code that he had actually committed, or which was part of a self-accusatory delusion; or for philosophical reasons, because he was unable to free himself from a feeling of the absurdity of life; or as a sacrifice to a cause he regarded as of greater importance than his own life, like the captain of a ship, the heroic soldier, or the Buddhist monks in Vietnam; was he drowned in trying to save someone dear to him, when neither had any hope of survival, or to save some unknown person simply because he was a fellow human being? Or in obedience to some law of his social group, or to hallucinations that commanded him to kill himself or carry out some fatal action, or, again, in order to escape from a delirious fear of death, like the alcoholic suffering from delirium tremens who jumps out of a window in order to flee some unreal danger and so meets with a real death?

Should we regard in the same light someone who has died in one of these situations, and someone who has made an attempt but who has remained in this world? Similarly, what should we think of someone who thinks or expresses suicidal thoughts without carrying them out, or someone who has never expressed, or even thought such thoughts, but who, in a few seconds, commits the fatal act? Again, what should we think of the harmless action, carrying with it little risk of death, committed by someone who has clearly expressed his intention of dying, or the action of someone who takes a massive dose of drugs, then telephones a friend in order to hear an affectionate voice before he dies, or because he no longer wants to die and wishes to be saved? Or, as J. Vedrinne has asked,[1] what are we to think of addicts who will probably be dead in fifteen years, but have so far made only unsuccessful attempts, and have been brought back to life in hospital?

From another point of view, what links are there between suicide and other more or less similar forms of behaviour? Should we regard as suicide the action of someone who voluntarily cuts off part of his body, someone who refuses all food on a hunger strike or in a state of anorexia without the context of traditional psychosis, or the schizophrenic who, in an extreme case, in a state of confirmed catatonia, settles into anorexia and complete immobility, letting life flow out of him, and dying if no one gives him the necessary treatment and care? And how should we regard the similar case of the sixty-seven-year-old woman who died as a result of multiple privations, because she only had four hundred francs a year to live on, and could not reconcile herself to accepting benefits and assistance to which she had a right?

Lastly, how are we to regard dangerous actions: the motorist who drives very fast without regard to the regulations and without due care, who is of course to be distinguished from the man who voluntarily throws himself into a river or drives his car into an obstacle; the mountain-climber who thinks he will succeed in his feat but cannot be sure whether he will arrive back safely from a dangerous ascent; the test pilot, or the soldier who always volunteers for dangerous raids, who also hope that they will return but who know that they have only a fifty-fifty chance of doing so? What are we to think of the 'game' of Russian roulette, actually performed with a revolver, or transposed into the various forms of 'heads or tails'? Or of the behaviour of the addict who gradually destroys himself with drugs or alcohol, and who answers the saying 'alcohol is a slow death' with 'I don't mind, I'm not in a hurry,' which, in fact, does not prevent such people, with not inconsiderable frequency, from killing themselves by a suicide act proper.

Beginning with the clear, simple definition of the Abbé Desfontaines, we have managed to complicate the question quite considerably. I have tried in the questions listed above to express the reaction that one might have on consulting various authors on the subject. All find the term 'self-murder' too vague and general, and have tried to circumscribe the problem by providing new definitions. Indeed, these same authors try to establish a new theory, or to adopt a theory of the causes of suicide. And since death of self affects man in his fundamental aspect as a living, mortal being, there are a great many disciplines involved: philosophy, ethics, sociology, metaphysics, psychology, psychiatry, psychoanalysis, economics, even aesthetics. It is hardly surprising to find a variety of explanatory theories, according to the mode of approach; but one might be forgiven for thinking that there would be some coincidence of theory and definition among specialists in the same discipline. This is often the case, but it is far from always being so, and it is a striking fact that on certain points the upholders of opposed theories agree, partly at least, on a definition.

This book is not concerned with suicide in general, and I have no intention of making a detailed study of the various theories and definitions. But I should like to recall those that have been current since the question began to interest specialists, in order to see in what context the theme that I am dealing with is situated. Later, we shall see whether any of them is suitable as a definition of the suicidal behaviour of the adolescent, or whether they must be considered in relation to our subject. Similarly, while realizing that definitions and theories do not coincide, we must realize that the authors' philosophical positions or other personal motivations intervene in the delimitation of the field and the elaboration of subjacent theory. This is, of course, a truism, since in any case it can hardly be otherwise. But this fact compels me, however briefly, to examine separately the current theories and the definitions and commentaries that accompany them, since the regrouping cannot be made identically in each case. I shall therefore make a traditional examination of the various theses before returning to the field of suicide itself.

All works concerned with suicide deal at length, and generally very ably, with the various theories as to the causes and mechanisms of suicide. They are too well known for me to need to go over them all in detail, and I would rather refer the reader to such works as the special number of the review *Problèmes*.[2] However, it might be useful at this stage to present them in abbreviated form. Furthermore, although they have until recently been presented under the three usual headings of psychiatric, sociological, and psychological, a movement has emerged in the last few years that has undermined the usefulness of this classification in understanding the development of the various theories. It would seem preferable, therefore, to group them into traditional theories on the one hand, and contemporary tendencies on the other. Such a distinction is as artificial as any other, and I am quite aware of its arbitrary character. The work of the most traditional nineteenth-century authors contains in many ways the roots of the most 'progressive' tendencies of the present day. But what matters is not only what these authors have written, but also the use that they made of their work, and above all the way in which this work was used by their contemporaries and their successors, the way in which it was integrated into the current ideas of the period. For that reason, the grouping of notions into traditional and contemporary may help us to trace more clearly the development of the notion of suicide, to free ourselves from *a priori* or alien preoccupations with the question, in particular moral preoccupations.

A. Traditional theses on suicide

The traditional psychiatric thesis was the first of the various scientific theses on suicide to be elaborated, following as it did on the literary and philosophical period of the eighteenth century. It should be emphasized that we are dealing here with *traditional* psychiatric theory. In many publications, psychiatric theory is presented with particular reference to nineteenth-centur

and early twentieth-century authors, without any suggestion
that psychiatry may have altered its positions and theories. What
is usually called the psychiatric theory of suicide is that of a
psychiatry whose main, if not sole, aim was, on the one hand,
to describe its manifestations and to group them in syndromes,
sometimes even in illnesses, and, on the other hand, to attach
symptoms or syndromes to organic constitutions or disorders,
that is to say, a resolutely descriptive and constitutionalistic or
organicist psychiatry. Such a starting point had an effect on all
later work, producing currents and counter-currents, controversies
and confrontations that are still to be found in the work of our
contemporaries.

The originator of this view was Esquirol, and it is often said
that for him, 'man makes an attempt on his life only when he is
mad, and that suicides are madmen';[3] and 'this categorical
affirmation was facilely accepted and repeated'.[4] French psychiatrists followed him, and the position was taken up by German
psychiatrists, thus reinforcing the position in France, where,
combined with the theories current at the beginning of the
twentieth century, it culminated in the thesis, propounded by
A. Delmas in 1932,[5] that suicide was always pathological and
linked with some constitutional organic disorder. Broadly
speaking, this view is based on three points:

1 Every suicide is mentally ill — this notion usually being
interpreted in its strongest, most traditional sense, as 'insane'
(délirant, aliéné). Sometimes, it extends to disorders involving
imbalance of character or neurotic imbalance, as when psychiatry is given a broader meaning than that of medicine for the
insane.

2 Suicide is a symptom, not a disease, a symptom that is
linked either with one of Delmas' psychopathic constitutions,
the cyclothymic constitution being the most important of these,
followed by the hyperemotive constitution, or with one of the
diseases within the usual nosological framework, the most
important of which are depression and melancholia. Sometimes,
too, specialists have spoken of suicide-disease, and attempts
have been made to create the category of suicide-monomania.
The association of these two points means that the only existence
of suicide that is valid as a symptom allows us to infer mental

illness, since one must be more or less mad to kill oneself.

3 According to Delmas, suicide is linked with 'organic' anxiety, this temperamental disorder being regarded as of biological origin, to be found in all the various mental diseases. This point gave rise to research in three directions: the study of constitutions, which was carried to the limit by Delmas; anatomo-pathological research into lesions of the nervous system or Paltauf's thymico-lymphatic status, which I mention by way of a reminder, since their interest to us today is mainly historical. Only the notion of the frequency of sexual activity in women during the suicide act has left any mark. The notion of suicide heredity is interesting in two respects, for the importance that it has had in the past, and for the fact that it is still current in both specialized and non-specialized contemporary circles, after being upheld by Ritti, Ribot, etc. It should be noted, however, that these anatomo-pathological or hereditary directions are to be found in all branches of the psychiatry of the period. Their application to suicide is merely one example among others.

The traditional sociological thesis, which emerged later, and which was probably influenced by pre-existing psychiatric views, has been presented, by virtue of this fact, 'as a reaction to psychiatric theories'.[6] It is based on statistical data, and regards the environment as the fundamental and sole cause of suicide; E. Durkheim[7] and M. Halbwachs[8] are its leading theoreticians. Here, too, their work is of historical interest, not only in itself, but also in so far as it has survived in the work of others. For Durkheim,[9] suicide is linked with the degree of integration of the subject in the group in which he lives. He distinguishes three main types of suicide: the egotistical, the altruistic, and the anomic. Two of these types may combine to form three mixed types (see table opposite).

His position is based on:

— the notion that 'the individual is dominated by a moral reality that transcends him: this is collective reality';
— the notion that suicide varies inversely to the degree of integration of the social groups of which the individual is a part;

Individual forms			
	Basic character		Secondary varieties
Ele-mentary types	Egoistic suicide	Apathy	Indolent melancholia with self-satisfaction Disillusioned composure of the sceptic
	Altruistic suicide	Energy of the emotions or of the will	With a calm sense of duty With mystical enthusiasm With quiet courage
	Anomic suicide	Irritation Disgust	Violent recriminations against life in general Violent recriminations against an individual
Mixed types	Ego-anomic suicide		Mixture of agitation and apathy, action and dreaminess
	Anomic-altruistic suicide		Exasperated excitability
	Ego-altruistic suicide		Melancholia tempered by a certain moral firmness

— religious, domestic, and political societies — changes in which are the principal cause of suicide;

— the positions of the individual in relation to society, which constitute the moral ideal, made up of a combination in 'proportions that vary from society to society, of egoism, altruism, and anomia . . . that incline man in three divergent and contradictory directions'. There is thus a state of balance, which, when disturbed by an increase in one of the tendencies, produces suicide tendencies. [10]

— the distinction between the suicide act and the method chosen, to which he attaches little importance;

— the fact that the most varied, and even contradictory events of life may also serve as a pretext for suicide, no one of them being the specific cause.

He bases his view on:

— the statistical notion of the constancy of suicide in relation to the much more variable rate of mortality in general;

— criticism of the psychiatric viewpoint, which he identifies with constitutionalist views of degeneracy. However, he does approach what he calls neurasthenia, and what we would now call neurosis, describes it correctly, but relates it to traditional psychiatric conceptions — to, in fact, a minor state of madness. He accepts that suicide is the result of a combination of personal and social factors, but considers that these factors operate at the level of individual cases as seen by the clinician, but do not affect the number of suicides.

Halbwachs's position differs on certain points:

— to the degree of cohesion of Durkheim's three social groups, whose importance he disputes, he adds 'way of life',[11] and wonders whether such a subject does not commit suicide because he is a peasant, Polish, or a Catholic;[12]

— he integrates individual factors, circumstances, and mental illnesses as causes of suicide, but regards them also as sociological factors. Thus, suicide is explained 'always by social causes . . . which are manifested sometimes as collective forces . . ., sometimes in the form of individual motives';[13]

— he considers the methods used to commit the act of suicide as significant as the act itself, because they too are related to social factors, and also because, being concrete facts, they constitute 'the sole means of setting out statistically information whose reality and even whose nature elude all discussion'.[14] For the same reasons, he excludes suicide attempts, which must always be interpreted with caution, and considers only deaths, which alone constitute certain proof of the intention to commit suicide.

— lastly, he sees as an immediate cause of suicide the growing complexity of social life.

B. Contemporary tendencies

I shall do no more than provide a broad outline of contemporary tendencies, for I shall be referring to them throughout this book, and being unable to describe them all, I shall confine myself to a few illustrations. The origins of these tendencies are to be found in the authors of the previous period; but they have moved away from their predecessors

more markedly in the last twenty years, and are now established side by side, curiously enough, with other views that
are very traditional in some ways. For example, notoriously
erroneous statistics, which have often been criticized, continue
to be used as if their data embodied the truth. This fact should
be stressed most strongly, and I shall return to it later.

The present renewal of interest is the result of two factors.
First, it reflects a change of attitude towards suicide. The
diminution of prohibitions has enabled authors, instead of
classifying in a static, abstract way, to concern themselves
with the intimate mechanism of the process, and with the
actual experience of potential suicides. By the same token, it
is now possible to concern oneself not only with those who
have died, but also with those who have survived suicide
attempts. Second, it is also part of a general change in ideas.
The extreme attitudes of the nineteenth and early twentieth
centuries, with their rigid scientism and excessive rationalization, yielding abstract classifications in which the part was
often taken for the whole, have been replaced by a desire to
grasp processes in their dynamic movement, their fundamental
movement, their fundamental unity, combined with the complexity of their various manifestations and determining factors.

Thus sociologists, no longer sheltering behind a tautology
that would seem to explain suicide by the fact that a certain
number of men commit suicide, are making their contribution
through an analysis of psycho-social factors, instead of combat-
ing the hypothesis of individual factors, which they would no
longer dream of denying. Psychiatrists, for their part, have
abandoned their position as purely dispensers of medicine to
the insane, and have dissociated themselves from the pressure
from representatives of other disciplines who have tended to
confine them within the closed field of psychosis alone. They
are beginning to see their discipline as a dynamic, pathological
psychology. As specialists in all aspects of psychical disorder,
they are now concerned with those factors leading to suicide
that they previously excluded. In an intermediate phase, the
elaboration of a psychological thesis on suicide made it
possible to avoid extremist theses and impassioned aetiological
positions. But, at present, the psychiatric and psychological

positions are coming together, since they are placing themselves in the same perspective - which does not mean that there is any confusion between normal and pathological.

At present, then, the notion of suicide can be approached in two ways: from the straightforward point of view of the suicide situation and suicide behaviour, and from the more complex one of the determining factors. These factors, which were originally divided into extrinsic and intrinsic factors, are grouped around the suicide situation, and constitute the social level and the individual level, each affecting the other. In giving preference to the one, contemporary work on suicide does not ignore the other, and tends to make frequent reference to it rather than denying its very existence.

Thus some specialists, such as H. Ey [15] and G. Deshaies, [16] aim above all at describing and explaining the various aspects of the suicide situation and suicide behaviour.

Others are more concerned with the social level, in particular with what are now called the psycho-social factors. This change of term, which often replaces that of sociological factors, is more than a mere change in terminology; it is an expression of a new approach which sees ethnic, cultural, and professional factors as collective phenomena that nonetheless leave their mark in the individual personality. *A fortiori*, age, sex, and marital status are studied in their social manifestations and in their role in the organization of personality. The work of J.C. Oeconomo[17] is a good example of this approach. A number of works by psychiatrists and psychologists refer to the psycho-social aspects of the problem, and take into account, without raising them to the rank of causes, temporary circumstantial factors that may trigger off suicide behaviour, or which may even, according to J. Nick and his colleagues,[18] have a determining role in what they describe as 'suicide of abandonment'.

While taking the psycho-social aspects into account, the psychiatrists and psychologists referred to above observe that the majority of psychotics do not commit suicide, and that all suicides cannot be regarded as belonging to the typical forms of psychosis of the traditional nosology, and, generally speaking, no longer use that nosology as their primary reference.

Some works set out to describe, in terms of the unity of suicide, the various processes which, according to the various schools of thought, are associated with a particular character disposition or personality structure (Deshaies, Ey, Vedrinne), while others set out to understand the signification of suicidal behaviour. Again, there are others who are studying certain aspects of the suicide process independently of the nosographical diagnosis: for example, the phenomenologists stress disturbances in 'experienced time' *(temps vécu),*[19] and a number of works emphasize that suicidal behaviour is an act, thus reviving the long-established parallel between suicide and delinquency.

The contribution of psychoanalysis seems minimal when one considers the suicide act itself. In 1955, Courchet[20] stressed that the bibliography was virtually non-existent, though as early as 1910 an entire conference was devoted to the subject. S. Nacht[21] gives only five references. This paucity of reference is certainly surprising, even if one adds chapters and paragraphs included in more general psychoanalytic works. The suicide act may seem to be insignificant in a psychoanalytic context, but in fact the processes and factors that may be at work in it have often been studied. The element of 'self-destruction' in the functioning of the psyche is a fundamental concern of psychoanalysts, and one that is constantly present in their work, from discussions as to its origin to discussions as to its development in the Oedipal relationship. A considerable proportion of psychoanalytic literature touches on the subject of this self-destructive element. However, I shall confine myself here to mentioning the beginnings in the work of Freud himself of the principal psychoanalytic concerns that relate to our subject. *Mourning and Melancholia*[22] and *Beyond the Pleasure Principle*[23] are the two main sources of the psychoanalytic theory of suicide. But these two texts belong to different stages in the development of Freud's thinking. They must be seen, therefore, in their chronological context.

The absence of any representation of death in the unconscious was the first important notion to emerge at the conference of 1910. This notion has received a good deal of attention ever since, in the course of which it has often been transformed into the nonexistence of death in the unconscious. It is one of the psychoanalytic concepts that has least evolved in the past fifty years. The confusion between the non-representation and the nonexistence of death in the unconscious is worth discussing. To begin with, it might be mentioned that Freud's own hypotheses do not contribute to this confusion.

The other root of our subject is masochism, which appeared very early on in Freud's work. In 1905[24] he laid down the fundamental features of masochism, above all its link with sadism   masochism being sadism directed against oneself, and auto-aggressivity being regarded as always secondary to repressed aggressivity.

These notions, linked with those of narcissism, object relation, and regression, and reinforced by the important contribution from K. Abraham,[25] were taken up again in 1917 in *Mourning and Melancholia.* By comparing the nature of the object loss - conscious and real in mourning, unconscious and possibly imaginary in melancholia - and noting the difference in the processes initiated by this object loss, Freud shows the role played in melancholia by narcissistic identification, reactivated sadism and the oral incorporation of the object, which makes it possible to recover the loved object on the fantasy plane, then to punish it for its abandonment through auto-aggressive behaviour. The melancholic's tendency to self-destruction, which appears to concern the subject, is in fact addressed to the incorporated object. By showing the differences with the work of mourning, he introduces the notion of the pre-depressive state that will give direction to the process at the moment at which the object is lost. The numerous psychoanalytic works based on this essay have since shown, over and above the unity of the depressions, what distinguishes them according to the mode and degree of regression.

The introduction, in 1920, of the notion of the death instinct or 'death impulse',[26] marked a turning-point of crucial importance. Freud now linked the sex instinct and the instincts of the ego (or instincts of self-preservation) in the life instinct (Eros), which he contrasted in a fundamental dualism with the death instinct (Thanatos).[27] He linked the latter with the tendency of every animate being to return to the inanimate state. In this irreducible dualism, aggressivity - the tendency to destroy, to fragment, to disunite living matter, represented by the Nirvana principle - is not secondary, but pre-exists all other processes, and is in conflict with the life instinct represented by the pleasure principle (and its derivative, the reality principle), which tends to unite, to bind, to maintain cohesion. In the various psychical activities, the two instincts are bound up with one another in variable forms that prevent either of them being manifested in a pure state. Hence the aggressive and destructive elements to be found in behaviour guided primarily by the pleasure principle, and, inversely, the libidinal element to be found in behaviour that is primarily destructive, and in a more extreme form of behaviour, in melancholia, is almost tantamount to 'a pure culture of the death instinct'.[28] Broadly speaking, the life instinct tends, in this dual process, to protect the human being by tying it down. One part is thus controlled by Eros, who directs it outwards, to its own satisfaction, in the form of aggressivity, conquest, etc., while the other part of the destructive forces remains, and, if it is not inhibited, continues its self-destructive activity. Freud, who took up these notions again and applied them more specifically to melancholia,[29] introduced no further modification of the fundamental conception of the life instinct/death instinct dualism, which he maintained to the end. Its effects on psychoanalytic theory have been considerable.

In particular:

Masochism, the turning of sadism upon the self, is now merely a secondary masochism, which is added to the original masochism, the source of aggressivity and sadism. The tendency to self-destruction is therefore the first fact of this sequence.

The notions of conflict and ambivalence, which are at the very heart of psychoanalytic theory, become the expression of the instinctual dualism. The death instinct is not a mere theoretical aspect; in its involvement with the life instinct it is the cornerstone of psychoanalytic theory, the woof of the organization of the personality. The tendency to self-destruction is situated in the central axis of the functioning of the psyche and 'finally, indissolubly binds every aggressive or sexual desire to the death wish'.[30]

Of all the concepts introduced by Freud, it is the most controversial among psychoanalysts themselves, the one that has aroused, and is still arousing, most criticism and most argument. Without wishing to examine it in detail, one might mention, by way of an example, the work of S. Nacht, who replaces the death instinct by a primary organic masochism that has its source in the tension created in the first few months of life as a reaction to frustration at not being able to express oneself sufficiently in aggressive behaviour. Since 'the child is for the moment organically incapable of such behaviour, it is neither repressed, nor deflected, but spreads over, penetrates, impregnates the whole organism'.[31] For Nacht, who is also a critic of Melanie Klein, the tendency to self-destruction is secondary to opposition to the pleasure principle, and, consequently, is attached to 'the forces that tend to maintain and defend life'.[32] Whatever the motives involved, it is disturbing that it should be around the question of the death instinct that controversy should be greatest, when it involves, on a philosophical plane, concepts that go beyond the question of the functioning of the psyche in its various manifestations.

Thus, whereas the self-destructive act has received little attention in psychoanalytic writings, the tendency to self-destruction has been studied at length. However, a number of works have attempted to examine the problem of suicide itself, or certain of its aspects. For example, the important work of Courchet,[33] which does more than merely state that suicide is an act, analyses the process that leads up to this act, and the relations of the act to disturbances in verbal elaboration, which have also been studied by Nacht,[34] who describes suicide as a 'psychotic act'.

Psychoanalysis has also thrown light on the varieties of the suicide act. It has been said that psychoanalysis has conceded victory to the sociological theses. It is true that it has thrown new light on so-called extrinsic conditions, as it has done on the clinical entities of the psychiatric nosography. It has shown that extrinsic factors, instead of being accepted or refuted as such, as causes may be understood in terms of the dynamic study of suicidal behaviour. Thus there emerges the role of the protective, structuring, or, on the contrary, destructuring social group. Similarly, through the interplay of narcissistic defences, identifications, and the repetition principle, we may understand the choice of the time, place, and method of the suicide. But, without denying the motivations that may intervene in these choices, one cannot have recourse to a simplistic, naive symbolism in order to explain, in a somewhat stereotyped way, each of the circumstances involved in a suicide, which may have little to do with psychoanalysis. It should be remarked, however, that such attempts are usually made by non-psychoanalysts.

Lastly, in elucidating the personality structures of suicides, and the dynamics of their behaviour, psychoanalysis has emphasized the role of pre-pathological states and factors favouring regressions and destructurations. Once these factors are no longer either posited or rejected as causes, they can be assigned a place in so far as they play a role in the experience of the potential suicide, and may help to deflect a process already in train.

C. The field of suicide: boundaries and definition

In approaching the definitions of suicide, that is to say, the conditions required for an act to be described as suicide, and its boundaries in relation to other more or less approximate behaviour, one might suppose that they would be grouped according to the theories outlined above. This is far from being the case; authors belonging not only to different disciplines, but to opposed theoretical positions, find themselves in agreement on all or part of the definitions, and vice versa. This disjunction exposes the subjective positions that lie behind apparently objective rational arguments. A. Bayet[35] emphasizes the extent to which moral aspects influence the opinion that one has of suicide, marking the gap 'between official and private attitudes', and their relative independence.

A good example of the influence of personal attitudes on scientific considerations is provided by sacrificial death. It is included in suicide by the sociologist Durkheim, the moralist

A. Bayet, the philosopher Landsberg, and the psychiatrists
H. Ey, P.B. Schneider, and Deshaies; all adopt as neutral an
attitude as possible, defining suicide as an act of voluntary
death whatever the motive. On the other hand, sacrifice is
excluded by Halbwachs, Esquirol, Blondel, A. Delmas, and
P. Janet, who regard death as suicide only when no ethical, or
any other, necessity is involved.[36] According to Bayet, the
attitude to sacrifice is bound up with the degree of tolerance
towards suicide. The more suicide is disapproved of, the more
it is felt to be an insult and an injury to the group, the less it is
likely to include sacrifice, which is strongly invested with
positive moral values; otherwise sacrifice would itself become
an insult and an injury, whereas 'society presides over
sacrifice'.[37]

The example of sacrifice throws light on the influence of
subjective, moral, or other preoccupations, and shows us how
others' views of the mechanism and causes of suicide decide
the delimitations of the suicide field, tracing a winding, and
sometimes surprising, dividing line between authors. This dual
influence is to be found at all the points that define and
delimit the suicide act; it is not necessarily apparent, but it is
always present in definitions whose strict formulation includes
beliefs that are sometimes opposed to one another. This is confirmed by a rapid survey of the opinions expressed on some
of these points.

— The hypothesis of the normal or pathological origin of
the suicide act is not written into the definitions, since each of
these definitions tries to confine itself objectively to the act
itself, but it places different significances on the act. For
Durkheim, Halbwachs and Delmas, it is because the cause is
in any case unique, whether sociological or psychiatric, whereas
for Deshaies the definition of the suicide act must include
those of pathological origin as well as normal ones that are
'the expression of a higher morality'.[38] For a number of contemporary authors, such as Barande,[39] Vedrinne, Colin,[40] and
Bayet, the present uncertainty as to the boundaries between
normal and pathological in psychiatry undermines any discussion based on such boundaries.

— Personal options appear even more clearly in such terms

as will, consciousness, intention, lucidity, which try to introduce the rational element but in fact merely add to the confusion and uncertainty. Whereas Deshaies and, of course, the
psychoanalysts (but with a different interpretation of the
notion of unconscious), do not regard consciousness of the
wish for self-destruction as necessary, Durkheim (who elsewhere makes an interesting distinction between unconscious
motivations and the rational justifications that conceal them),
Halbwachs, Landsberg, and Delmas agree that the subject must
have clearly expressed his intention of dying, and decided to
do so quite lucidly. The latter therefore exclude the mentally
subnormal. Schneider does not demand consciousness of
intention, but excludes subjects whose desire to die does not
appear clearly at the inquest, or who are obeying a delirium
when the act that is 'imposed on them by hallucination'[41] is
not an order to commit suicide; such acts are regarded as
accidents due to an error of judgment, a possibility that is
often emphasized by authors who obviously wish to place
the suicide act on the level of rational decision. This tendency
is also to be found in the case of children and adolescents,
whose self-destruction is often regarded as accidental owing to
an error of judgment regarding the consequences of the act
committed, arising out of the fact that the child has as yet no
knowledge of death. Many contemporary authors have described the frequency with which children play with death.

— Playing with death, the intention of dying, consciousness,
bring us to the question of blackmail, which is subject to the
same influences. Traditionally, the notion of blackmail and
even of simulation was unanimously accepted by psychiatrists
and sociologists; all agreed that blackmail should be classified
among the pseudo-suicides, and excluded from the field of
suicide proper. At present, there is a diversity of attitude.
Blackmail is still frequently excluded from the suicide field,
its exclusion being supported sometimes by the 'admission of
the subject', after the event or on circumstantial appearance.
Deshaies contrasts blackmail with simulated suicides and 'their
high degree of sincerity'.[42] Other authors, such as Vedrinne,[43]
show the weakness of the usual criteria, since some acts that
seemed like blackmail proved fatal, while others, apparently

sincere, proved to be quite harmless. Certain authors retain this category, but treat it as a modality of suicidal behaviour. Lastly, several authors resolutely reject this category and its pejorative application to subjects who, in any case, have committed the act of self-destruction, whether successfully or not.

— The same diversity of attitude is to be found on the subject of attempted suicide. Vedrinne[44] notes that for a long time interest was directed solely to the suicide death. Publications on cases of attempted suicide contained a distinction between 'serious' attempts, which proved non-fatal only because of some fortuitous intervention, and 'non-serious' (even simulated) attempts. Specialists in anti-poison centres stress the non-correlation between the toxic gravity of the attempt and the psychological gravity of the act, whereas for Halbwachs[45] death is the sole proof. The situation at present is that some authors (Deshaies, Vedrinne, Gorceix, Schneider) refuse to distinguish between successful and unsuccessful attempts, and believe that there is a single 'suicide illness', whose development is subject to innumerable factors, including that of medical progress, by which many individuals who committed the suicide act and who, some years ago, would have died, are now alive. Other authors have revised the tendency to distinguish between successful and unsuccessful attempts,[46] basing their thesis on the study of psycho-social factors, which would appear to be different in either case.

But whether suicides and suicide attempts are regarded as distinct or similar, they at least have one thing in common: in both cases the subject has committed an act of self-destruction. This notion of resorting to action, which is regarded as fundamental by a number of authors - notably Courchet,[47] Schneider,[48] and Deshaies[49] - marks a definite stage in the idea of suicide. But whereas for some, from Esquirol[50] to Gorceix,[51] the idea of suicide cannot be regarded as suicide until it has been expressed in action, others, such as Schneider[48] and Deshaies,[49] treat both the idea of suicide and the suicide act as suicidal behaviour, while distinguishing between the idea of suicide, which is common enough, and the suicide act, which is committed by only a few individuals.

Opinions are most divided on the subject of the various forms of self-destructive behaviour that do not belong to suicide in the strict sense of the term: certain accidents, acts of self-mutilation, certain disorders culminating in physical destruction. Such behaviour is excluded from the suicide field by authors like Gorceix and Schneider and, of course, Halbwachs,[52] because it does not express a death wish, and accepted by others, such as Colin[53] and Deshaies, who refer to it as suicide equivalent, parasuicide, or partial suicide. Psychoanalytic work since Freud[54] has stressed the significance of unsuccessful acts and their role in certain accidents that constitute unconscious suicides. Every unsuccessful act that reveals a self-destructive tendency expresses to a greater or lesser degree the emergence of the death impulses.

The interpretation of acts of self-mutilation is particularly delicate. While some have an undoubtedly suicidal significance, others seem to represent a sacrifice consented to in exchange for having one's life saved; they appear to have the same signification as the castration anxiety, and this would obviously be so in genital self-mutilations. Nevertheless, experiencing the castration anxiety is not the same thing as really castrating oneself. Is self-mutilation an exchange for life itself, or is it the self-destructive tendency failing in its total purpose and settling for a part of the body only?

Equally debatable is the significance of behaviour that does not involve acts of direct self-destruction but which leads to death. It is a fact that both mental anorexia and toxicomania lead to death, but some authors deny that toxicomania is a 'chosen' mode of behaviour, while others regard both as equivalent to unconscious suicide. Deshaies[55] extends the concept of the suicide equivalent to even more distant forms of behaviour, such as the abusive quest for surgical operations for disorders of a more or less real kind or for psychosomatic diseases.

The dividing line between behaviour that realizes an unconscious wish for suicide and behaviour that has a different significance is certainly difficult to determine. Such as the difference between accidents that express a suicidal tendency, and dangerous behaviour that involves an acceptance of fatal risk, not out of a desire for death, but to convince oneself that one is strong enough to overcome this risk; or between psychogenic somatic diseases whose aim is death, and those where suffering is imposed in exchange for the right to live. But this raises the question of the difference, or the similarity, of the two types of motivation.

I have demonstrated, I think, how uncertain the delimitation of the suicide field can be. Between the strict suicide death, with consciously expressed intention, and the inclusion within the definition of suicide of any act leading directly or indirectly to total or partial self-destruction, there is room for an infinite number of gradations, involving innumerable factors. The great complexity of the concepts, the extreme difficulty in finding precise limits for suicide, the confusion that continues to reign over the question, are not without significance. The some-times paradoxical positions adopted by authors can only con-firm the interference of extra-scientific factors, and the importance of personal, especially philosophical and moral, factors, and individual attitudes to death.

Under these conditions, the choice of a definition of suicide is very difficult and demands the utmost care. There is a great gap between the explicit meaning of certain definitions, the implicit content of those definitions, and the theory of which they are part. Without going over all the definitions that have been offered, or settling for the vague 'self-murder', we have a choice between the definition of Durkheim,[56] who considers that 'for an act to be suicide, it is enough that the act, which must necessarily result in death, should have been performed by the victim with full knowledge'; or that of Gorceix,[57] 'an overall auto-aggressive act' which excludes partial self-mutilation and suicide equivalents; or that of Deshaies,[58] 'the act of killing oneself in a normally conscious manner, by taking death as means or as end'; that of Landsberg,[59] 'the act by which a human being voluntarily brings about what he believes to be an efficient and adequate cause of his own death'; or, lastly, that of Janet,[60] for whom 'suicide is when an individual seeks to escape from life simply because it is life'. The definition that we finally adopt must be sufficiently flexible, and must go beyond the bounds of excessive objectivity which would prevent·us from taking into account innumerable unconscious motivations. But it must not include unnumerable modes of human behaviour which would dilute the concept of suicide, and, in the last resort, would be an obstacle to understanding.

Notes

1. J. Vedrinne, *L'intoxication aiguë volontaire*, Paris, Masson, 1965, 38.
2. *Problèmes*, Numéro spécial sur le suicide, No. 58-59, April-May 1959.
3. Esquirol, *Des maladies mentales*, Paris, Baillière, 1838, t. I, 665.
4. G. Deshaies, *Psychologie du suicide*, Paris, P.U.F., 1947, 98.
5. A. Delmas, *Psychologie pathologique du suicide*, Paris, Alcan, 1932.
6. Vedrinne, *op. cit.*, 62.
7. E. Durkheim, *Le suicide*, Paris, P.U.F., 1960, new edition.
8. M. Halbwachs, *Les causes du suicide*, Paris, Alcan, 1930.
9. Durkheim, *op. cit.*, 332.
10. *Ibid*, 363.
11. *Ibid*, 6.
12. *Ibid*, 8.
13. *Ibid*, 13.
14. *Ibid*, 43.
15. H. Ey, 'Le suicide pathologique', *Études Psychiatriques*, t. II, Paris, Desclée de Brouwer, 1948, 341-77.
16. Deshaies, *op. cit.*
17. J.C. Oeconomo, 'Le comportement suicide et le problème de la tentative', *Revue de Science criminelle et de droit pénal comparé*, Paris, Librairie Sirey, 1959, 805·28, no. 4.
18. J. Nick, A. Moinet, A. des Lauriers, A' Guilland and M. Nicolle, 'Le suicide d'abandon', *Annales M.P.*, t. II, No. 1, June 1966, 131.
19. Digor, *De l'ennui à la mélancolie*, mémoire dactylographiée, 1942, 5-17.
20. L. Courchet, 'Le suicide. Essai d'étude psychanalytique', *L'Évolution Psychiatrique*, 1955, No. III, 467.
21. S. Nacht, 'Les états dépressifs', *La Présence du psychanalyste*, Paris, P.U.F., 1963, 121.
22. S. Freud, standard edition of the *Complete Psychological Works*, London, Hogarth Press, vol. XIV, 237-58.
23. Stand. ed., vol. XVIII, 7-64.
24. *Three Essays on the Theory of Sexuality*, stand. ed., vol. VII.
25. K. Abraham, *Selected Papers*, Int. Psychoanalytic Lib., no. 13, London, Hogarth Press, 1927, 418-507.
26. J. Laplanche and J.P. Pontalis, *Vocabulaire de la Psychanalyse*, Paris, P.U.F., 1967, 371.

27. S. Freud, *Beyond the Pleasure Principle*, stand. ed., vol. XVIII, 34-64.
28. S. Freud, *The Ego and the Id*, stand. ed., vol. XIX, 53.
29. *Ibid.*
30. Laplanche and Pontalis, *op. cit.*, 377.
31. S. Nacht, 'Les états dépressifs', 131; 'Instinct de mort ou instinct de vie', 158, in *Présence du psychanalyste*, Paris, P.U.F., 1963.
32. *Ibid*, 154.
33. *Op. cit.*
34. *Ibid*, 123.
35. A. Bayet, *Le suicide et la morale*, Paris, Alcan, 1922, 19.
36. Delmas, *op. cit.*, 104; P. Janet, *De l'angoisse à l'extase*, Paris, Alcan, 1928, t.II, 365.
37. Halbwachs, *op. cit.*, 475.
38. Deshaies, *op. cit.*, 331.
39. R. Barande, 'La conduite suicidaire', *Problèmes, op. cit.*, 14.
40. M. Colin, 'Je vous annonce . . .', *Problèmes, op. cit.*, 69.
41. P.B. Schneider, *La tentative de suicide*, Neuchâtel, Delachaux et Niestlé, 1954, 12.
42. Deshaies, *op. cit.*, 181.
43. Vedrinne, *op. cit.*, 82.
44. *Ibid.*, 37.
45. Halbwachs, *op. cit.*, 89.
46. L.M. Raymondis, Y. Shektan, P. Moron and L. Gayral, 'Une enquête psycho-sociale sur les tentatives de suicide', *Annales Méd-Psychol.*, no. 4, t. II, 1965, 563-607.
47. Courchet, *op. cit.*, 468.
48. Schneider, *op. cit.*, 11.
49. Deshaies, *op. cit.*, 6 and 239.
50. Esquirol, *op. cit.*, 596.
51. A. Gorceix, 'Le suicide, l'adolescence et le poison', *Semaine des Hôpitaux*, 39th year, no. 50, 8 November 1963, 2372.
52. Halbwachs, *op. cit.*, 452.
53. Colin, *op. cit.*, 15.
54. S. Freud, *Psychopathology of Everyday Life*, stand. ed., vol. VI, 191.
55. Deshaies, *op. cit.*, 151.
56. Durkheim, *op. cit.*, 246.
57. Gorceix, *op. cit.*, 2372.
58. Deshaies, *op. cit.*, 5.
59. P.L. Landsberg, *Essai sur l'expérience de la mort*, Paris, Le Seuil, 1951, 126.
60. Janet, *op. cit.*, 365.

2·The notion of adolescence

Adolescence offers certain analogies with suicide. Like suicide, it seems easy, but is in fact very difficult, to define, and it has been and remains a favourite theme for literature, the press, and the cinema; it concerns specialists in a number of disciplines: philosophers, sociologists, moralists, psychologists, psychiatrists, psychoanalysts, biologists. But it differs from suicide in other respects: the teacher occupies an important place among its specialists; although each of these specialists has studied adolescence often almost exclusively from his own point of view, the divergences of opinion between the representatives of the various disciplines is nothing like as sharp, at least on the theoretical plane, as in the case of suicide. Furthermore, whereas suicide is an unusual fact which concerns only a minority of human beings, adolescence concerns them all. Lastly, the participation of the organic factor is evident and beyond dispute. These different aspects appear very clearly in the historical development of the concept of adolescence.

Up to the nineteenth century, only philosophy and literature were concerned with adolescence: they lent support to educational theory and practice and were strongly inbued with moral preoccupations. Thereafter, they evolved, integrating knowledge gained from the human sciences but retaining this moral colouring. Morality continues to affect the scientific approach to adolescence in a number of disciplines, in education in particular.

In the nineteenth century, the efforts of psychiatrists to dismember the mass of 'insanity', their concern to create a nosography, their interest in the clinical and developmental aspects of mental illnesses often led them to adolescence, the age at which so many mental illnesses become manifest. But their position as mental specialists concerned only with psychoses, their constitutionalist and organicist approach, hindered the integration of their undoubtedly interesting observations into the psycho-social current of adolescence, which, in any case, it was obviously impossible to identify with a mental illness. Thus, although their direct influence was minimal, their indirect influence was considerable and can still be felt. On the one hand, their attitude to mental health in adolescence was imbued with moral concerns to a quite remarkable degree, thus reinforcing the pre-existing current of thought. On the other hand, their development of nosographical entities on the basis of symptoms culminated in the following association: behaviour = illness = a more or less irreversible constitution or organic disorder. The latter helped to spread serious diagnoses and prognoses based on the adolescents' behaviour alone, which did nothing to further the understanding of the process of adolescence. It also added to the confusion concerning the boundaries between the normal and the pathological, which in the case of adolescence, as in that of suicide, gave rise to important controversies.

Furthermore, important progress in biology revealed the physiology of puberty. But this helped to establish the confusion between puberty, a physical process, and adolescence, a bio-psycho-social process, to the detriment of the latter. This resulted in contradictory statements: on the one hand, everything becomes irremediably fixed at puberty, thus denying the psycho-social aspects of adolescence; on the other, everything falls into place as a result of biological upheaval, thus denying the psychological development of the child. This attitude reigned until the work of G. Heuyer[1] stressed the importance of the past and of social factors in adolescence.

At the beginning of the twentieth century, adolescence became of concern to most of the modern disciplines. This seems to have retarded the establishment of a scientific approach, and the extreme diversity of viewpoints helped to maintain a literary and moral dominance over the question which it is only now beginning to throw off. But the subject escaped the inflexible, impassioned attitudes that were adopted on the question of suicide. Even though the various works on the subject were clearly orientated towards the author's own

particular discipline, they did take into account the attitudes
of other disciplines, and made frequent reference to them.
Thus the psychological works of S. Hall, published in 1905,
were followed in France by those of Mendousse in 1907, and
of Debesse in 1937. In seeking to decipher the riddle of behaviour, these works tried to link it to the 'inner life' of the adolescent, while ignoring the unconscious aspects of that life. However, they did take into account the environment and psychiatric
factors.

Similarly, juvenile delinquency, which was one of the first
problems to be approached as it expresses in a concrete way
the conflict between the adolescent and society, was studied
by the psychiatrist G. Heuyer,[2] who emphasized the role of
the environment; and specialists in the field of delinquency,
jurists, and social psychologists often appeal to psychological,
psychoanalytic, and psychiatric data. Again, anthropology has
revealed important points concerning the adolescent in primitive societies - points to which I shall refer later.

The psychoanalytic study of the question began with one of
Freud's *Three Essays on the Theory of Sexuality*.[3] In this essay,
Freud refers a great deal to the roles of the constitution and
the environment. Since then, a number of works have referred
to a variety of factors. Among the more recent, mention might
be made of those by Bloch and Niederhoffer,[4] by Roumajon
on teenage gangs, which set up a permanent confrontation
between individual and social *données*,[5] and the work of
Aichorn and Friedlander on juvenile delinquency. There are
also the psychoanalytic works of Anna Freud, Eissler and
Lampl de Groot, while Male and Kestemberg deal extensively
with the life of adolescents today, its psychological context
and the social *données,* thus achieving a fruitful union of
psychology and sociology.

However, until recent years scientific work on adolescence,
as opposed to work of a more popularizing character, has been
rare. This rarity is reflected in psychoanalytic work on the
subject - so much so that Anna Freud[6] remarked that adolescence was the poor relation of psychoanalysis. If one wished
to classify existing works on the subject according to discipline,
one could certainly do so, but their approach, and the con-

clusions that they arrive at, are often similar. They could also be classified by dividing them into, on the one hand, those concerned with a comparison of internal and external, present and past, conscious and unconscious, physical and psychical, *données,* and in doing so emphasizing one of the factors, and, on the other hand, those that make a study of what adolescents consciously think of the personal and social factors, such as the work of Gesell[7] and the inquiry into the 16-24 age group.[8] What, in the present state of research, do we know about adolescence? It is this that I shall now try to outline.

A. The field of adolescence

Most contemporary authors agree that we do not understand adolescents. This important fact is reflected in the difficulty in providing a definition of adolescence - from whatever angle we look at the problem we are faced by a lack of precision.

Chronological limits: the lack of precision as to age limits is particularly apparent in the upper limit.

There is virtual unanimity that adolescence begins with the onset of puberty, and I have no hesitation in sharing that opinion. I do not believe, as has sometimes been suggested, that the beginning of adolescence can be situated during puberty, or even at nubility. This would ignore the earliest stages of adolescence, which are important even though their outward manifestations are not very obvious. The beginning of puberty is relatively fixed, with little variation within the same geographical zone and the same cultural group; that is, for populations of a Western type living in temperate zones, at 10-12 years for girls and 12-14 years for boys. But as Male[9] has pointed out, this still leaves the problem of precocious and retarded puberty, with their consequent uneven development. In cases of precocious puberty, it seems preferable to regard adolescence as beginning with puberty. Its appearance over the final period of childhood certainly has lasting repercussions, and the experience of this early adolescence is a very special one, but it is adolescence nonetheless. The problem is a more delicate one in cases of retarded puberty. It seems preferable, when the delay is longer than a year or two, to regard adolescence as beginning at the age at which it would normally have done so. Experience shows that subjects who remain psychically infantile are rare, but the anxiety that results from the retardation may have profound repercussions.

Another problem is that posed by children who behave in an apparently adolescent way well before puberty. Such children are not necessarily precocious, or to be regarded as adolescents. Beneath pseudo-maturity, there often exists an archaic mode of identification, and neurotic attitudes of a hysterical type that find expression, in actual fact, in the retardation of maturation.

Such extreme cases show that one certainly cannot reduce adolescence to puberty, but that puberty constitutes the basic reference for determining its beginning. To ignore puberty would be to ignore the importance of genital maturation and the basic role of its integration. Psychical reactions to sexual maturation, its precocity or its retardation, are always the dominant factor in the process of adolescence.

At what age does adolescence end? For some authors, adolescence has the same duration as puberty, of which it is the psychological reflection. This is tantamount to taking biological development, a partial aspect of adolescence, as the whole, thus denying the many psycho-social factors whose rhythm of development is different. On the other hand, those who accept only the social factor fix the end of adolescence at the age of penal majority, eighteen, or civil majority, twenty-one. Either classification involves a denial of the development of the personality and of the relational system.

Among the authors who take internal development into account, some confine their attention to the integration of the pubertal transformation, which means placing the upper limit of adolescence at approximately the end of puberty, about eighteen (in boys). But if one takes into account all factors and their integration into the personality, the duration remains imprecise. Many authors believe that it lasts about ten years, that is, that it ends between twenty and twenty-five approximately. Confronted by so much uncertainty, one is tempted to evade the whole issue with the old formula, 'It's different for everyone; some people remain adolescents all their lives'. But it has proved necessary to have some limits, since society, those who have to respond to certain behaviour, and the doctor who has to weigh up the significance of that behaviour, will not approach the subject of seventeen, twenty-two, or thirty in the same way.

A few years ago, some colleagues and I[10] proposed that the end of military service should be taken as the upper limit for boys, because of the way in which the young man experiences that event, the way in which he sees himself and is seen by others. But this criterion is clearly not applicable to girls; in any case, the age at which young men perform military service has become increasingly varied in recent years, and at present a great many young men no longer do so at the legal age because of the large number of exemptions and deferments. Moreover, terminal crises, which are becoming more and more frequent, take place over the age of twenty-one, and it now seems desirable to situate the end of adolescence between twenty and twenty-five for young men, and twenty and twenty-three for young women. In view of this considerable extension of adolescence, there has been a revival in recent years of a tendency to fix the upper limit at eighteen, to be followed by an intermediary period, 'youth' (*la jeunesse*), thus creating a category of young adults. We shall see later what the advantages and disadvantages of this approach are.

To sum up, the beginning of adolescence, apart from a few minor variations, is accepted as being relatively fixed, but there are a great many variations and imprecisions as to its end, depending on the particular aspect under consideration. So we must now try to introduce a little precision into our delimitation of the field.

The qualitative definition of adolescence. This is as fraught with imprecision as the attempt to lay down the chronological limits of adolescence. It is tempting, therefore, to attribute this impression to the very nature of adolescence, to the fact that the adolescent does not know himself who he is. But this would simply be an expression of our own ignorance. E. Kestemberg[11] quotes the negative definition provided by Littré's dictionary (*'l'âge compris entre l'enfance et l'état adulte'*), and suggests 'someone who is no longer a child, and not yet an adult'. Socio-

logical definitions that regard adolescence as 'the period of
life between biological and social maturity'[12] are appealing to
the same *données,* the adolescent no longer having the status
of a child, but not yet having that of an adult. P. Pichot[13]
stresses the importance, from the point of view of social psychology, of the transition from the role and status of a child
to the role and status of an adult.

Such definitions refer us back to that of the adult. One
might turn the question round and say that an adult is someone who has emerged out of adolescence. And where does that
take us? From the social point of view, an adult is someone
who is given the right to assume responsibility for his own
person, 'and to assume, within the limits laid down by society
for normal adult behaviour, (a) sexual, (b) economic, and (c)
civic and religious responsibilities'.[14] But it seems to me that
such a definition is useful only if it is made clear that the
individual must assume this right permanently, so that adaptation to the circumstances of daily life does not lead, over a
fairly long period, to decompensation, and psychical or social
disorders. Moreover, this right is granted at the age at which
one is usually capable of assuming it, and not according to
individual capacity. If individual capacity was taken into
account, the notion of adolescence would have to be extended to include maladjusted and sick adults.

From the psychological point of view, I propose to regard
as adulthood the age at which one can normally choose, the
choice being not only the option for satisfaction, but, more
important, the renunciation of other simultaneous desires, the
subject being capable of bearing the frustration involved without profound or prolonged disturbance to the functioning of
the psyche.

Let us look at the etymology of the term adolescent.[15] It implies the notion of growth, transformation, development, movement. All those who have written on the subject stress this
movement, which is, after all, its essential characteristic. With
the integration of new *données,* it expresses a calling into
question of the *données* of childhood, and, in accordance
with a paradox that is a reflection of the state of the adolescent himself, he is someone who is no longer a child but not

yet an adult, and, at the same time, still a child and already an adult.

To sum up, we can define adolescence from the psychological point of view as the period during which, under the impact of sexual maturation in its biological, psychological, and social aspects, the individual begins to reshape the image that he has of himself and of others, and the relational system of his ego to the environment, including the definitive organization of his personality. From the social point of view, it is the period during which the individual gradually abandons his infantile attitudes to other members of the group, and achieves a perception and acceptance of reality that enable him to be admitted into the group on an equal footing with others. But these definitions are still unsatisfactory, because they do nothing to remove the imprecision as to chronological limits.

B. *The work of adolescence*

Neither a child nor an adult, still a child and already an adult, the adolescent is a child-becoming-man. Adolescence is the most intense phase of development, bringing with it more changes than are produced in the rest of life put together, just as, after birth and death, puberty is the period that produces the most important and the most rapid physical changes.

Involving the integration of both internal and external *données,* present acquisition and a calling into question of the past, 'investments' and 'disinvestments' that express the difficulty of knowing and recognizing oneself, adolescence is above all movement, contrast, contradiction. Difficulties 'of identity and identification',[16] and the movement that gives adolescence its fragmented aspect, are responsible, paradoxically enough, for its fundamental unity. This work enables the adolescent to run through the whole field of psychical life from one end to the other, with astonishing rapidity, with effects not only on overt behaviour but also on conscious and unconscious experience. He is caught up in his own contradictions, his own paradoxes, to the perplexity of those around him, especially if they fail to recognise the continuity beneath so much apparent disconnexion.

The paradoxical work of adolescence

The transition from childhood to adulthood is both necessary and desirable, but it is also a cause of fear and refusal, thus setting up defences and resistances in a paradox that reflects the diversity of the impulses expressed, and the diversity of the defence mechanisms involved.[17] The pivot of the process is, of course, the maturation of the genital organs, and the resumption of the Oedipal situation. But it presupposes a re-shaping of the whole organism and the whole psyche, so that 'the erotogenic zones become subordinated to the primacy of the genital zone' by means of a series of 'transformations that bring the infantile sexual life to its normal definitive form'.[18] As many authors have insisted,[19] all the *données,* even the most archaic, most varied pregenital ones, are react-ivated and called into question during genitalization, with con-sequent effects upon one another.

Thus, the same fact may express successively, or even sim-ultaneously, instinctual *données* as well as the defences that become attached to them and shape the impulses, adolescent *données,* and reactivated archaic *données.* Any attempt to see them as a whole results in a constant difficulty in grasping the significance of adolescent behaviour, and an impression of paradox; but failure to do so produces a fragmented view of the situation, and of the individual subject. For example, an archaic manifestation may be a regressive defence against the Oedipal genital problem, but it may also be the authentic expression of a reactivated archaic *donnée.* Similarly, a defence may be erected against the revival of archaic *données,* but also against their increasing eroticization.

A number of examples illustrate this confusion. The adoles-cent's attitude to parents and parent-substitutes, his audacity and his fears, his revolt and his submission, his intense activity and his voluntary passivity (sometimes described as asthenia), his need for autonomy and his search for a model, are all features that express his ambivalence, and the simultaneous emergence of *données* at very different levels.

A typical example is to be found in the adolescent's behaviour towards his own body. The maturation of the gerital

organs both awakens pride and revives the anxiety of the
Oedipal conflict, which, with its impulses and defences in the
process of being reshaped, is to be the woof of the adolescent's
relational development. The extra-genital physical transformations are eroticized, and become the support of the displacement of the Oedipal conflict. But at the same time they are
experienced at a more archaic level, where they affect the
consciousness of one's own body and cause a disturbance to
the body image. A sudden alteration in muscular strength and
in the dimensions of the segments of the body, call into
question the perception of one's own dimensions and those
of the human and material environment in which the adolescent develops. This loss of the instrument of measurement
that is the perception of one's own body constitutes a temporary, but important, psycho-motor deficit, for it has a
definite role to play in the tendency to resort to action. I
shall be returning to this point in greater detail.

Again, the feeling of no longer recognizing one's voice
when it is breaking is both fear of acquiring a male voice, and
a genuine difficulty in recognizing it, an impression that the
new intonations are coming from someone else. Similarly, the
adolescent's preoccupation with his face, which reflects the
sexual transformation that he is undergoing, is at the same
time a displacement of his genital preoccupation, pride in its
acquisition, a desire to please, and a fear that his face will
betray his masturbatory activities. It is also an expression of
his disarray at being confronted by a face that is not entirely
his, without however being another's, and when he looks at
himself in the mirror it is to make sure that he is attractive,
and, at the same time, to acquaint himself with this face that
changes from week to week.

Interest in sport, or its rejection, expresses a desire to show
off and to develop one's body, in a mixture of exhibitionism
and inhibition of more direct conquest behaviour, sometimes
by a narcissistic approach towards the sexual impulse, but
sometimes by means of a deeper narcissism. It may also be an
attempt to divert energy, to avoid sexual desire, to exhaust
oneself enough to avoid in particular the anxiety-inducing
solitude of pre-sleep that is favourable to desire and to mastur-

bation, in the hope of falling, exhausted and already half-
asleep, on to one's bed. The desire to excel at sport, to go to
the utmost limits of physical resistance, may express a desire
either to prove one's virility, or to destroy it, or, again, it may
express the more archaic pleasure in the play of muscle
and sinew.

Behaviour connected with eating also has meaning on
several different levels. Bulimia may express either a desire to
be stronger, to hasten growth, or a refusal to be attractive,
to confine oneself within a passive obesity. Its opposite,
anorexia, may express a desire to be slim, to accord with
certain canons of beauty in order to increase one's value as a
sexual object, but it may also express a refusal to grow up, to
become stronger; or it may express a rejection of 'instinct'
in toto, an attack on alimentary needs being a displacement
of the struggle against the sexual instinct. It may also be
regressive defence behaviour, or a resurgence of oral preoccupations that have so far remained subjacent.

All these forms of physical behaviour, of experience of the
body, express at one and the same time the perception of
genital maturation, whether accepted or rejected, preoccupations of various kinds, anxiety, a confused attitude towards a
new physical identity, and the resurgence of pregenital
impulses.

The language of adolescents is also expressive of the number
and diversity of the *données.* Language is a means of communication for a personality suddenly enriched by a rediscovered
world; it is also a reflexion of the uncertainties and confusions
of the adolescent's experience. The hazards of language development are also relevant to our subject, and I shall return to them
later.

Adolescence: a bio-psycho-social confrontation

The great merit of much modern work on adolescence, in particular in the fields of psychoanalysis and genetic psychology,
is that, in addition to describing adolescence - which has already
been done, well or ill, during the 'literary' period - it has shown
that adolescence is neither a mere continuation of childhood,

nor a beginning without a past; it is, at the same time, an integration of new factors and a reshaping of the structures of childhood. Similarly, modern studies stress the mutual interaction of biological, psychological and social factors, and, from this point of view, adolescence is a privileged period for the study of this confrontation. It is absolutely necessary, therefore, to take into account the congenital factors of equipment, factors of personal history (not in terms of 'events', but in terms of the process of integration that produces the organization of the personality), and present factors, internal and external, individual and collective. If one confined one's attention to only one of these factors, one would be guilty of taking the part for the whole, of producing an abstraction that would do nothing to help us understand the young person with whom we wish to communicate. Although one must be aware of all the various factors I cannot do more than touch on a few of them here, and the reader is referred to more exhaustive works, such as those by P. Male, who has shown in particular the effects of infantile development on the experience of the adolescent. Similarly, I shall be making no more than a passing reference in this chapter to some of the factors proper to adolescence: these will reappear at various points throughout the book.

For the same reason I shall deal briefly with the psycho-affective factors of childhood. The resumption of the Oedipal situation, the peculiar dynamics of the instinctual drive, the development of the superego and the ego ideal take place on the basis of a reshaping of childhood structures. Thus the earliest stages of infancy will be brought back into play, from the maternal relationship, which is the foundation of self-love and of basic energy capacity, then to the mother/child defusion, which makes it possible to know the other and to achieve autonomy, then to control over aggressivity and the feeling of omnipotence, with its expression in the megalomaniac ego ideal, which are characteristic of the anal development of the second year, and, finally, to identification and the flowering of the Oedipal situation.

We must stress the importance of the latency period that follows these early stages, when control over one's impulses is

achieved. For some years now stress has been laid on the role
of the latency period, especially by authors concerned with
adolescents. Though less has been said about it, it also plays
a major role in the preparation of adolescence. Freud[20] has
shown, in particular, how important it is in the formation of
social feelings and sexual barriers, which play a crucial role in
adolescence. The adolescent draws on them in part as a source
of energy and material for a new organization, but may also
find in them the nuclei for neurotic developments.

Cognitive factors have been the subject of studies by Piaget
and, in America, by Gesell, and their followers. I shall mention
only the excellent summary by Osterrieth[21] of the development from childhood to adolescence, and the place of cognitive
factors in the bio-psycho-social confrontation. After the cognitive development of childhood, we are again brought up
against the importance of the latency period. The older child
is intellectually remarkably active, at ease and receptive, with
a considerable capacity for apprehension and logical structuration of whatever is concrete. From pre-adolescence onwards,
the child passes from concrete thought to 'hypothetico-
deductive' abstract thought; he acquires the power of logical
reasoning, together with a body of laws and principles, and
becomes capable of formal thought and generalization.

At what age does intellectual structuration end? Most
authors believe that it is about the age of fifteen, and Osterrieth
rightly observes that it is at that age that one reaches the
summit of the various intelligence scales. Fifteen to sixteen is
also precisely the age at which the process of intellectualization
accelerates rapidly, to reach its summit two or three years
later. Its earliest manifestations certainly occur prior to this
age, but these can scarcely be regarded as intellectualization
as such. It would appear that intellectual capacities are quantitatively acquired about the age of fifteen, but not qualitatively,
and intellectual structuration continues for some years. But
this is a difficult question to answer on account of the complex
signification of intellectual activity and the intrication of cognitive and other factors.

The adolescent reasons about everything; he generalizes not
only on the basis of subjective personal experience, but also

on the basis of an idea, a hypothesis, a phantasy, which would be reminiscent of certain paranoiac modes of reasoning if the rapid shifts in his ideas did not introduce an element of constant movement. We are familiar with his predilection for large-scale theories that can be applied to all spheres of human activity, his categorical affirmations, and his definitive positions, which last no longer than the time it takes to change his mind, his feeling of having discovered ideas that are obvious enough to older people, but which, in fact, are discoveries for him. He talks for the sake of talking, thinks for the sake of thinking, argues for the sake of arguing, but what for the adult is just so much hot air is a basic need for the adolescent, a highly structuring activity.

For the adolescent, this intellectual activism is the principle way in which he becomes aware of his new intellectual equipment; it expresses a need to know himself in his newly acquired inner richness, to test what he has acquired, to apply these new instruments to taking the measure of the world, to seeing it anew. But this intellectualization also plays a role in the struggle against reactivated impulses. The role of intellectualization as a means of defence[22] is so important that I shall be returning to it later. We are also familiar with the role that cognitive development plays in relations with parents and parent-substitutes, when an adolescent feels as capable as they of judging, evaluating, penetrating, and understanding the material, cultural, social, and political world, and is seen by them to have a desire to do so. The over-investment of intellectual activity applied to school work is evidence of this.

It may be, then, that the end of the phase of intellectualization is explained by the fact that once this new equipment has been tested it is no longer the object of a privileged activity, that the new organization of the impulses makes intellectual defence less indispensable. But it may also be that this phase is an integral part of cognitive development, and is necessary to the setting up of new intellectual structures. We certainly have here an example of the intrication of present and past, and of the interaction of all the bio-psycho-social factors.

As far as the biological factors are concerned, there is certainly no need to stress the importance of the pubertal

process, and the physical and psychical changes that occur as
a result of hormonal impregnation. I have already mentioned
the unevenness of pubertal development, which is a good
illustration of the interaction of the biological, psycho-
affective, and social spheres, and the rapid changes in stature
and weight that occur, whose effects can sometimes extend
to the temporary instrumental deficit of the adolescent. The
whole past affects the way in which these upheavals are experienced and assumed - upheavals which, in turn, reshape
this past, just as the physical past affects all factors of the
personality.

Thus heredity, not as a fixist, explicative notion, but in the
contemporary sense of genotype and phenotype, which corresponds to 'experienced heredity',[23] seems to have an effect
on childhood from the mere fact of resemblances. It will be
present therefore when the adolescent has to confront the
problems of identity, identification, and autonomy. Similarly,
in childhood, certain handicaps of the initial equipment,
whether hereditary or as a result of illness, affect the perceptivo-motor organization, and possibly the process of identification and the relational system, owing to adult attitudes of
rejection or over-protection and their refusal to grant independence. But at adolescence, in addition to the direct effect of
these handicaps, which enhance the temporary disturbance of
the body image, the compensations of these handicaps may
diminish or become stronger, and this goes even for physical
bearing; they also intervene when one is embarking on one's
professional life. At a deeper level, there are major infirmities;
their persistence, in spite of the physical reshaping that leaves
a body mutilated and incomplete, is an invitation to the adolescent to experience this fragmentation as a reality, to confirm
rejection by others by provoking it, or, on the contrary, to
induce behaviour involving either suppression or exhibitionism
of the infirmity.

Taking a broader view, one could mention the long or
repeated illnesses of childhood that have promoted regression
and passivity but effected certain secondary benefits, as well
as causing a fixation on bodily preoccupations. At adolescence,
concurrent illnesses may recall certain advantages which the

child gained as a result of constant ill health, and encourage the return of passivity or somatic preoccupations to the detriment of the adolescent dynamism. Sometimes, on the other hand, this past may motivate hyperactive behaviour, desperate attempts to improve one's health, a rejection of parental over-protection, and a negation of intercurrent illnesses.

And we should not forget the relationship between the parents and the physical history of their child. Their ambivalence, which is composed of their satisfaction at their child's good health or dissatisfaction at his illness, and their reactions to the frustrations aroused by a child who does not conform to their projective model (which may or may not resemble him), or who is ill, come into play in the conflictual relations with the adolescent.

The social factors of childhood are characterized by their entirely external origin; they later come into play only in so far as they have left their mark on the developing personality. At adolescence, they appear as internal factors, integrated into experience, and as such are called into question. But these social factors of childhood are peculiar in that they are not perceived directly by the child. The few adults who are responsible for his upbringing are obligatory intermediaries; the most important of these is the father, and in recent years much stress has been laid on his role as a support of the reality principle, and as a factor in the organization of the ego ideal and superego. In the child, then, there is a coalescence between the paternal image and social factors, whether these factors induce the behaviour of the parents or parent-substitutes by constraint, or whether they constitute the parents' own ideal, which they then project on to the child.

Throughout adolescence, the social factors act directly, and the subject perceives them without intermediaries. This new view of the world must necessarily confront the one that he has been given, with the result that the adolescent separates himself from the parental image. The importance of the action of these social factors cannot be doubted, and the subject is at present a much discussed and highly controversial one, but in the present state of our knowledge it seems to be very difficult to evaluate. Between the position that sees in adolescence a

merely social phenomenon, and the one that regards it solely
as an internal process that is very little influenced by social
conditions, there remains the need to define what, in adolescent experience, is fundamental and irreducible, and what
varies according to socio-cultural development. We lack docu-
mentation about adolescents in societies other than our own,[24]
though recent work has provided us with some interesting
notions.[25] Without wishing to overemphasize social factors it
is obvious that some of these present problems. We need only
take the example of the recent extension of the school-leaving
age in France, which is having repercussions at the deepest
level of adolescent experience, and of the adolescent's relationships with others, especially with his parents.

C. Is adolescence a crisis?

This brief survey of the process of adolescence leaves a number
of points in doubt, but one fact is clear: above all, adolescence
involves an enormous upheaval. But what is its value and signification?

One point must be made clear at the outset, namely, what
we are to understand by upheaval. The term 'crisis of adolescence' has been given wide currency, but it is unsuitable for
at least one reason: one can hardly use the term crisis of a
process that extends over about ten years. Debesse, who makes
great use of the term, emphasizes this fact and points out that
as well as storms there are periods of calm: in the crisis of
juvenile originality he describes two phases that may be separated by several years. Another term, then, might be better
suited to describe adolescence as a whole. Nevertheless, the
adolescent does undergo critical moments (in every sense of
the term), during which certain characteristic features of adolescence come to a climax. One cannot speak of the crisis of
adolescence, but one can say that crises occur during adolescence. Two questions now arise: what place do these crises
occupy in the upheaval of adolescence as a whole, and what
is the signification and value not of the crises in isolation but
of that whole?

The evolutive phases of adolescence

The attempt to reduce adolescence to a crisis illustrates the common tendency to describe adolescence in an overall way. The same is true if one describes only the factors that partic- ipate in the upheaval, or only the behaviour of the adolescent. Such a one-sided approach leads either to an abstract model, or to a partial view of adolescence, and prevents one from approaching the experience of the adolescent at grips with his own self-questioning. Adolescence has, of course, a funda- mental unity: upheaval, self-questioning, and their consequence, mobility. But another fundamental factor is the structuring dynamics of this mobility, which plays an 'organizing' role.[27] The adolescent is 'becoming', and at the end of this adventure he finds himself different from what he was at the beginning. If we see only the crisis or the mobility we may fail to recognise the changes that occur: the young person does not live his life in the same manner, and is not perceived in the same way, at fifteen, nineteen and twenty-three. It would be preferable, then, not to describe adolescence in an overall way, but to distinguish between the different phases in the process that leads from childhood to adulthood. It would certainly be much more difficult to speak of phases in adolescence than in the case of childhood, for one cannot clearly establish what distin- guishes adolescents from one age to another. We would appear to be dealing with phases whose characteristics are even more interpenetrated than in childhood.

The notion of crises may help us, for these crises do seem to occur as hinges between the different phases, corresponding to transitions, to moments of accelerated change in the internal and psycho-social organization: the beginning and end of puberty, modification of the sexual life, the change from one school year to the next, school-leaving, starting work, the acquisition of adult autonomy. At these moments, ambivalence becomes more marked, with a fear of committing oneself to the unknown and of losing certain benefits on the one hand, and a desire to move forward with the structuring process on the other. Incidentally, greater knowledge of the terminal crisis will enable us to have a better understanding of the last phase of adolescence.

But the description of adolescence according to these phases and crises remains a delicate question. Debesse[28] has demonstrated these difficulties in an excellent study. The most difficult problem is to determine the differential criterion of the phases. There are several possibilities. Certainly the most judicious is based on the sexual life of the adolescent, for the question is basically concerned with his evolution towards a maturity that involves 'an exact convergence of the affectionate current and the sensual current, both being directed towards the sexual object and the sexual aim'.[29] From a social point of view, one can measure the progression in the degree of independence and autonomy; this makes it possible to evaluate the evolution in the adolescent's attitudes to the world, but ignores the evolution in his deeper experience. I believe that by taking as our basis sexual maturation in its instinctual, affective, and social aspects, it should be possible to describe the successive phases of adolescence in conjunction with the development of the relational system, that is, the development of the redefinition of self and of the world through one's relations with others. Such a description would require more evidence than is at present at our disposal, but it is a task that I hope to turn to in a later work.

Is the upheaval of adolescence necessary?

This question is raised by all our authors, but because so many present it in terms of crisis it tends to confusion. Some question whether the actual process of adolescence - the upheaval - is necessary, while others simply question the necessity for particular crises that occur throughout this upheaval. The confusion is lessened if one considers the crises in conjunction, not with their outward manifestations, which are to a greater or lesser degree a source of irritation to the adult environment, but with the accentuation of the fundamental conflicts of adolescence.

Most authors regard the upheaval and its conflicts as a fundamental factor in adolescence: it is not only necessary, but 'inevitable, welcome and beneficial',[30] a sign of progressing maturity. Others do not share this point of view. In particular, K. Eissler[31] does not regard the crisis as being of fundamental importance, and believes that conflicts need not arise if there are no internal or external obstacles to the satisfaction of heterosexual instincts. But 'such conditions are so ideal that they practically never exist in conjunction'.[32] I will even go further and ask whether it is not precisely the confrontation of these sexual instincts and these obstacles that constitutes the process of adolescence. Both are fundamental constituent elements of man, whose development is essentially a conjoint integration or a maturing confrontation of these factors. To postulate an adolescent without conflicts is to postulate an adolescent lacking one side of the confrontation, or lacking the dynamism necessary to the confrontation, and therefore pathological. One is reminded of Anna Freud's opinion that therapy is of the greatest help in such cases. It is certainly true that the upheaval is dangerous, and that adolescence is a difficult and hazardous period, but that is no reason to see it as an atypical, even pathological, phenomenon. To this question are linked two others that are also important enough to be mentioned here.

Is present-day youth in a bad way?

The hypothesis of the atypical character of the 'crisis' is paralleled by that of an increase in its frequency and the generally expressed assertion that youth is in a worse way than before. Such an assertion should be treated with the utmost caution. The first hypothesis, banal and vulgar as it is, is nonetheless obvious: each generation of adults has long declared that the younger generation is in a worse way than the last. If this were true, and there is nothing to prove that it is, a gradual decline in man would have taken place and mankind would now be in a catastrophic condition. Furthermore, on what basis can one declare that youth is in a good or a bad way? It depends partly on what the adult can stand, and such an assertion shows above all that the adult feels uncomfortable because he is disturbed by the adolescent, which is not a new phenomenon either.

This type of declaration would seem to be due mainly to a confusion of form and content, as Roumajon,[33] Bloch and Niederhoffer,[34] and Anna Freud[35] have pointed out. The adult makes a pejorative interpretation of adolescent behaviour according to the narcissistic wounds that he thinks he can see in it - an important question that I shall deal with in greater detail later. In no way does present-day youth seem to be in a worse way than its predecessors. On the contrary, if anything it would appear to be in a better way than either the 'conformist' youth or the rebellious youth of the past. Maturation seems to take place more rapidly and more harmoniously; the present-day adolescent seems to have greater insight, and finds it easier to assume his own experience and to work out his own attitudes to things, which in current terms might be called a greater degree of authenticity. With the decline in certain prohibitions he finds it easier to express his unease and his conflicts, which makes them more obtrusive in the eyes of the adult, and perhaps gives the impression that young people are in a bad way, whereas in fact it is a sign of progress.

It is nonetheless true that certain questions are presenting problems. The extension of the school age, the appearance of the young as a class of consumers, the technological and moral development of our society, to take only a few, are bound to affect the experience of adolescents. Indeed, they are a good illustration of the interaction of internal and social factors during adolescence. Undoubtedly, we are living through a profound mutation in society and human relations, but we do not possess the necessary distance to judge either its effects or the significance of the behaviour of adolescents placed in these conditions. We are even less qualified to judge such behaviour in value terms.

—*The boundary between the normal and the pathological* poses once again the question of the signification of the crisis. Its interest is not purely theoretical; for specialists in the field of mental health, it forms part of everyday practice. Their major preoccupation is to detect mental illness at the time that it is forming, or as soon afterwards as possible. Therapy may alter the course of the illness at the point at which the prepsychotic subject becomes psychotic. By the same token, it is useful to help certain adolescents at the moment at which their conflicts are beginning to crystallize, to become fixated, to set up an obstacle to maturation, and to block future development. On the other hand it is just as important not to psychiatrize youth as a whole, to avoid over-hasty interference that will run counter to the aim in view by 'freezing' or even preventing the progressive spontaneous process.

Indeed, it is undoubtedly a difficult distinction to establish. It is often said that the behaviour characteristic of the process of adolescence resembles the symptoms of mental illnesses. This is only one step away from saying that adolescence is an illness, which allows us to liken it to a psychosis, a neurosis, a perversion, etc., as the case may require; this step has sometimes been taken. But many authors, P. Male[36] in particular, have stressed the need to distinguish between what is and what is not pathological in the process of adolescence, and not to extend the notion of illness in an abusive way. To do so would, on the one hand, dilute the concept of illness by applying it to a constant and inevitable process that forms an integral part of man's development towards maturation, whereas illness is, by definition, a particular phenomenon that diverts or impedes that process. On the other hand, it would be to judge of adolescence according to criteria that are, to say the least, arguable, and which are not unconnected with the embarrassment felt by the adult. I would agree with those authors who regard as pathological whatever, in the course of adolescence, impedes or holds back the process, and *a fortiori* whatever tends to fixate earlier disturbances around which the personality will organize itself, thus blocking the way to future development, the way by which things may always become other and more than they are.

Notes

1. Cf. in particular, *Introduction à la psychiatrie infantile*, Paris, P.U.F., 1952, 228-40.
2. G. Heuyer, *Enfants anormaux et delinquants juvéniles*, thesis, Paris, no. 371, Steinheil ed., 1914.
3. S. Freud, 'The transformations of puberty', in *Three Essays on the Theory of Sexuality*, stand, ed., vol. VII.
4. H. Bloch and A. Niederhoffer, *Les bandes d'adolescents*, Paris, Payot, 1963.
5. Y. Roumajon, 'Comportements inadaptés de l'adolescent normal', *Psychiatrie de l'enfant*, vol. IV, fasc. 1, Paris, P.U.F., 1961, 229-78.
6. A. Freud, 'Adolescence', *The Psychoanalytic Study of the Child*, vol. XIII, New York, Int. Univ. Press, 1958, 259.
7. A. Gesell, *L'adolescent de 10 à 16 ans*, Paris, P.U.F., 1959.
8. J. Duquesne, *Les 16-24 ans*, Inquiry of I.F.O.P., Paris, Le Centurion, 1963.
9. P. Male, *Psychothérapie de l'adolescent*, Paris, P.U.F., 1964, 84-9.
10. P. Sivadon, M. Schweich and A. Haim, 'L'adolescent à l'hôpital psychiatrique', *L'hygiène mentale*, no. 3, 1955, 81-95.
11. E. Kestemberg, 'L'identité et l'identification chez l'adolescent', *Psychiatrie de l'enfant*, vol. V, fasc. 2, Paris, P.U.F., 1962, 443.
12. Bloch and Niederhoffer, *op. cit.*, 35.
13. P. Pichot, Preface to Bloch and Niederhoffer, *op. cit.*, 12.
14. *Ibid*, 35.
15. Kestemberg, *op. cit.*, 444.
16. *Ibid*, 448.
17. A. Freud, *op. cit.*, 267-75.
18. S. Freud, *Three Essays on the Theory of Sexuality*, *op. cit.*, 207.
19. Especially, in France, P. Male; cf. Étude psychanalytique de l'adolescent', *La Psychanalyse d'aujourd'hui*, Paris, P.U.F., 1956, 242.
20. S. Freud, *Three Essays ...*, *op. cit.*, 176-7 and 238-9.
21. P.A. Osterrieth, 'L'adolescence: aspects psychologiques'. *L'abord psychiatrique de l'adolescence*, Excerpta Medica Found., 1966, 114-20.
22. A. Freud, *The Ego and the Mechanisms of Defence*, London, Hogarth Press, 2nd ed., 1942, 172-80.
23. Male, 'Étude psychanalytique de l'adolescent', *op. cit.*, 240.
24. Kestemberg, *op. cit.*, 446.
25. Cf. in particular Bloch and Niederhoffer, *op. cit.*
26. M. Debesse, *La crise d'originalaté juvénile*, Paris, P.U.F., 1948, 8.
27. Kestemberg, *op. cit.*, 456.
28. Debesse, *op. cit.*, 23-5.
29. S. Freud, *Three Essays...*, *op. cit.*, 207.
30. A. Freud, 'Adolescence', *op. cit.*, 264.

31. K. Eissler, 'Notes on problems of technique in the psychoanalytic treatment of adolescents', *The Psychoanalytic Study of the Child,* vol. xiii, New York, Int. Univ. Press, 1958, 224-5.

32. E. Kestemberg, 'La psychanalyse des adolescents', *Psychiatrie de l'enfant,* vol. iii, fasc. 1, Paris, P.U.F., 1961, 298.

33. *Op. cit.,* 271 ff.

34. *Op. cit.,* 19.

35. 'Adolescence', *op. cit.,* 264.

36. Male, 'Étude psychanalytique de l'adolescent', *op. cit.,* 226.

3·General numerical data

A. Position of the numerical question

An examination of the figures is often placed at the beginning of studies on suicide. By virtue of the apparent precision and incontrovertibility of figures compared with the uncertainties of the theories concerning the causes of the process of the suicide act, they often form the main part of such studies. This is even more the case where adolescents, rather than adults, are concerned. But what value do these figures have? In spite of reservations as to their supposed precision, I shall follow the tradition, because:

1)   Although the published statistics do not express the real number of suicide acts, they do provide us with useful information for an interesting approach to the question. But they can lead one into error, and must be used with care.[1]

2)   The official figures are used in various ways to constitute the basic reference of the number of suicides, whereas in fact they make no claim to be so. The persistence of their use in such a context is itself worthy of interest, and constitutes one of the *données* of the question.

It is for these two reasons that the numerical data have been included in the first part of this book. But in referring to them as numerical, rather than statistical data, I wish to emphasize that I do not consider that they express the real number of suicide acts among adolescents. No exact statistics exist, to my knowledge, in France or in any other country. For similar reasons, although I refer to personal experience in my study of causes and processes, I am unwilling to publish personal statistics. As such they would be invalid, for my figures would concern only those cases that I have had the occasion to examine, and would not form a representative sample of the population of suicidal adolescents, whether in terms of the overall number, the means used, or the relative proportion of the sexes. Any extrapolation would be mere conjecture, and such a statistic would be devoid of value.

I have made use therefore only of numerical data from official sources, treating these not as the real number of suicides, but as the number of declared suicides. Figures published by the following sources have been used:

— The I.N.S.E.E. (Institut national de la statistique et des études économiques), which makes it clear that these statistics represent only the number of declared suicides on the basis of medical death certificates, and make no claim to express the real number of suicides. Nevertheless, they are the official statistics of deaths in France used by national and international authorities. Among the information supplied by the I.N.S.E.E., the absolute number of deaths for each cause of death, and the proportion attributed to each cause per thousand deaths, enable us to appreciate the relative importance and the position of suicide in relation to the various causes of death. But only the death rate per 100,000 inhabitants enables us to evaluate its absolute importance by eliminating factors of error arising from demographic variations, and to make comparisons between different years and different ages.

— The Compte Général de l'Administration de la Justice Criminelle records suicide acts, successful or unsuccessful, brought to the knowledge of the Courts. The number of deaths is higher than that indicated by the I.N.S.E.E., by virtue of the fact that certain suicides are recognized as such only after the judicial inquiry, and are not indicated as such on the death certificate (the source used by the I.N.S.E.E.).

— The statistics of the Département de la Seine provide information for the Paris area. The number of attempted suicides recorded there is higher than in the Compte Général de la Justice, because some have involved intervention by the Paris police, but have not led to a judicial inquiry.

— For the situation outside France, we have a number of sources, in particular the publications of the World Statistical Organization (W.S.O.), which collates the official data supplied by various countries.

— Scientific publications deal very little with overall estimates of deaths; they often draw on premature official sources or make use of incomplete data. On the other hand, they provide very interesting material about the means used, the anamnesia, and the psychological and social context of suicide attempts. However, each study is valid mainly for the group studied, and can hardly be extrapolated to general quantitative laws about suicide; each refers to a particular population sample, according to the place of recruitment (psychiatric hospital, prison, specialised institution), the activity of the subjects (students, servicemen), or the mode of hospitalization, which is often connected with the means used, such as, for example, the surgical units, which see only cases involving wounds, or the poison units, which see only cases involving serious, but not immediately fatal, intoxication.

In view of the object of my research, and the difficulties encountered in the study of the numerical data, I shall present these data over three chapters.

In the first chapter, I shall present the quantitative data for all ages, with a view to situating the suicide of adolescents in relation to suicide in general; this may help us to discern the similarities and differences. In the second, I shall present the numerical data for adolescent suicides as a whole, and in the third, I shall present the numerical data according to sex and according to the method used. Lastly, I shall supply a brief account of the available international data, and examine the possibility of estimating the real number of suicide acts among young people.

I have separated the numerical study from a consideration of possible causes, which I take up in Part III, so as to deal with them side by side with the theories and hypotheses advanced as to these causes.

B. Death by suicide: all ages

The position of suicide among the causes of death

In 1966, according to the I.N.S.E.E., 7,668 deaths by suicide were declared. In Table 1,[2] in which the main causes of death are classified in order of importance, we see that suicide occupies eleventh place, with a rate of 15 per 1,000 deaths and 16 per 100,000 inhabitants. It comes just after diabetes mellitus and before tuberculosis of the respiratory system, and accounts for a third more deaths than alcoholism, more than double the number from nephritis or leukaemia, over three times that from all infectious diseases, and two hundred and seven times more than that from poliomyelitis. It comes well behind acc:dents, which account for 67 deaths out of every 1,000 and 71 per 100,000 inhabitants. But if one takes road accidents alone, which accounted for 12,277 deaths, it represents 62% of that figure. This difference did not exist a few years ago: In 1963, there were 6,571 suicide deaths and 7,166 deaths from road accidents: the gap that has occurred is due to a greater increase in road deaths (about 5,000) than from suicide (about 1,000).

Table 1. Frincipal causes of deaths, all ages, in decreasing order of importance in 1966 (I.N.S.E.E.).

		Total	*per 100,000 inhabitants*	*per 1,000 deaths*
	Total number of deaths	525,497		
1	Heart diseases	98,622	200	188
2	Cancers	98,605	200	188
3	Cerebral vascular lesions	63,380	128	120
4	Accidents and other violent deaths	35,303	71	67
5	Vascular disorders	17,813	36	34
6	Cirrhosis of the liver	17,178	35	33
7	Diseases of respiratory system	15,649	32	30
8	Diseases of digestive system	14,228	29	27
9	Pneumonia, bronchitis	9,622	19	18
10	Diabetes mellitus	8,540	17	16
11	*Suicide*	*7,668*	*16*	*15*
12	Respiratory tuberculosis	5,950	12	11
13	Alcoholism	5,635	11	11
14	Various tumours	4,297	9	8
15	Leukaemia	3,444	7	7
16	Nephritis	3,311	7	6
17	Influenza	3,116	6	6
18	Infectious diseases	2,414	5	5
...				
	Poliomyelitis	37		

Table 2. Number of suicide deaths, all ages, per 100,000 inhabitants and position from 1953 to 1966 (I.N.S.E.E.).

Years	1953	1954	1955	1956	1957	1958	1959	1960	1961	1962	1963	1964	1965	1966
total number	6571	6973	6903	7577	7268	7391	7571	7223	7305	7112	7434	7207	7352	7668
number per 100,000 inhabitants	15	16	16	17	17	17	17	16	16	15	16	15	15	16
position	12	12	11	11	12	11	12	12	11	11	13	12	12	11

The figures for the last fourteen years (see Table 2[3]) show that the total number of declared suicide deaths increased from 1953 to 1966, but the rate per 100,000 inhabitants varies only between 15 and 17. Similarly, its rank among the causes of death varies only minimally between 11 and 13. And even these variations can be explained by the very variable role played by influenza in different years, suicide being placed before or after influenza according to the size of the epidemics. Respiratory tuberculosis, however, has diminished by 50%, and from being double the figure for suicide is now well below it, while diabetes mellitus is increasing and has exceeded suicide since 1963 (cf. I.N.S.E.E.). On the other hand, if we examine the proportion for 100,000 inhabitants over a long period (Table 3[4]), we see that it has tended to fall.

Table 3. Number of suicide deaths, all ages, per 100,000 inhabitants from 1906 to 1952 *(Problèmes)*.

1906	1907	1908	1909	1910	1911	1912	1913	1914	1915	1916	1917	1918	1919
20	23	21	22	22	22	23	23	22	16	15	14	16	17

1920	1921	1922	1923	1924	1925	1926	1927	1928	1929	1930	1931	1932	1933
19	19	–	–	–	19	19	19	19	18	19	19	21	20

1934	1935	1936	1937	1938	1939	1940	1941	1942	1943	1944	1945	1946	1947
22	20	20	–	–	–	19	18	13	11	11	12	11	13

1948	1949	1950	1951	1952
14	15	15	16	15

Table 4. Principal causes of death, for men of all ages, in decreasing order of importance in 1966 (I.N.S.E.E.).

		Total	per 100,000 inhabitants	per 1,000 deaths
	Total number of deaths	271,304	1,123	
1	Cancers	54,151	224	199
2	Heart diseases	48,772	202	179
3	Cerebral vascular lesions	27,991	116	103
4	Accidents	21,519	90	79
5	Cirrhosis of the liver	11,917	49	44
6	Diseases of respiratory system	8,987	37	33
7	Vascular disorders	8,693	36	32
8	Diseases of digestive system	7,013	29	25
9	Suicide	5,626	23	20
10	Alcoholism	4,422	18	16
11	Respiratory tuberculosis	4,388	18	16
12	Pneumonia, bronchitis	4,347	18	16
13	Diabetes mellitus	3,198	13	12
14	Various tumours	2,213	9	8
15	Hyperplasia of the prostate	1,922	8	7
16	Leukaemia	1,847	8	7
17	Nephritis	1,769	7	6
18	Infectious diseases	1,226	5	4
19	Influenza	1,186	5	4
20	Non-respiratory tuberculosis	327	1	1
...	....	...		
	Poliomyelitis	19		

During each of the world wars it diminished considerably — this is a well known fact — and then began to rise gradually. However, it never reached the figures of the previous period. Thus before 1914 it was about 22 per 100,000 inhabitants, between the two wars 20, and since 1950 between 15 and 17. What is the reason for this decline? Do the figures represent a real falling off in the number of suicides, a decline only in the number of declared suicides for reasons that remain unclear, or the appearance of other forms of voluntary deaths that do not appear in the statistics for suicide?

Suicide deaths according to sex

The difference in the number of suicide deaths according to sex is a very ancient notion and one that is worth mentioning here.

Table 5. Principal causes of death, for women of all ages, in decreasing order of importance in 1966 (I.N.S.E.E.).

		Total	per 100,000 inhabitants	per 1,000 deaths
	Total number of deaths	254,193	1,007	
1	Heart diseases	49,732	197	195
2	Cancers	44,454	176	175
3	Cerebral vascular lesions	35,389	140	139
4	Accidents	13,438	54	53
5	Vascular disorders	9,120	36	36
6	Diseases of digestive system	7,215	29	28
7	Diseases of respiratory system	6,662	26	26
8	Diabetes mellitus	5,342	21	21
9	Pneumonia, bronchitis	5,275	21	21
10	Cirrhosis of the liver	5,261	21	21
11	Various tumours	2,084	8	8
12	*Suicide*	*2,042*	*8*	*8*
13	Influenza	1,930	8	7
14	Leukaemia	1,597	6	6
15	Respiratory tuberculosis	1,562	6	6
16	Nephritis	1,542	6	6
17	Alcoholism	1,213	5	5
18	Infectious diseases	1,188	5	5
19	Non-respiratory tuberculosis	272	1	1
...	....	...		
	Poliomyelitis	18		

For the male sex, we see (Table 4[5]) that suicide ranks as the ninth most important cause of death, with 20 deaths out of 1,000 and 23 per 100,000 inhabitants, i.e. 25% more deaths than for tuberculosis or alcoholism (excluding cirrhosis of the liver), 75% more than diabetes mellitus, 3 times more than nephritis, hyperplasia of the prostate, or leukaemia, and over 4 times more than infectious diseases. In 1963, it occupied eleventh place, but has since exceeded pneumonia/bronchitis and respiratory tuberculosis, which have declined.

For the female sex, we see (Table 5[6]), that suicide occupies twelfth place, with 8 deaths out of 1,000 and 8 per 100,000 inhabitants, coming just before leukaemia, nephritis, and respiratory tuberculosis, with 60% more deaths than alcoholism, and 70% more than all infectious diseases.

In this brief examination of the figures for suicide for all ages, two factors minimize their real importance:

1) In terms of absolute value, I used only the declared deaths published by the I.N.S.E.E., with no mention of the possible real number of suicide deaths. It is true that the figures for all the causes contain numerical errors; there is a relatively high figure for undetermined causes, and some causes, such as influenza or diabetes, are more open to question than others. But it is fair to suppose that the error is greater in the case of suicide than for other causes of death.

2) In terms of relative value, some of the causes of death shown in the tables have been grouped together in categories, such as respiratory diseases, digestive diseases, tumours, infectious diseases. Detailed tables would give a relatively more important place to suicide.

Nevertheless, it is clear that suicide occupies an important place among the causes of death, and a more important one for men than for women (3 to 1), which we already knew, with a similar position to that of diabetes mellitus or respiratory tuberculosis, and a more important one than alcoholism, nephritis, leukaemia, or infectious diseases. Similarly, while it does not have the same importance as road accidents, it does represent an appreciable proportion.

What is the real importance of the number of suicide deaths? What is the real place of suicide among the causes of death? We are not in a position to answer these questions at present, but they should be asked. If we take the figures published by the Compte Général de la Justice[7] for 1964 (the latest year for which we have figures), we have 8,563 deaths (as against the I.N.S.E.E.'s 7,207), which would give 17 deaths per 1,000 (as against 14), and 18 deaths per 100,000 inhabitants (as against 15), and place it tenth in order (as against twelfth).

Lastly, an examination of the causes of death over a period of years shows that they tend to fall into two groups: on the one hand, those that decline as a result of diagnostic and therapeutic progress, such as tuberculosis, infectious diseases and surgical diseases, and on the other, those that are increasing. Among the latter, some are entirely increasing in real terms, accidents or diabetes mellitus, for example, while in other cases a real increase is accompanied by one due to an improvement in clinical and diagnostic knowledge. Moreover, the increase in certain causes is related to a decrease in others. Thus the treatment of certain children's diseases, which were once fatal, allow people to reach the age at which they may contract heart diseases or cancer. 'The increase in the number of cancers is a sign of improved health in the population.' Suicide is among the causes of death that are increasing and gaining in importance. This needs stressing, since, although the prohibition that prevented people from declaring suicide as a cause of death is certainly decreasing, it is doing so less rapidly than the improvements in diagnosis and treatment for other causes of death are increasing. Moreover, suicide among the elderly is not increasing, as we shall see.

C. Suicide attempts

Whatever reservations we may have in regard to the official number of suicide deaths these figures do exist, and, although lower than the real figures, they make possible the sort of comments that I have made above. Our information about suicide attempts is much more inadequate. The Compte Général de la Justice, the only official source, deals only, it should be remembered, with cases that have appeared before the courts. And this occurs far more frequently for deaths than for attempts — indeed, the figure for attempts is so low as to have no relation to reality.

Table 6[8] shows that for the whole of France the number of attempts recorded is 1/5 that of deaths for men and 3/5 for

Table 6. Suicide deaths and suicide attempts in 1964 (Compte Général de la Justice et Statistiques du Département de la Seine).

	Suicide attempts			Suicide deaths			Total suicide acts		
	M	F	All	M	F	All	M	F	All
France (Justice)	1216	1587	2803	6135	2428	8563	7351	4015	11,366
Seine (Justice)	449	830	1279	739	501	1240	1188	1331	2519
Seine (département)			2236			903	1483	1656	3139

Table 7. Number of suicides (deaths and attempts) in the departement de la Seine from 1954 to 1961.

Year	1954	1955	1956	1957	1958	1959	1960	1961
Total	3,069	3,012	2,954	2,623	2,622	2,732	2,744	2,831
Male	1,500	1,458	1,318	1,241	1,286	1,353	1,346	1,397
Female	1,569	1,554	1,436	1,382	1,336	1,379	1,398	1,434

women. On the other hand, in the Département de la Seine the number of attempts is over half that for deaths in the case of men, and well above the number of deaths in the case of women. This difference between France as a whole and the Seine is still more marked if we take the figures in the third line of Table 6, since they represent the number of attempts notified to the police but not brought before the courts; the fact that the number of deaths is lower in the departmental statistics than in those of the Ministry of Justice is explained, as I have already said, by the fact that some deaths are recognized as being due to suicide only after investigation.[9]

Oeconomo[10] has shown that the number of attempts recorded is proportionally higher in the Seine than in the rest of France, and explains this by the existence in the Seine of better means of recording attempts. In other words, the number of officially known attempts varies above all in relation to the administrative means of recording them. The lack of figures concerning attempts is not peculiar to France; in 1954, P.B. Schneider[11] insisted on this point, and deplored the fact that such figures did not exist, in particular in Switzerland. Without wishing to consider at this point the reasons for such a lack, it is perhaps worth mentioning that when Schneider tried to carry out a poll in French-speaking Switzerland, he was forced, somewhat bitterly, to admit defeat. No official document enables us to have even an approximate idea of the total number of attempts, either for a whole country or for a particular area. It is quite impossible therefore to evaluate the relationship between suicide attempts and suicide deaths. Thus, for the Seine, the published figures, which do not distinguish between deaths and attempts, strike me as being markedly lower than the number of attempts alone made in Paris each year.

If, putting official publications to one side, we refer to the
many scientific works on the subject, a few notions do seem
to emerge; but these are in the nature of hypotheses and
probabilities rather than affirmations. As far as the deaths/
attempts ratio is concerned, it would seem, according to
Deshaies,[12] to vary considerably: 2:1 in Italy, 5:1 in New
York, 4 or 5:1 in France. In his view, this ratio may vary
according to place, circumstances and factors of various
kinds, between 1 and 10. In France, according to a number of
authors, the ratio is often estimated at 10 attempts to 1 death.
This variation would have a certain importance if such
figures concerned the real number of suicide attempts, but
this is not the case. As we saw in Chapter 1, suicide deaths
and attempts must be studied separately, because some authors
use the same terms with different meanings, while in the case
of other authors, one cannot distinguish between the terms.
What I propose to do, then, is to examine the question as a
whole, making a distinction between the terms only at certain
points.

The partial studies on suicide attempts have also yielded
certain hypotheses as to the efficacity of the methods used:
hanging appears to be the most successful, and intoxication
the least — intoxication therefore figures highest in the number of attempts. This has even made it possible to establish
coefficients of efficacity according to method. Similarly, a
comparison between men and women has been possible, on
the supposition that the suicide attempt is proportionally
more frequent among women. Whereas women kill themselves less (sometimes quite considerably so), than men, the
gap is narrowed when deaths and attempts are taken together,
and for attempts alone women sometimes even exceed men.
It can be said that women try to kill themselves, but men do
kill themselves, more often. Lastly, it has been possible to
make observations on the relation between age and the
degree of success achieved. I shall return to this aspect in the
next chapter.

If we return to the relation between deaths and attempts
(in France from 5 or 10 to 1, according to different authors),
we have, for 1965, taking only the official figures of deaths

issued by the Compte Général de la Justice, between about 42,000 and 85,000 suicide attempts in France, which represents about 1 or 2 attempts per 1,000 inhabitants, a figure that is already quite high, and one that should be made much higher in relation to the real number of suicide deaths. But in any case we have seen that this relationship must be studied in relation to age, and this will lead us to our main subject, the suicide act among adolescents.

Notes

1. In particular, I should like to thank Dr Aubenque, the administrator of the I.N.S.E.E., for the indispensable information that he has provided.
2. I.N.S.E.E., *Études et Conjonctures*, Paris, P.U.F., no. 9, September 1967, 181, 188, and 196.
3. I.N.S.E.E., *op. cit.*, 195, and *Études statistiques*, Paris, P.U.F., no. 3, July—September 1964, 240.
4. M. and C. Moine, 'Étude statistique sur le suicide', *Problèmes*, Numéro spécial sur le suicide, no. 58-59, April—May 1959, 24.
5. I.N.S.E.E., *Études et Conjonctures*, 181, 189, and 196.
6. *Ibid.*, 181, 188, and 196.
7. Compte Général de l'Administration de la Justice civile et de la Justice criminelle, Melun, Imprimerie Administrative, 1966, 266.
8. *Ibid.*, 266.
9. *Annuaire statistique de la Ville de Paris et de la Seine, année 1964*, Paris, Imprimerie Municipale, 1967, 541.
10. 'Le comportement suicide et le problème de la tentative, *Revue de Science criminelle et de droit pénal comparé*, Paris, Librairie Siray, 1959, 814-16.
11. *La tentative de suicide*, Nauchâtel, Delachaux et Niestlé, 1954, 69-71.
12. *Psychologie du suicide*, Paris, P.U.F., 1947, 22.

4·Numerical data on adolescent suicides

In this chapter I shall examine the numerical data on the suicide act among adolescents as a whole, both sexes taken together. Deaths and attempts will be examined separately, as the conditions of enumeration of each are so different that no overall study is possible.

A. Adolescent suicide deaths

According to the figures issued by the I.N.S.E.E. for 1966, there were 17 declared deaths by suicide of persons between 10 and 14 years old, 153 for those between 15 and 19, and 256 for those between 20 and 24, that is, 409 for those between 15 and 24. This is obviously a small number in relation both to the total number of subjects of that age living in France in 1966, and to the total number of suicide deaths. But if we wish to situate these figures more precisely, and draw some kind of information from them, we can study them according to three parameters, which I shall now examine in turn: the total number of suicide deaths at different ages, suicide in relation to other causes of death at adolescence, and the development of the suicide death of adolescents in time.

The suicide death at adolescence and at other ages

In Table 8,[1] we see that for both sexes taken together the rate of suicide deaths increases steadily with age; those of adolescents represent only a small proportion of the total number of suicide deaths, that is, 2% between 15 and 19, 3.3% between 20 and 25, or 5.33% of the total of suicide

Table 8. Suicide deaths in 1966, according to age: absolute number, rate for each age group in relation to the total number of suicide deaths, rate per 100,000 inhabitants (I.N.S.E.E.).

Ages		all ages	10-14	15-19	20-24	25-29	30-34	35-39	40-44
Suicide deaths		7,668	17	153	256	325	452	493	667
% of total suicides			0.2	1.9	3.3	4.2	5.8	6.4	8.7
Suicides per 100,000 inhabitants		16		4	8	11	14	20	21

Ages	45-49	50-54	55-59	60-64	65-69	70-74	75-79	80-84	85+
Suicide deaths	582	705	935	895	787	515	390	308	182
% of total suicide	7.5	9.2	12.2	11.6	10.2	6.7	5.0	4.0	2.2
Suicides per 100,000 inhabitants	24	29	34	35	37	36	40	56	57

deaths; this figure corresponds to only 2/5 of the theoretical average of 6.25% by five-year groups, or 12.5% by ten-year groups. The difference is even sharper if one makes the comparison not by means of the general theoretical average, but with the number of suicide deaths at later ages. Adolescent suicides then represent only 24% of those between 50 and 60, or 60 and 70, and 58% of those between 75 and 85; if one compares the death rate per 100,000 inhabitants between 15 and 25, that is, 6, to that of older age groups, the proportion is still lower: it represents only 18% of the rate of 32 for the 50-60 age group, 16% of the rate of 36 for the 60-70 age group, and 12% of the rate of 53 for the 75-85 group.

This merely confirms the traditional notion that adolescence is the period of life during which one dies least from suicide and partly explains why the matter has attracted so little attention. But it is seen in a different light if we examine it according to other parameters.

The suicide death in relation to other causes of death in adolescence.

Out of 1,256 deaths of persons aged between 10 and 14, 17 were declared to be by suicide; out of 3,147 between 15 and 19, 153; and out of 3,578 between 20 and 24, 256.

The tables[2] summarizing the main causes of death in adolescence show that, between the ages of 10 and 14 (Table 9), suicide occupies only eleventh place, coming well behind the main causes of death: accidents, cancer, leukaemia, heart diseases, etc.; it occupies a position similar to that of nephritis and cerebral vascular lesions, and is well ahead of diabetes mellitus, tuberculosis, and poliomyelitis.

In the 15-19 age group (Table 10), it comes immediately after accidents and cancer but is 20% more common than leukaemia, double the figure for heart diseases, 4 times that for nephritis, 11 times that for influenza, 15 times that for respiratory tuberculosis, 25 times that for other forms of tuberculosis, and 51 times that for poliomyelitis.

Table 9. Principal causes of death, in decreasing order of importance, in the 10-14 age group, 1966 (I.N.S.E.E.).

		Total	per 100,000 inhabitants	per 1,000 deaths
	Total number of deaths	1,256	31	
1	Road Accidents	275	13	218
2	Other Accidents	234	13	186
3	Cancers	98	3	78
4	Leukaemia	96	3	76
5	Various tumours	44	1	35
6	Diseases of digestive system	33	1	26
7	Heart diseases	31	1	24
8	Infectious diseases	26	1	20
9	Diseases of respiratory system	22	1	17
10	Nephritis	18	1	14
11	*Suicide*	*17*	*1*	*13*
12	Cerebral vascular lesions	16	1	12
13	Vascular disorders	14	1	11
14	Pneumonia, bronchitis	13	1	11
15	Influenza	8	—	6.3
16	Diabetes mellitus	5	—	3.9
17	Cirrhosis of the liver	3	—	2.3
18	Respiratory tuberculosis	1	—	0.7
19	Non-respiratory tuberculosis	1	—	0.7
..	. . . .	. . . . .		
	Poliomyelitis	2	—	1.5

In the 20-24 age group (Table 11), it comes immediately after accidents, and is 20% higher than cancer, 3 times higher than heart diseases, 4 times higher than leukaemia, 5 times higher than nephritis, 16 times higher than respiratory tuberculosis, 32 times higher than other forms of tuberculosis, 51 times higher than influenza, and 256 times higher than poliomyelitis. Only accidents are higher than suicide.

Thus, if one excludes deaths by accident, the number of declared deaths by suicide for the 15-19 age group is second after cancer, and, for the 20-24 group, first among all causes except accidents. If one takes the figures in percentage form, we see that declared suicides accounted for 4.9% of all deaths in the 16-19 age group, and for 7.1% in the 20-24 age group.

Table 10. Principal causes of death, in decreasing order of importance, in the 15-19 age group, 1966 (I.N.S.E.E.).

		Total inhabitants	per 100,000	per 1,000 deaths
	Total number of deaths	3,147	73	
1	Road accidents	1,063	43	338
2	Other accidents	725	43	230
3	Cancers	182	4	58
4	*Suicide*	*153*	*4*	*48*
5	Leukaemia	128	3	41
6	Heart diseases	74	2	23
7	Various tumours	64	2	20
8	Diseases of digestive system	46	1	14
9	Infectious diseases	38	1	12
10	Nephritis	36	1	11
11	Cerebral vascular lesions	34	1	11
12	Diseases of respiratory system	34	1	11
13	Vascular disorders	25	1	8
14	Pneumonia, bronchitis	25	1	8
15	Influenza	14	1	4.4
16	Diabetes mellitus	10	1	3.1
17	Respiratory tuberculosis	10	1	3.1
18	Non-respiratory tuberculosis	6	—	1.9
19	Cirrhosis of the liver	5	—	1.6
20	Alcoholism	2	—	0.6
...	....	....		
	Poliomyelitis	3	—	0.9

If one excludes death by accident, which for reasons that I shall return to later should be studied separately, declared suicides account for 11.2% of non-accidental deaths in the 15-19 age group, and for 16.7% in the 20-24 group. Taking the two groups together to form a 15-24 group, suicide accounts for 6% of all deaths, and 14% of non-accidental deaths.

It now becomes interesting to take up once again the question of the place of the suicide death in adolescence in relation to other age groups, not in terms of absolute number, nor of death rate per 100,000 inhabitants, but in proportion to other causes of death (Table 12). Whereas adolescent suicide deaths represent a relatively unimportant proportion of the total number of suicides, and a small ratio per 100,000

Table 11. Principal causes of death, in decreasing order of importance, in the 20-24 age group, 1966 (I.N.S.E.E.).

		Total	per 100,000 inhabitants	per 1,000 deaths
	Total number of deaths	3,578		
1	Road accidents	1,311	60	366
2	Other accidents	737	60	205
3	*Suicide*	*256*	*8*	*71*
4	Cancers	201	6	56
5	Heart diseases	75	3	2.1
6	Diseases of digestive system	67	2	1.9
7	Leukaemia	62	2	1.7
8	Nephritis	46	1	1.2
9	Various tumours	45	1	1.2
10	Infectious diseases	43	1	1.2
11	Cerebral vascular lesions	42	1	1.2
12	Vascular disorders	36	1	1
13	Diseases of respiratory system	22	1	0.6
14	Respiratory tuberculosis	15	1	0.4
15	Pneumonia, bronchitis	11	1	0.3
16	Diabetes mellitus	10		0.3
17	Non-respiratory tuberculosis	8	—	0.2
18	Alcoholism	8	—	0.2
19	Influenza	5	—	0.1
20	Cirrhosis of the liver	3	—	0.1
..	Poliomyelitis	1	—	0.02

inhabitants (4 for the 15-19 age group, and 8 for the 20-24 age group, compared with the 35 in the 60-64 age group, 40 in the 75-79 group, and 57 in the over 85 group), it occupies a most important place among the causes of adolescent death after accidents. The percentages indicated in Table 12 show that it is in youth that suicide represents the higher proportion of deaths, according to a progression that reaches its peak not in adolescence but between the ages of 30 and 34. Thereafter this percentage declines, and at 50 is merely half what it was at 20, and 1/10 what it is among the over 70s, for in that group it represents only .8% of all deaths. If we exclude accidental deaths, we accentuate not only the propor-

Table 12. Suicide deaths in 1966: absolute number, rate per 100 deaths, including and excluding accidents, position including accidents (I.N.S.E.E.).

Ages	All ages	10-14	15-19	20-24	25-29	30-34	35-39	40-44	45-49
Total deaths	525,497	1,256	3,147	3,578	3,513	4,741	7,298	10,575	11,894
Suicide deaths	7,668	17	153	256	325	452	493	667	582
Accidental deaths	34,957	509	1,788	2,048	1,549	1,591	1,711	1,679	1,434
Non-accidental deaths	490,540	747	1,359	1,530	1,964	3,150	5,587	8,899	10,460
% with accidents	1.5	1.3	4.9	7.1	9.2	9.5	6.8	6.3	4.9
% without accidents	1.5	2.3	11.2	16.7	16.5	14.3	8.8	7.5	5.6
Position	11	10	3	2	2	3	5	5	5

Ages	50-54	55-59	60-64	65-69	70-74	75-79	80-84	85+
Total deaths	18,527	31,985	46,226	59,367	65,485	76,558	77,795	83,435
Suicide deaths	705	935	895	787	515	390	308	182
Accidental deaths	1,650	2,136	2,205	2,217	2,088	2,754	3,201	4,388
Non-accidental deaths	16,877	29,849	44,021	57,150	63,397	74,804	74,594	79,047
% with accidents	3.8	2.9	1.9	1.3	0.8	0.5	0.4	0.2
% without accidents	4.2	3.1	2	1.4	0.8	0.5	0.4	0.2
Position	6	6	10	12	13	14	15	15

tion of deaths due to suicide, but also the difference between the age groups.

While the exclusion of accidents considerably alters the relative importance of suicide among the young, especially in the 25-29 age group, it does not do so in the older age groups. Thus, while on average, for all ages, 1.5 deaths out of 100 is declared to be by suicide, the corresponding figure for the 15-25 age group is 6. It can be said therefore that although in absolute terms, and in relation to the adolescent population as a whole, suicide does not play an important role, and that adolescence is the period when one dies least from suicide, it is nevertheless the most important cause of death after accidents. These facts are revealed in Fig.1, which shows the position of suicide in the death rate per 100,000 inhabitants, and as a percentage of deaths, in terms of age.

Fig. 1. Suicide, according to age: rate per 100,000 inhabitants, rate per 100 deaths from all causes, including and excluding accidents.

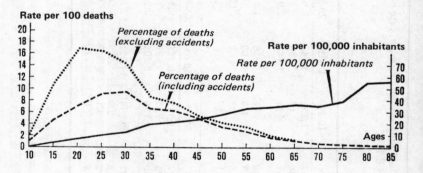

The development in time

The development in time of the quantitative importance of adolescent suicide deaths is difficult to estimate: in addition to the usual difficulties involved in the use of old statistics, there are the difficulties caused by variations in the age limits from one publication to another; some include children, others stop at 15, 16 or 18, thus making all comparison impossible.

I can thus do no more than provide an incomplete picture of the situation.

The limitation of the research carried out in recent years makes it possible to use figures that are mutually comparable. But there is still the danger of dealing with insignificant periodical variations. Thus, in figures for 1963 one notes a sudden increase (from 10 to 20) in suicide deaths in the 10-14 age group. But a study of 12-year-olds, based not on absolute numbers but on the proportion per 100,000 inhabitants, shows that this increase hardly exceeds the periodical variations, shown in Fig.2.

Fig. 2. Variations in the suicide rate per 100,000 inhabitants from 1954 to 1965.

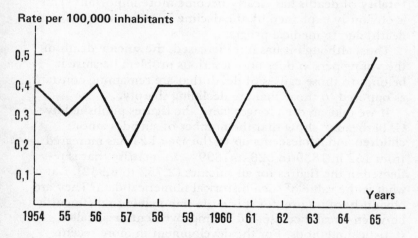

Even if we confine ourselves to the last seven years, the death rate per 100,000 inhabitants, which eliminates errors due to demographic variations (Table 13), shows that for the 10-25 age group the number of declared suicide deaths varies very little.

Taking a longer view we see in Table 14 that for the years 1936, 1946, 1957 and 1966, the death rate by suicide per 100,000 inhabitants declined, but then tended to rise again,

Table 13. Rate of suicide deaths per 100,000 inhabitants in the 10-14, 15-19 and 20-24 age groups.

Ages	1960	1961	1962	1963	1964	1965	1966
10-14	0.2	0.4	0.4	0.2	0.3	0.5	0.4
15-19	3.7	4.3	3.4	3.7	3.0	3.6	3.5
20-24	6.4	6.7	6.8	7.5	7.7	6.9	8.2

and that the proportion of suicide deaths of young people per 100 suicide deaths of all ages varied only in the 20-24 age group, where it declined, and then tended to rise again.

On the other hand, the number of declared suicide deaths out of 100 deaths from all causes doubled or tripled. Table 14 confirms that in absolute terms the number of declared suicide deaths has not increased over the past thirty years, and sometimes has even declined, but that its place in the totality of deaths has clearly become more important. This is obviously explained by the decline in other causes of death, due to medical progress.

Thus, although it has not increased, the suicide death of the young person does pose a serious problem because it belongs to those causes of death that are remaining constant, as opposed to those that are declining sharply.

If we take an even longer view, the figures published by G. Barbeaux[3] show that the number of suicides among children and adolescents up to the age of 21 has increased from 152 in 1839 to 526 in 1899 — an increase that is reflected in the figures for all suicides (2,752 to 8,952). But what is the value of such historical numerical data? They are obviously of no use, for it is quite impossible to distinguish between a real increase and an improvement in so-called statistical methods. For the development in more recent years, notably with regard to the quantitative decrease after World War II, the same questions present themselves as for suicide deaths at all ages. Does the decrease represent a real decline in the number of suicide deaths, a greater gap between the real number and the number declared (for reasons that remain to be elucidated), or the appearance of new means of voluntary death that are necessarily excluded from the statistics on suicide deaths?

Table 14. Rate of suicide deaths in the 10-14, 15-19, and 20-24 age groups, per 100,000 inhabitants, per 100 suicides, and per 100 deaths, for the years 1936, 1946, 1957, and 1966.

	10–14			15–19			20-24		
	per 100,000 inhabs.	per 100 suicides	per 100 deaths	per 100,000 inhabs.	per 100 suicides	per 100 deaths	per 100,000 inhabs.	per 100 suicides	per 100 deaths
1936	0.4	0.15	0.3	5.9	2	2.5	9.9	4	2.6
1946	0.5	0.20	0.2	2.5	2.2	1.6	6.5	4.6	2.3
1957	0.2	0.10	0.6	3.5	1.5	4.8	6.0	2.7	6.6
1966	0.4	0.22	1.3	3.5	1.99	4.9	8.2	3.3	7.1

Table 15. Total number of suicides (deaths and attempts) up to the age of 21 in 1963 and 1964 (Compte Général de la Justice).

		16			16–18			18–21		
		All	M	F	All	M	F	All	M	F
1963	France	55	21	24	153	78	73	394	229	165
	Seine	7			23			47		
1964	France	59			117			540		
	Seine	6			21			45		

B. Adolescent suicide attempts

The absence of numerical data is even worse in the case of adolescent suicide attempts than for suicide attempts in general. The Compte Général de la Justice[4] does not, for the different age groups, distinguish between the sexes; it does, however, distinguish between deaths and attempts. But the number of attempts shown is so low as to be hardly worth taking into account. Thus Table 15 shows that the courts dealt with 602 suicide acts (deaths and attempts taken together) in 1963, and 716 in 1964 for the whole of France, and 87 in 1963, and 72 in 1964 for the Département de la Seine. It is clear that the number of cases brought before the Courts bears no relation to the real number of suicide acts. One has only to recall that between 1 May 1961 and 1 May 1962 Gaultier and his colleagues[5] at the Hôpital Fernand-Widal dealt with 95 subjects under the age of 21, that is, more than the number indicated by the Compte Général de la Seine. And it should be added that the Hôpital Fernand-Widal deals only with serious cases of intoxication that are not immediately fatal, which excludes less serious cases of intoxication, and attempts by other means. Similarly, in my own work and that of colleagues who deal with suicidal adolescents, the number that each of us examines is close to, or even exceeds, that indicated by the Compte Général de la Justice.

In estimating the number of attempts and the ratio of attempts to deaths, one can do no more than suggest hypotheses. These vary from author to author, but all agree that the ratio of attempts to deaths is between 1:10 and 1:50. To take only the declarations of death collected by the I.N.S.E.E., we have between 4,000 and 20,000 suicide attempts in the 15-25 age group.

Although I have no adequate means of checking the figures, it seems to me that the truth is much nearer to 20,000 than to 4,000, excessive as that may seem. According to a number of polls — they have of course no statistical value — it would seem that among those attending French *lycées* alone there are over 5,000 suicide attempts a year. This estimate concerns only subjects for the most part under the age of 18 attending a state secondary school. If one adds those aged between 18 and 25, and those who are not attending such an establishment, one would very probably reach the highest figure that I have proposed.

Scientific publications have provided me with a great deal of information that I shall use in later chapters. But two points are worth mentioning here.

— *The frequency of recidivism.* Out of a group of 167 cases, Duché[6] notes recidivism in 35% of the cases, distributed as follows:

		Boys	Girls	Total
2nd attempt	25%	12	31	43
3rd attempt	6%	5	5	10
4th attempt and +	4%	4	3	7

The recidivist is therefore not rare, and we find a similar proportion in the figures published by Fau and his colleagues,[7] and by Gaultier and Gorceix.[8] Launay and Col[9] estimate that recidivists survive in 10 to 20% of cases. A number of authors emphasize the fact that a first attempt may be harmless and subsequent ones serious and even fatal.

— *The number of attempts in relation to age.* It would seem, as Oeconomo[10] has shown, that the number of attempts is proportionally, and even absolutely, higher among the young, and that with age the number of attempts diminishes while the number of deaths increases. One might say with Deshaies, then, that the propensity of suicide is as high among the young as the old, but that the old are more successful in their attempts at self-destruction. The increase in the number of deaths would reflect, therefore, a greater efficacity in the means used, and not an increase in the number of suicide acts. 'A phenomenon of maturation would seem to lead to suicide, while a state of maturity would seem to guarantee its successful execution.'[11]

The numerical change in the number of attempts in accordance with age is the kind of question that is of particular interest to me, for it goes well beyond the statistical framework, and penetrates to the very heart of the significance of the suicide act. If we take the various figures suggested, and add the suicide deaths to the suicide attempts, to produce the rate of suicide acts per 100,000 inhabitants, we have, according to the deaths/attempts ratios used, from 140 (a ratio of 1:10) to 650 (1:50) suicide acts in the 15-25 age group, and from 92 (1:4) to 230 (1:10) in the 40-50 age group. I have chosen the 40-50 group as a term of comparison because the deaths/attempts ratio decreases with age, and this age group seemed to correspond most closely (according to the graphs) to the average ratios suggested. Thus, although these figures have only an indicative value, and do not represent definite facts, they do suggest that people in the 15-25 age group commit at least as many suicide acts as those in the 40-50 group, and, quite probably, as those in any other age group. They would seem to confirm that what differentiates older subjects from younger subjects is their greater efficacity, and not a great number of suicide acts. Of course, this consideration is of little interest if one regards the suicide death and the suicide attempt as being different in nature. But it takes on a particular, and very important significance if one accepts the notion of the unity of the suicide act.

Notes

1.   I.N.S.E.E., *Études et conjonctures,* Paris, P.U.F., no. 9, September 1967, 184 and 186.

2.   *Ibid.,* 183-6 and 188-9.

3.   G. Barbeaux, *Le suicide chez les enfants,* thesis, Paris, 1910, no. 175.

4.   Compte Général de l'Administration de la Justice civile et de la Justice criminelle, Melun, Imprimerie Administrative, 1966, 266.

5.   M. Gaultier, E. Fournier, A. Gorceix and N. Zimbacca, 'Etude clinique et statistique d'un groupe de mineurs suicidants', *Semaine des Hôpitaux,* no. 50, 8 November 1963, 2375.

6.   D.J. Duché, 'Les tentatives de suicide chez l'enfant et l'adolescent', *Psychiatrie de l'enfant,* Paris, P.U.F., 1964, vol. vii, fasc. 1, 51.

7.   R. Fau, R. Château, and M. Machu, 'Le suicide chez l'adolescent, à propos de 23 observations medico-psychologiques', *Annales Médico-psychologiques,* t. I, no. 1, January 1965, 13.

8. Gaultier *et al.*, *op. cit.*, 2378.
9. C. Launay and C. Col, 'Suicide et tentative de suicide chez l'enfant et l'adolescent', *Revue du Praticien*, t. xiv, no. 6, 21 February 1964, 623.
10. J.C. Oeconomo, 'Le comportement suicide...,' *Revue de Science criminelle et de droit pénal comparé*, Paris, Librairie Sirey, 1959, 821.
11. G. Deshaies, *Psychologie du suicide*, Paris, P.U.F., 1947, 22.

5. Numerical data according to sex and method

A. Numerical data according to sex

We have seen that in 1966, 5,624 suicide deaths were declared
for men and 2,042 for women, that is, a ratio of 2.75 men to
1 woman. For the 10-24 age group, the figure is 299 boys and
127 girls — a ratio of 2.35 to 1. The difference in suicide
deaths according to sex, although slightly less, is to be found
among the young as among other age groups; the figure
varies from year to year, but in 1965 it was 3 men to 1
woman for all ages, and 1.87 boys for 1 girl in the 10-25 age
group. Can a study according to sex help us to uncover the
signification of these facts? I propose to take the three
parameters that I have already used: the importance of
suicide among the young in relation to suicide as a whole,
the rank of suicide among the causes of death, and the proportion of suicide to be found in 100 deaths for each age
group.

Male suicide deaths among the young

Table 16[1] shows that in 1966, for the male sex, there were
15 declared suicide deaths in the 10-14 age group, 106 in the
15-19 group, and 178 in the 20-24 group. These figures follow
a familiar progression that reaches its maximum at about the
age of 55. They represent a small proportion of the total
number of suicide deaths, namely, .26% of the 10-14 group,
1.88% in the 15-19 group, and 3.16% in the 20-24 group, of
the 5,624 male suicide deaths.

Table 16. Male sex, total number of deaths, total number of suicides, rate per 100,000 inhabitants, proportion of suicides per 100 deaths, including and excluding accidents, position in 1966 (I.N.S.E.E.).

Ages	All ages	10-14	15-19	20-24	25-29	30-34	35-39	40-44	45-49
100,000 inhabitants	23	1	5	10	16	20	22	32	35
Total deaths	271,304	772	2,238	2,258	2,484	3,256	4,860	7,010	7,793
Total suicides	5,624	15	106	178	252	344	380	523	433
Total accidents	21,519	359	1,400	1,663	1,261	1,365	1,431	1,379	1,149
% with accidents	2	2	4.7	7	10.1	10.6	7.8	7.5	5.6
% without accidents	2.3	3.6	12.6	19.9	20.6	18.4	11	9.2	6.5
Position	9	8	4	3	3	3	5	6	6

Ages	50-54	55-59	60-64	65-69	70-74	75-79	80-84	85 +
100,000 inhabitants	43	52	53	57	53	65	94	98
Total deaths	12,275	21,762	30,916	37,309	33,742	34,989	30,824	26,856
Total suicides	517	707	660	570	325	217	220	120
Total accidents	1,286	1,681	1,631	1,463	1,062	1,106	1,004	1,042
% with accidents	4.2	3.2	2.1	1.5	1	0.8	0.7	0.4
% without accidents	4.7	3.5	2.2	1.6	1	0.8	0.7	0.5
Position	7	7	12	13	14	15	14	14

Table 17. Principal causes of death, in decreasing order of importance, for males in the 10-14 age group in 1966 (I.N.S.E.E.).

		Total	per 100,000 inhabitants	per 1,000 deaths
	Total number of deaths	772	37	
1	Other accidents	203 ⎫	17	263
2	Road accidents	156 ⎭		202
3	Cancers	60	3	78
4	Leukaemia	55	3	71
5	Various tumours	19	1	25
6	Diseases of digestive system	18	1	23
7	Heart diseases	16	1	21
8	*Suicide*	*15*	*1*	*19*
9	Infectious diseases	14	1	18
10	Diseases of respiratory system	14	1	18
11	Vascular disorders	13	1	17
12	Cerebral vascular lesions	10	1	13
13	Nephritis	9	—	12
14	Pneumonia, bronchitis	6	—	8
15	Influenza	4	—	5
16	Diabetes mellitus	3	—	4
17	Cirrhosis of the liver	1	—	1.3
18	Non-respiratory tuberculosis	1	—	1.3
19	Respiratory tuberculosis	0	—	
..	. . . .			
	Poliomyelitis	2	—	2.6

But if, as for suicide deaths as a whole, we place them among the various causes of death, we see that:

In Table 17,[2] suicide occupies eighth place among boys between 10 and 14 — which, despite a small absolute number, is similar to the position it occupies for males of all ages, namely ninth.

It accounts for 5 times more deaths than diabetes mellitus, 7 times more than poliomyelitis, while there are no deaths from respiratory tuberculosis and only 1 from other forms of tuberculosis.

In Table 18,[2] it occupies fourth place among boys between 15 and 19, that is, second place among the non-accidental

Table 18. Principal causes of death, in decreasing order of importance, for males in the 15-19 age group in 1966 (I.N.S.E.E.).

		Total	per 100,000 inhabitants	per 1,000 deaths
	Total number of deaths	2,238	102	
1	Road accidents	785 ⎫	64	351
2	Other accidents	615 ⎭		275
3	Cancers	115	5	51
4	*Suicide*	*106*	5	47
5	Leukaemia	76	4	34
6	Heart diseases	47	2	21
7	Various tumours	41	2	18
8	Diseases of digestive system	32	2	14
9	Nephritis	25	1	11
10	Infectious diseases	21	1	9.4
11	Cerebral vascular lesions	21	1	9.4
12	Diseases of respiratory system	20	1	8.9
13	Vascular disorders	16	1	7.1
14	Pneumonia, bronchitis	15	1	6.7
15	Influenza	8	—	3.6
16	Respiratory tuberculosis	4	—	1.8
17	Diabetes mellitus	4	—	1.8
18	Non-respiratory tuberculosis	2	—	0.9
19	Alcoholism	2	—	0.9
20	Cirrhosis of the liver	2	—	0.9
..	....			
	Poliomyelitis	2	—	0.9

causes of death, immediately after cancer, with a number 20% higher than that for leukaemia, twice that for heart disease, 13 times that for influenza, 26 times that for respiratory tuberculosis, and 53 times that for poliomyelitis or non-respiratory tuberculosis.

In Table 19,[3] it occupies third place among male deaths in the 20-24 age group, or first place among non-accidental causes of death, accounting for half as many more deaths as cancer, nearly 4 times more than heart disease, 20 times more than respiratory tuberculosis, 25 times more than other forms of tuberculosis, 35 times more than diabetes mellitus, while no deaths were due to poliomyelitis. It emerges that although

Table 19. Principal causes of death, in decreasing order of importance, for males in the 20-24 age group in 1966 (I.N.S.E.E.).

		Total	per 100,000 inhabitants	per 1,000 deaths
	Total number of deaths	2,558	147	
1	Road accidents	1,057⎫	96	413
2	Other accidents	606⎭		437
3	*Suicide*	*178*	*10*	*70*
4	Cancers	126	7	49
5	Heart diseases	46	3	18
6	Leukaemia	44	3	17
7	Diseases of digestive system	31	2	12
8	Various tumours	26	2	10
9	Nephritis	25	1	10
10	Infectious diseases	21	1	8.2
11	Vascular disorders	19	1	7.4
12	Cerebral vascular lesions	13	1	5.1
13	Diseases of respiratory system	13	1	5.1
14	Respiratory tuberculosis	9	1	3.6
15	Non-respiratory tuberculosis	7	—	2.7
16	Pneumonia, bronchitis	7	—	2.7
17	Alcoholism	6	—	2.3
18	Diabetes mellitus	5	—	2
19	Cirrhosis of the liver	3	—	1.2
20	Influenza	3	—	1.2
..	....			
	Poliomyelitis	0	—	0

declared suicide among young males is low in terms of absolute number, or in relation to the death rate for 100,000 inhabitants, it occupies a high place among the non-accidental causes of death, the second in the 15-20 age group, first in the 20-35 group, thereafter gradually declining until it occupies a very low place among the older age group.

If we translate the figures into percentages, we see that declared suicide accounts for 2% of deaths in the 10-14 age group, 4.7% in the 15-19 group, and 7% in the 20-24 group. If we exclude accidental deaths, it represents 3.6% of non-accidental deaths in the 10-14 age group, 12.6% in the 15-19 group, and 19.9% in the 20-24 group, the highest proportion

Table 20. Female sex, total number of deaths, total number of suicides, rate per 100,000 inhabitants, proportion of suicides per 100 deaths, including and excluding accidents, position in 1966 (I.N.S.E.E.).

Ages	All ages	10-14	15-19	20-24	25-29	30-34	35-39	40-44	45-49
100,000 inhabitants	8	—	2	5	5	7	7	9	12
Total deaths	254,193	484	909	1,020	1,029	1,505	2,438	3,565	4,101
Total suicides	2,042	2	47	78	73	108	113	144	149
Total accidents	13,438	150	388	385	288	226	280	300	285
% with accidents	0.8	0.4	5.2	7.6	7	7.2	4.6	4	3.6
% without accidents	0.8	0.6	9	12.3	9.9	8.4	5.2	4.4	3.9
Position	12	14	5	3	4	3	5	5	6

Ages	50-54	55-59	60-64	65-69	70-74	75-79	80-84	85 +
100,000 inhabitants	15	15	17	17	16	15	18	20
Total deaths	6,252	10,223	15,310	22,058	31,743	41,569	46,971	56,579
Total suicides	188	228	235	217	190	119	88	62
Total accidents	364	455	574	754	1,026	1,648	2,197	3,346
% with accidents	3	2.2	1.5	1	0.6	0.3	0.2	0.1
% without accidents	3.2	2.3	1.6	1	0.6	0.3	0.2	0.1
Position	6	8	11	12	15	18	18	17

Table 21. Principal causes of death, in decreasing order of importance, for females in the 10-14 age group (I.N.S.E.E.).

		Total	per 100,000 inhabitants	per 1,000 deaths
	Total number of deaths	484	24	
1	Road accidents	119	6	246
2	Leukaemia	41	2	85
3	Cancers	38	2	78
4	Other accidents	31	2	64
5	Various tumours	25	1	52
6	Heart diseases	15	1	31
7	Diseases of digestive system	15	1	31
8	Infectious diseases	12	1	25
9	Nephritis	9	1	18
10	Diseases of respiratory system	8		16
11	Pneumonia, bronchitis	7		14
12	Cerebral vascular lesions	6		12
13	Influenza	4		8
14	*Suicide*	2		*5*
15	Diabetes mellitus	2		5
16	Cirrhosis of the liver	2		5
17	Respiratory tuberculosis	1		2
18	Vascular disorders	1		2
19	Non-respiratory tuberculosis	0		0
..	. . . .			
	Poliomyelitis	0		0

being in the 25-29 group, namely 20.6%. We are a long way, then, from the 1.96% of deaths from all causes, and the 2.12% of non-accidental deaths attributed to suicide for all ages.

Female suicide deaths among the young

Table 20[4] shows that in 1966, 2 deaths were declared to be by suicide in the 10-14 age group, 47 in the 15-19 group, and 78 in the 20-24 group, thus following the same progression in relation to age as for males. In percentage terms, these figures represent respectively .1%, 2.3%, and 3.82% of the 1,865 declared suicide deaths among females.

Table 22. Principal causes of death, in decreasing order of importance, for females in the 15-19 age group (I.N.S.E.E.).

		Total	per 100,000 inhabitants	per 1,000 deaths
	Total number of deaths	909	43	
1	Road accidents	278⎫	19	306
2	Other accidents	110⎭		121
3	Cancers	67	3	74
4	Leukaemia	52	3	57
5	*Suicide*	47	2	*52*
6	Heart diseases	27	1	30
7	Various tumours	23	1	25
8	Infectious diseases	17	1	19
9	Diseases of respiratory system	14	1	15
10	Diseases of digestive system	14	1	15
11	Cerebral vascular lesions	13	1	14
12	Nephritis	11	1	12
13	Pneumonia, bronchitis	10		11
14	Vascular disorders	9		10
15	Respiratory tuberculosis	6		7
16	Influenza	6		7
17	Diabetes mellitus	6		7
18	Non-respiratory tuberculosis	4		4
19	Cirrhosis of the liver	3		3
20	Alcoholism	0		0
··	·······················			
	Poliomyelitis	1		1

Table 21[4] shows that in the 10-14 age group suicide occupies fourteenth place among the causes of death. Yet, despite its low position, it accounts for as many deaths as diabetes mellitus and double the number for poliomyelitis or non-respiratory tuberculosis.

Table 22[3] shows that for the 15-19 age group it occupies fifth place, or second place among non-accidental causes of death, after cancer and leukaemia, but before heart disease, accounting for 8 times more deaths than diabetes mellitus, influenza or respiratory tuberculosis, 12 times more than other forms of tuberculosis, and 47 times more than poliomyelitis.

Table 23[3] shows that for the 20-24 age group it occupies

Table 23. Principal causes of death, in decreasing order of importance, for females in the 20-24 age group (I.N.S.E.E.).

		Total	per 100,000 inhabitants	per 1,000 deaths
	Total number of deaths	1,020	63	
1	Road accidents	254 ⎫	25	249
2	Other accidents	131 ⎭		128
3	*Suicide*	*78*	*5*	*76*
4	Cancers	75	5	74
5	Diseases of digestive system	36	2	35
6	Heart diseases	29	2	28
7	Infectious diseases	22	1	21.6
8	Nephritis	21	1	20.5
9	Cerebral vascular lesions	19	1	18.6
10	Various tumours	19	1	18.6
11	Leukaemia	18	1	17.6
12	Vascular disorders	17	1	16.7
13	Diseases of respiratory system	9		8.8
14	Respiratory tuberculosis	6		5.9
15	Diabetes mellitus	5		4.9
16	Pneumonia, bronchitis	4		3.9
17	Influenza	2		2
18	Alcoholism	2		2
19	Non-respiratory tuberculosis	1		1
20	Cirrhosis of the liver	0		
..	. . . .			
	Poliomyelitis	1		1

first place after accidents, accounting for 4 times more deaths than leukaemia, 13 times more than respiratory tuberculosis, 15 times more than diabetes mellitus, with only 1 death from non-respiratory forms of tuberculosis.

The same observations can be made about the figures for the female as for the male sex: though low in absolute terms, and in relation to the death rate per 100,000 inhabitants, suicide deaths occupy an important position among the causes of death in the 15-25 age group, third in the 15-19 group and first in the 20-24 group among the non-accidental causes of death, while occupying a very low place in older age groups.

Fig. 3. Suicide according to age, for the male sex: rate per 100,000 inhabitants, rate per 100 deaths from all causes, including and excluding accidents.

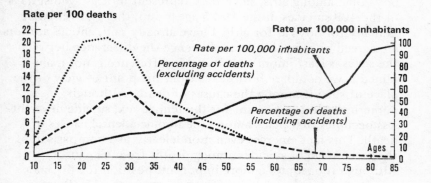

Fig. 4. Suicide according to age, for the female sex: rate per 100,000 inhabitants, rate per 100 deaths from all causes, including and excluding accidents.

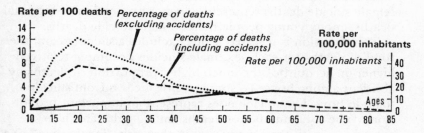

Figs. 3 (for males) and 4 (for females) show the difference according to whether one regards suicide in terms of its rate per 100,000 inhabitants, or in terms of its importance per 100 deaths in each age group.

In relation to all deaths in each age group, suicide represents .4% in the 10-14 group, 5.2% in the 15-19 group, and 7.6% in the 20-24 group. Of non-accidental deaths, suicide represents .6% in the 10-14 group, 9% in the 15-19 group, and 12.3% in the 20-24 group. Again, we are a long way from the .8% of all causes and .84% of non-accidental deaths for all ages.

Comparison of male and female suicide deaths among the young

On the whole, suicide deaths are much more frequent among
boys than among girls, since they represent 69% as against 31%
of the 409 suicides in the 15-25 age group, that is, over twice
as many for boys as for girls. I have already said, and all authors
are agreed on this, that at adolescence the difference between
the sexes is least important. But this difference is not maintained if we compare both sexes from the point of view of the
place of suicide among the causes of death. Although
numerically less important for the female sex, suicide nevertheless occupies first place among the non-accidental causes of
death. This fact emerges even more clearly in a comparison of
the percentage of suicides among deaths from all causes.
Although it occupies a more important position for the male
sex, it accounts for only 4.76% of deaths in the 15-19 age
group and 6.12% in the 20-24 group, while for the female sex
it accounts for 5.2% of deaths in the 15-19 group, and 7.6% in
the 20-24 group. So, although lower as a death rate for 100,000
inhabitants (5 and 10 on the one side, 2 and 5 on the other),
female suicide deaths represent a higher proportion of the total
deaths among young people than do male suicide deaths.

This situation is reversed if one excludes accidents from the
total of deaths for each sex, male suicides becoming relatively
higher on account of the much higher proportion of deaths by
accident among boys. To sum up, girls die less from suicide
than do boys, but suicide does represent an important proportion of the total number of deaths among girls. This is in
accordance with the general notion that girls die less than boys
- the number of male deaths between the ages of 15 and 25 is
over double that for girls. But here we are touching on
questions that lie outside the scope of this book, questions
concerning the frequently discussed notion that mortality is
higher among males than among females, whatever the cause,
and that the difference is even more marked at adolescence
than at other periods. For if one excludes deaths by accident,
the difference is far smaller, namely, 1,733 male deaths as
against 1,156 female deaths between the ages of 15 and 25.
The fact remains, therefore, that the cause that is responsible

for the higher number of deaths among boys in relation to girls is violent death, whether by accident or suicide.

Comparison of male and female suicide attempts among the young

The difficulty in making a numerical estimation of suicide attempts is more than usually apparent when one wishes to make a comparison of the two sexes. We cannot refer to any overall figure, official or otherwise. All we have at our disposal are figures provided by scientific publications on the basis of particular samples. And it is quite impossible to take these as evidence of a general relation in the number of suicide attempts between the sexes. I would refer the reader to these various publications, in particular to that of Duché,[4] who quotes figures suggested by various other authors. In general, three points emerge.

1) The boy-girl ratio. For some authors, attempts are more frequent among boys, but most authors find that girls equal or well exceed boys in the proportion of 2 to 1. But any numerical study based on the method used by a sample should be treated with reserve, for we do know the frequency of various suicide methods used according to sex. There are works such as those by Gaultier *et al.,*[5] Jacobnizer, Tuckmann, etc., that deal exclusively with attempts by poisoning; since poisoning is a particularly female method, it is normal to find a majority of girls among those using it. For six years I have myself examined subjects admitted into a surgery department after suicide attempts, and I have always found a majority of males, both among adolescents and adults. Then there are publications based on samples collected in a general hospital that deals with all forms of suicide attempts, or in a psychiatric department. These correspond more to the overall picture, but again we have to know the criteria of hospitalization used in each case if we are to discover whether the sample is representative of suicide attempts as a whole, and whether it can help us in making any comparison between the sexes.

2) The number of attempts appears to increase at a later age

among girls than among boys, but when it increases it does so to a greater degree.

3) The dramatic increase in the number of attempts in recent years would thus seem to be due mainly to the increase of the number of attempts among females. Several hypotheses may throw light on this apparent numerical increase on the female side:

The present psycho-social development of girls may provide more grounds for attempts than previously. But it may also be that the various harmless attempts made by girls by excessive, but not really dangerous use of medicaments for example, lead more frequently than they used to to a psychiatric examination, either out of fear of the possible toxic results of the product absorbed, or out of a concern to understand the psychological significance of even a harmless attempt.

In any case, whatever the exact figures may be, it seems that girls attempt suicide relatively more often than boys, but that the death/attempt ratio is markedly different for each. In other words, although there are more suicide attempts among adolescent and adult females, the males die more often. In the absence of real figures, we have only hypotheses to go on, the possible significance of which has still to be elucidated.

B. Suicide methods

The various methods used in the suicide act have always been a source of lively interest to specialists. But I intend to be brief on this point, indicating simply the numerical data provided by the usual documents and the obvious lessons that can be derived from them. I shall leave over to the next chapter any discussion of the possible use of these figures to estimate the real proportion of the methods used, or to throw light on the suicide act itself.

Despite the abundant literature on suicide in general, we possess very few documents on the numerical data according to method - or rather, very few that are of any use here.

— *For all suicide acts,* deaths and attempts taken separately and together, we have at our disposal the Compte Général de la Justice, whose findings are summarized in Table 24. It does

Table 24. Suicide methods for attempts, deaths and total number of suicide acts (according to age: all ages, 16-18 and 18-21). (Compte Général de la Justice.)

Total: all methods	All ages			16-18			18-21		
	Attempts	Deaths	Total	Attempts	Deaths	Total	Attempts	Deaths	Total
	2803	8563	11366	100	77	177	227	313	540
1-2 Analgesic and soporific substances	23.65	7.22	11.28	41	18.18	31.07	33.03	11.50	20.55
3 Gas	26.82	14.04	16.29	10	14.28	11.86	18.50	8.30	12.77
4 Hanging, strangulation	12.70	41.67	35.41	–	14.28	6.21	4.84	34.82	22.22
5 Drowning	10.06	17.42	15.60	19	24.67	21.46	17.18	23.64	20.92
6 Firearms	8.45	12.11	11.20	14	15.84	14.67	7.04	11.50	9.64
Sharp or pointed instruments	6.42	1.77	2.92	6	1.29	3.95	7.92	1.27	4.07
Falling from a high place	4.49	4.30	4.35	7	6.49	6.77	7.04	6.07	6.48
Others	5.77	2.59	3.38	3	5.19	3.95	4.40	2.55	3.33

Table 25. Suicide methods (deaths) according to age in 1963 (I.N.S.E.E.).

Total suicide deaths	All ages			15-19			20-24		
	All	M	F	All	M	F	All	M	F
	7,434	5,543	1,891	138	87	51	212	139	73
1 Barbiturates	2.75	1.73	5.76	4.34	0	11.76	4.24	2.87	6.84
2 Other analgesic and soporific substances	0.82	0.61	1.42	1.44	2.29	0	2.35	0.71	5.47
3 Gas	6.44	4.61	11.79	8.62	5.74	13.72	8.96	7.19	12.32
4 Hanging/strangulation	49.93	55.42	33.89	27.60	36.78	11.76	26.41	34.53	10.95
5 Drowning	13.45	10.21	22.95	13.76	9.19	21.56	13.20	10.79	17.80
6 Firearms	11.39	14.43	2.48	23.91	28.73	15.68	18.86	23.73	9.58

not distinguish between males and females according to age
group. Although it does distinguish between deaths and
attempts, it cannot be used to determine the real number of
attempts, or the ratio of attempts to deaths, on account of the
particularly low proportion of attempts recorded.

—*For suicide deaths alone,* we have the data provided by the
I.N.S.E.E. These, which are reproduced in Table 25, corrobo-
rate the situation as outlined by the various authors on the
subject.

Hanging is the most frequent method used, followed by
firearms, drowning and gas, with poisoning coming last. In
relation to suicide deaths at all ages, firearms appear with
markedly greater frequency, as does poisoning; gas is a little
less frequent; while hanging/strangulation and drowning are
markedly less frequent, nearly half as much. The preference
according to sex is similar for the young and all ages, though
in sometimes different proportions. Thus the number of
deaths by firearms is shown to be greater for boys than for
girls, but with less wide a difference than that between adult
men and women. The greater frequency of male deaths
caused by hanging/strangulation is more marked among adolescents than among adults. Poisoning, whether chemical or
by gas, appears more often among girls than boys, and with
a more marked difference than among adults. On the other
hand, the number of deaths by drowning is higher for women
than for men, but the ratio remains constant at all ages.

— Is any comparison possible between the figures issued
by the Ministry of Justice and those of the I.N.S.E.E.?
Theoretically, such a comparison should enable us to make
a study of both deaths and attempts. But we always come up
against the same obstacle: the figures published by the Ministry
of Justice are far from representative of the number of attempts
and such a study would bear no relation to reality.

— We are particularly lacking in numerical data on the
methods used in attempts. The only figures are to be found
in the scientific publications. There are certainly a great
many of these, but very few are suitable for my purposes.
For various reasons, they have had to be discarded:

Very few provide figures for the age group with which we

Table 26. Percentage of various methods in suicide attempts according to certain authors.

Authors	Ages	Means in %										
		Total number	Toxic substances	Gas	Hanging/ strangulation	Drowning	Firearms	Sharp or pointed instruments	Falling	Cutting of veins	Combined methods	Various
Fau et al.	13–23	23	56.5	8.6	—	—	—	—	8.6	21.7	—	—
Szymanska	10–18	100	44	12	14	2	—	2	6	17	—	1
Duché	13–18	141	47.5	4.9	13.4	—	—	1.4	—	7.8	19.8	—

are concerned. When specifying the means used, they include adolescents either with adults or with children. Only the study carried out by Fau and his colleagues[6] concerns adolescents alone, but this refers only to 23 subjects. Duché's study[7] combines children and adolescents, but it is presented in such a way that it is easy to distinguish subjects over the age of 13; but, again, it would be extremely hazardous to draw conclusions as to the use of the various methods on the basis of such a sample.

To my knowledge, no work has been done on adolescents admitted to a general hospital. Such a sample would appear to be more representative, but it would still be subject to strong reservations. Apart from the fact that only certain attempts are brought to the attention of the hospital, the socio-demographic characteristics of the area of recruitment are not without their influence; the work of B. Castets[8] is a fine example of this. Although it deals with all cases of attempted suicide admitted to the Hôpital Necker, the characteristics of the area are such that the majority is made up of adolescent or young adult women of a social status in which poisoning is likely to be more than usually frequent.

However, in Table 26, by way of illustration I have reproduced the figures to be found in three publications. They have no more than an indicative value, and cannot be regarded as statistical evidence, since they are all influenced by special conditions. Those of Fau and his colleagues[9] concern only a small number of cases, and these were all admitted into a single specialized hospital department, and therefore with a prior selection. The same can be said of those published by Duché,[10] while those of Szymanska and Zelazowska[11] do not distinguish between children and adolescents. As one can see, poisoning ranks first, followed by the cutting of veins, hanging/strangulation, falling, and gas.

Compared with the figures for deaths, we see, as we already knew, that the various methods occupy a different place, sometimes in inverse order. This only goes to confirm the obvious fact that certain methods are more lethal than others.

Can we derive more precise information from this numerical data on the suicide act, whether death or attempt? This question contains two others:

1) Can we estimate the real proportion of the various methods, whether for death or for attempt? This apparently simple question is in fact highly complicated. Generally speaking, it is on the subject of methods that the statistics seem to me to be most open to question. So many factors intervene that would first have to be analysed before we could go on to interpret the existing numbers. On the other hand, this analysis might help us to understand the errors contained in the other statistics on suicide.

2) Can the numerical data help us to understand the nature and significance of the suicide act? Some authors consider that the study of methods and their frequency would make it possible to explain the suicide act, and in particular to distinguish between the suicide death and the suicide attempt; the choice of method would indicate whether death was really desired or not. Similarly, some authors have tried to establish a relation between method and personality, and even the psychological process, to ascertain whether or not it is pathological.

It can be stated, because it is obvious enough, that certain methods require less preparation, and are therefore more likely to be resorted to on impulse than as a result of a long premeditated decision to commit suicide. It is also known that the methods that require least preparation are also the least lethal, and fit in therefore with the various conditions just referred to. Similarly, as we saw in the preceding chapter, the adolescent makes as many suicide attempts as the adult, but dies less, and appears to make greater use of the less lethal methods. But is it the inadequacy of the method that prevents him from killing himself, or his desire to live that makes him choose a less lethal method? At this stage, it does not seem that we can carry this investigation much further. Before we can answer the two questions, we must first criticize the numerical data as a whole.

Notes
1.   I.N.S.E.E., *Études et conjonctures*, Paris, P.U.F., No. 9, September 1967, 184 and 188.
2.   *Ibid.*, 183, 184 and 188.
3.   *Ibid.*, 185, 186 and 189.
4.   D.J. Duché, 'Les tentatives de suicide chez l'enfant et l'adolescent', *Psychiatrie de l'enfant*, Paris, P.U.F., 1964, vol VII, fasc. 1, 17-18.
5.   M. Gaultier *et al.*, Étude clinique et statistique d'un Groupe de mineurs suicidants', *Semaine des Hôpitaux*, no. 50, 8 November 1963, 2376.
6.   R. Fau, R. Château and M. Machu, 'Le suicide chez l'adolescent, à propos de 23 observations médico-psychologiques', *Annales Médico-psychologiques*, t.1, No. 1, January 1965.
7.   *Op. cit.*
8.   Castets, 'Note sur 350 observations de tentatives de suicide', *Recherches sur les Maladies Mentales*, vol. II, 1963, Paris, Imprimerie Municipale, 273-93.
9.   *Op. cit.*, 13.
10.   *Op. cit.*, 38-43.
11.   Z. Szymanska and S. Zelazowska, 'Suicides et tentatives de suicide des enfants et des adolescents', *Revue de Neuropsychiatrie infantile*, No. 12, December 1964, 731.

6· Foreign numerical data and a critique of the numerical data

I will later attempt to make some kind of critique of various figures for suicide among young subjects in France, and will examine to what extent it is possible, on the basis of existing figures, to estimate the real number of suicides. But before doing so, it might be useful to take a brief look at the figures for other countries; it may be that certain comparisons will lend support to our hypotheses.

A. Foreign numerical data

The numerical data for other countries, as for France, always concern the number of declared suicides, and not the real numbers; their correct use would necessitate a prior detailed study for each country of the conditions in which they are collected. A full statistical study is therefore not possible within the limits of this book and would merely extend it to a quite disproportionate degree, to doubtful advantage. I shall confine myself, then, to providing a brief examination of the situation in a number of countries, on the basis of the figures published by the World Health Organization, and to making a few comparisons, whose value is only of an indicative kind and which should be treated with caution. For as the W.H.O. report puts it, 'the real frequency of suicide is difficult to determine. Because of the diversity of the methods of certifying the causes of death, of recording, and of coding, as well as other factors that impair the universality and completeness of the data, any comparison between countries is impossible.'[1] For the same reasons, I shall deal only with suicide deaths; I shall not approach the subject of attempts, for it is quite impossible to establish an adequate critique of the various publications on the suicide attempt in each country.

— *The general position of suicide.* 'Suicide comes third, fourth or fifth, according to country, in a list of the causes of death among persons aged between 15 and 44, in certain countries of North America, Europe and Oceania; in 1964, it accounted, on average, for about 6.5% of all deaths in that age group, with an average death rate of 10 per 100,000 inhabitants.'[2] This is confirmed in Table 27,[3] which also shows that suicide is among the first ten causes of death, even for subjects in the 5-14 age group in six countries. As in France, then, suicide is one of the chief causes of death in industrialized countries.

— *Suicide rates per 100,000 inhabitants.* The overall trend is shown in Table 28.[4] For all these countries taken together, the suicide rate per 100,000 inhabitants increases with age, that of the 15-24 group being lower than that for all ages taken together. Compared with 1956, 1965 shows a slight increase in the rate for all ages. But, and this fact needs stressing, this increase is due solely to the increase among young subjects aged between 15 and 44, the rate for the older age groups being on the decrease. Moreover, it concerns male subjects, the rate for female subjects having only slightly increased.

The position for subjects in the 15-24 age group is similar in each of the countries shown in Table 29,[1] but in variable proportions; in certain countries, such as Japan, the figures for this age group are roughly equal to those for all ages, while in others the ratio goes from 2:3 to 1:2, or, as in Belgium, Denmark, France, the Netherlands, and Sweden, the ratio is markedly wider.

If we compare the rates per 100,000 inhabitants of declared suicide deaths, according to the 27 countries shown, we see that for all ages, both sexes taken together, the first ten countries come in the following order: West Berlin, Hungary, Austria, Czechoslovakia, West Germany, Finland, Denmark, Sweden, Switzerland, with France and Belgium sharing tenth place. This order is noticeably different if we compare the rates in the 15-24 age group. West Berlin and

Table 27. Position of suicide among the ten principal causes of death in certain countries (W.H.O.).

Countries	All ages	5—14	15—44
North America, Europe, Oceania			
Canada	10	—	4
U.S.A.	10	—	4
Austria	7	10	3
Belgium	10	—	4
Denmark	6	—	3
Finland	6	10	3
France	8	—	4
West Germany	7	9	3
Greece	—	—	6
Hungary	7	9	3
Republic of Ireland	—	—	10
Italy	—	—	6
Netherlands	—	—	4
Norway	10	—	4
Poland	—	—	5
Portugal	—	—	6
Sweden	6	—	3
Switzerland	7	7	3
England and Wales	8	—	4
Northern Ireland	—	—	5
Scotland	—	—	4
Australia	7	—	4
New Zealand	10	—	4
Africa, Central America, South America, Asia			
Mauritius	—	—	—
U.A.R.	—	—	—
Chile	—	—	9
Colombia	—	—	10
Costa Rica	—	—	9
Guatemala	—	—	—
Mexico	—	—	—
Nicaragua	—	—	—
Panama	—	—	6
Paraguay	—	—	10
Porto Rico	—	—	6
China	8	10	2
Hong Kong	9	—	5
Israel	10	—	4
Japan	8	—	3
Philippines	—	—	—

Table 28. Average mortality rates through suicide per 100,000 inhabitants, according to sex and age for certain countries in 1956 and 1965 (W.H.O.).

Year	All ages	15-24	25-34	35-44	45-54	55-64	65-74	75+
1956								
All	10.4	5.4	8.5	12.8	22.1	25.8	27.3	26.9
M	15.7	6.4	12.7	17.6	30.0	34.8	44.1	46.2
F	7.2	4.0	4.6	8.1	13.0	16.3	16.4	9.6
1965								
All	10.8	6.4	11.2	13.5	19.4	23.2	26.1	24.2
M	15.6	9.3	15.9	19.0	28.6	35.5	36.8	44.4
F	7.3	3.7	6.9	9.3	12.1	16.6	14.1	13.8

Hungary remain in the lead, but other countries enter the list: Japan (4th), Venezuela (8th), and Australia (10th). France falls to 18th.

— *Rate of suicide deaths per 1,000 deaths.* In Table 30,[5] we see that in all countries, as in France, suicide deaths account for an important proportion of deaths from all causes in the 15-24 age group, and that the proportion decreases with age. For all countries taken together, the proportion is second highest in this 15-24 group, that for the 25-34 group occupying the first place. The proportion for the 15-24 group also occupies the same second position in a number of countries, and in some, such as West Berlin, Greece, Hungary, Poland, and Switzerland, it even occupies the first position. It occupies only the third place, after the 35-44 group, in Denmark, France, Sweden, Northern Ireland, Australia, and New Zealand.

It should also be noted that it represents over 10% of deaths from all causes in the 15-24 age group in 10 countries out of 27, rising to 25% in Hungary and 37% in West Berlin.

— *Difference in the number of suicide deaths, according to sex.* If we take the rate of suicide deaths per 100,000 inhabitants, the proportion for all ages taken together is 2 male suicides to 1 female suicide. This disproportion is even more marked in the 15-24 age group, where it reaches almost 3:1 for all countries, with variations from country to country, the ratio often being 2:1, 3:1 and even 4:1. The only exceptions

Table 29. Mortality rate per 100,000 inhabitants for certain countries, all ages, and 15-24 age group, sexes taken together and separately (W.H.O.).

Countries	All ages			15—24		
	All	M	F	All	M	F
All countries	10.8	15.6	7.3	6.4	9.3	3.7
Canada	8.8	12.9	4.5	5.7	9.0	2.3
U.S.A.	11.1	16.3	6.1	6.2	9.4	3.0
Venezuela	6.4	9.2	3.5	10.2	13.1	7.4
Israel	6.6	7.7	5.5	4.1	5.9	2.1
Japan	14.7	17.3	12.2	13.5	15.3	11.7
Austria	22.8	32.0	14.7	11.9	18.7	4.9
Belgium	15.0	20.7	9.6	6.5	9.1	3.9
Czechoslovakia	21.5	31.2	12.3	16.6	13.6	9.4
Denmark	19.3	24.0	14.7	8.0	10.4	5.4
Finland	19.8	32.2	8.1	9.4	14.7	3.9
France	15.0	23.0	7.5	5.0	6.2	3.6
West Germany	20.0	26.8	13.8	12.6	18.1	6.7
West Berlin	41.3	51.7	33.5	24.7	32.9	15.4
Greece	3.2	4.4	2.1	3.7	3.8	3.5
Hungary	29.8	42.6	17.9	21.1	30.3	11.6
Italy	5.4	7.8	3.1	2.7	3.3	2.0
Netherlands	6.9	8.5	5.3	2.7	4.2	1.1
Norway	7.7	11.8	3.6	3.8	5.8	1.8
Poland	9.0	14.9	3.4	8.0	12.3	3.6
Portugal	9.1	14.9	3.7	4.0	5.5	2.7
Sweden	18.9	27.7	10.1	8.1	10.9	5.2
Switzerland	18.4	27.5	9.7	11.7	17.6	5.7
England and Wales	10.8	12.7	9.0	4.5	6.3	2.6
Northern Ireland	4.8	5.9	3.7	2.5	4.1	0.8
Scotland	8.0	9.3	6.8	3.6	3.7	3.6
Australia	14.9	18.8	10.8	8.6	10.6	6.4
New Zealand	9.1	12.1	6.1	4.9	5.9	3.8

to the rule are Japan, Greece and Scotland, which record almost as many suicides among women as among men.

On the other hand, this difference is less marked if one refers, in Table 31,[5] to the rate of suicide deaths per 1,000 deaths. For all countries, and for all ages, the figure for male suicides is double that for female suicides, and this proportion is also found in most countries, with the exception of Japan and Northern Ireland, where the figures for the sexes are

Table 30. Suicide rate per 1,000 deaths in certain countries, sexes taken together (W.H.O.).

Countries	All ages	15–24	25–34	35–44	45–54	55–64	65–74	74+
All countries	11	67	83	51	28	14	6	2
Canada	11	59	86	59	31	14	4	1
U.S.A.	11	55	80	51	27	13	6	2
Venezuela	10	79	48	30	13	9	4	1
Israel	10	55	92	45	28	13	4	1
Japan	21	151	117	50	30	19	12	6
Austria	18	133	154	109	56	28	11	4
Belgium	12	75	87	56	33	18	9	4
Czechoslovakia	22	175	158	110	54	24	11	5
Denmark	19	118	212	137	74	30	8	3
Finland	20	119	166	98	53	21	9	1
France	15	61	94	65	42	23	10	4
West Germany	17	130	141	92	53	24	9	4
West Berlin	23	372	339	160	82	31	12	5
Greece	4	42	26	19	16	4	2	1
Hungary	30	249	218	143	85	33	14	8
Italy	6	33	34	26	16	9	4	1
Netherlands	9	37	78	36	30	13	6	2
Norway	8	59	99	60	27	12	4	1
Poland	12	93	83	55	29	11	4	1
Portugal	9	45	52	37	26	14	7	2
Sweden	20	143	206	152	83	32	9	3
Switzerland	19	162	153	119	61	26	11	3
England and Wales	9	66	94	58	28	12	6	2
Northern Ireland	5	49	71	55	15	8	2	0
Scotland	6	52	69	36	20	10	3	1
Australia	16	73	137	89	43	16	7	2
New Zealand	10	51	41	56	39	14	6	1

Table 31. Suicide rate per 1,000 deaths, all ages and for the 15—24 age group, sexes taken together and separately (W.H.O.).

Countries	All Ages			15—24		
	All	M	F	All	M	F
All countries	11	15	8	67	61	73
Canada	11	15	7	59	66	39
U.S.A.	11	15	7	55	58	49
Venezuela	10	13	6	79	69	96
Israel	10	12	8	55	59	48
Japan	21	22	19	151	130	192
Austria	18	25	12	133	145	99
Belgium	12	16	9	75	75	74
Czechoslovakia	22	29	13	175	169	190
Denmark	19	22	16	118	113	130
Finland	20	29	11	119	116	127
France	15	21	8	61	59	65
West Germany	17	22	13	130	131	129
West Berlin	23	28	18	372	400	300
Greece	4	5	3	42	31	67
Hungary	30	40	19	249	253	240
Italy	6	7	3	33	30	41
Netherlands	9	10	7	37	39	33
Norway	8	11	4	59	59	56
Poland	12	19	5	93	103	69
Portugal	9	13	4	45	36	61
Sweden	20	27	12	143	134	165
Switzerland	19	27	11	162	171	137
England and Wales	9	10	8	66	65	70
Northern Ireland	5	5	4	49	32	85
Scotland	6	8	5	52	52	54
Australia	16	18	13	73	61	105
New Zealand	10	12	9	51	33	108

almost equal, and Poland, where female suicides represent only a quarter of male suicides.

If we take the 15-24 age group, the gap is considerably narrowed. Of the 27 countries listed, it is lower than 20% for 7 countries, and is even inverted, the number of female suicides being higher than that of male suicides in 13 countries and in all the countries taken together.

This brief examination of the data for other countries has revealed data similar to those for France. In many countries, the number of male suicides is higher than the number of female suicides of whatever age; but the rate per 1,000 deaths alters this situation, since women die less whatever the cause of death. Similarly, we find that the number of suicides is lowest in the younger age groups, but that it is the most important cause of death in those age groups. It can be said, therefore, that declared suicide deaths represent one of the major causes of death among the young in all industrialized countries.

B. The possibilities of estimating the real number of suicides

I have used the official numerical data, while repeatedly emphasizing that they represent only the number of declared suicides, and not the real number of suicides. Because of the gap that exists between the two, we should ask ourselves what value can be placed on the information derived from them, and whether they can be regarded as scientific facts or as mere hypotheses. We should also ask ourselves whether it is possible to estimate even approximately the real number of suicide acts.

— *The value of the known numerical data.* The gap between the official number and the real number depends on various factors, two of which are immediately apparent. The first concerns the quality of the statistical methods generally employed. As these methods improve, it is reasonable to expect (though not, of course, certain) that the figures for suicide will benefit as much as any other set of figures. In France, for example, the number of deaths from unspecified causes decreases each year in favour of precise causes. The other factor depends on the possibility of estimating the number of concealed suicides, whether deliberately concealed by those close to the person concerned or by the suicide himself, or cases where the method used leaves a degree of uncertainty as to intention, as, for example, in certain voluntary violent deaths that may look like accidents.

Can one agree with Oeconomo[6] that one can make comparisons and establish accurate relations on the basis of erroneous numerical data, because the error acts in a constant, identical manner over the various terms of the factors? I do

not think so, and I believe that factors of error affect calculations in a variable way and undermine the validity of certain
studies and comparisons; these can only have value as hypothetical indications and not as certainties. I shall not refer
again to all the numerical data that I have used, but will
illustrate this point with three examples; comparisons in time,
comparisons according to the method used, and comparisons
between countries.

As for comparisons in time, it is a fact that the absence of
true statistical methods in earlier periods renders earlier figures
suspect, and the apparent increase in the number of suicides
between 1839 and 1899 is evidence above all of improved
methods of recording. But I have also said that present-day
conditions have made possible the appearance of new methods
of suicide that elude the statistics. In any case, comparisons
in time are open to question, on account of the secondary
consideration of motive, as A. Bayet[7] has shown: 'We are
absolutely ignorant as to whether the Stoic attitude that
reigned in Rome within a certain elite appreciably increased
the total number of suicides, nor do we know whether suicide
was rare in the Middle Ages or merely concealed . . . Suicide
comes out into the open when repression declines . . . but
nothing allows us to say whether it has really become more
common.'

The same can be said of comparisons between countries.
If the industrialized countries record more suicides than others
it may be because only they have anything resembling proper
statistical methods. Similarly, there are sociologists who,
observing that countries with Protestant majorities have a
higher rate than countries with Catholic majorities, have con-
cluded that Protestantism favours suicide. But it may simply
be that Protestant countries are more honest in the compilation
of their figures on suicide, either because they are more
rigorous and scrupulous in face of a disagreeable truth, or
because Protestantism is less severely condemnatory of suicide.

The numerical data on suicide methods seem to me to be an
even better illustration of the influence of the errors they contain as to the known number of suicides and the interpretation
of the suicide act. It is obvious that certain methods are fully

indicative of the suicidal nature of the act, whereas others are open to doubt. Thus hanging can hardly leave much doubt as to intention; firearms can leave much more (it can be ascribed to an accident); drowning and poisoning may often leave some doubt. It is quite possible that the known proportion of certain methods may be related, not only to their efficacity and to the real frequency of their use, but to the fact that their use leaves no doubt as to the subject's intentions, whereas others may be included among accidents, miscellaneous diseases or unknown causes, and may appear in the official records under these three headings. They exercise an influence, therefore, on the total number of suicides recorded and on the proportion attributed to the various methods.

Equally questionable, it seems to me, is the attempt to establish a dichotomy between death and attempt in relation to method. To the affirmation that some do not die because they use harmless methods, one could answer that they do not die because the method used has proved less effective. This is certainly true, of course, but it becomes erroneous if placed in a general context. This is particularly important in the case of adolescents, who, as we have seen, commit as many suicide acts as adults, but who die less. Many factors intervene in the death rate, and to attribute it to the choice of harmless methods alone would be over-hasty. And, indeed, all authors insist on the need to use great care in estimating this choice. In particular, Gaultier and his colleagues[8] stress the non-correlation between the size of the dose taken of a toxic substance and the intention to die - the taking of an inadequate dose may be due to lack of information. We have also seen that impulsive, emotive suicides are less well prepared and use less effective methods. And this is often the case with young suicides, which might partly explain the higher proportion of non-fatal acts in the younger age groups.

The attempt to correlate personality and method is no less questionable. It is purely illusory in the case of deaths, especially in relation to adolescents, the majority of whom were not regarded as pathological before the act and had not therefore been examined. Thus diagnosis can only be *post mortem*, and the dangers of such an approach are well known.

For example, we know how often a pre-schizophrenic may be regarded as normal by those around him, and this very lack of recognition may play a role in the determination of the act.

Thus we can see that the numerical study of methods teaches us more about the means by which suicide is detected than about suicide and the person committing suicide. Generally speaking, the numerical data provide us with certain information, but they also contain within themselves causes of error that are an obstacle to the understanding of suicide; these causes of error seem to play an even more important role in the figures for adolescent suicide than in those for suicide as a whole.

— *Estimating the gap between the official and the real number of suicides.* Is it possible, then, to estimate, even approximately, the real number of adolescent suicides in France - that is to say the approximate number of concealed suicides that should be added to the 409 suicide deaths in the 15-24 age group declared in 1966? I have found no study that deals with this subject, and much of the information needed is lacking. Thus we are reduced to our own personal reflexions and those collected orally from various specialists.

The first question that presents itself is whether there are as many, fewer or more suicides concealed among adolescents than among adults. Some specialists believe that the proportion is about the same in each case, while others believe that suicide is more often concealed in adolescent cases. Personally, I share the second position. Suicide death in the young may be more often concealed for three reasons:

— The family, especially the parents, have stronger motives for concealing the suicide of an adolescent than have the family and/or neighbours of an adult.

— In the case of young people below the age of 21, there is the fear on the part of those responsible for the young person that they will also be held responsible, to a greater or lesser degree, for the suicide of that person. Not only do the adults in the environment in which the adolescent was living at the time of the suicide act feel, rightly or wrongly, concerned, and fear being held morally responsible, but there is also the question of legal responsibility, especially when the adolescent is in an educational or specialized institution. This possibility often places the heads of such establishments in a difficult position with regard to suicide.

— Finally, the young person is more inclined than the adult to perform acts that may give the act of suicide the appearance of an accident, in particular accidents involving driving or sporting activities. All those who, for one reason or another, have to deal with adolescent suicide have come up against a greater number of suicides attributed to 'accidental' death among adolescents than among adults; indeed, the accident has often been announced in advance by the individual concerned. There would appear, then, to be more concealed suicides among the young than among adults - and this does not take into account unconscious suicide, which, in the form of an unsuccessful act, provokes an unconsciously desired accident. This last aspect is not only particularly difficult to estimate on the statistical level, but on the theoretical plane it poses the delicate problem of the concept of suicide.

So we do not know by how much we should increase the official figure to approach the real number of suicide deaths in the 15-24 age group. Opinions vary between 25% and 100%.

According to the hypotheses shown in Table 32, the number of suicide deaths in the 15-24 age group would seem to be between 510 and 800, depending on the proportion of concealed suicides proposed. But these are merely hypotheses that cannot at the moment be verified. At most one can regard them as probable and suppose that the real number of suicide deaths in the 15-24 age group represents between 7.5% and 12% of the total number of deaths, which would make suicide for this age group the biggest cause of non-accidental death, and either close to or in excess of the figure for accidental death, since the latter would decrease to the degree that real suicide deaths were attributed to accident.

If we try to estimate the real number of suicide attempts, our hypotheses will be even less rooted in fact; the number of deaths indicated by the I.N.S.E.E. may be subject to caution, but at least it exists. We saw earlier that there is no official figure, accurate or inaccurate, of the annual number

Table 32. Declared suicide deaths (I.N.S.E.E.) increased by 25% and 100% in absolute numbers and in proportion per 100 deaths from all causes in 15-24 age group.

Ages	I.N.S.E.E.		+ 25%		+ 100%	
	Absolute number	% total deaths	Absolute number	% total deaths	Absolute number	% total deaths
15—19	153	4.9	201	6.3	306	9.7
20—24	256	7.1	320	8.9	512	14.3
Total 15—24	409	6	511	7.5	818	12.1

of suicide attempts in France. We have seen that different authors estimate that in the case of adolescents there are between 10 and 50 times more attempts than deaths. But should the basis for such an estimate be the number of declared deaths or the real number of deaths? If we take the declared deaths, we know that the number of attempts may be regarded as being between 4,000 and 20,000. If we apply the same percentage to the supposed number of real deaths, the number of attempts is, if we increase the official number of deaths by 25%, between about 5,000 and 25,000, and if we increase the number of official deaths by 100%, between about 8,000 and 40,000. But we lack so many elements necessary to an estimate that these figures can only be regarded as pure supposition, and we are in no position to say whether, in 1966, the number of suicide attempts among young people was nearer 4,000 or 40,000.

So we are presented with figures ranging beteeen 409 and 818 deaths and between 4,000 and 40,000 attempts. And no scientific fact exists to enable us to decide what the real figures are. So much uncertainty must give us pause. Of course, it would be quite impracticable ever to obtain rigorously accurate statistics. But such gaps go well beyond the usual margin of uncertainty in statistics. This margin of uncertainty may well be especially important where suicide is concerned, and we inevitably ask why. Furthermore, it seems to me that this margin is even wider in the case of adolescent suicide. Again, why? Earlier, I suggested two reasons: the inadequacy of the statistical methods and the concealment of suicide either by the individual himself or by those around him. Are these the only reasons? It would not seem so. The experience described by Oeconomo [9] concerning the statistics of attempted suicide in Paris is very instructive; as soon as proper methods of registration were set up, the number of known attempts increased considerably. Yet these methods of registration had long been technically feasible, and the obstacle represented by concealment of suicide by those around the individual could not have diminished so much in so short a time. We may presume, therefore, that there are other reasons that prevent us from setting up the methods necessary for the discovery of the real number, even an approximate one, of suicides in general, and of adolescent suicides in particular. Furthermore, I would suggest that these reasons are more general, and go much deeper, than those mentioned so far, since they do not seem to have changed very much. It is this aspect of the subject that I should like to approach in Part II.

Notes

1. *Rapport de Statistiques sanitaires mondiales*, O.M.S., Geneva, vol. 21, no. 6, 1968, 365.
2. *Rapport épidémiologique et démographique*, O.M.S., vol. 20, nos. 1 and 2, 1967.
3. *O.M.S., Statistiques mondiales, op. cit.*, 365.
4. *Ibid.*, 392-6.
5. *Ibid.*, 366 and 409-11.
6. J.C. Oeconomo, 'Le comportement suicide et le problème de la tentative', *Revue de Science criminelle et de droit pénal comparé*, Paris, Librairie Sirey, 1959, 809.
7. A. Bayet, *Le suicide et la morale*, Paris, Alcan, 1922, 807.
8. M. Gaultier, E. Fournier and A. Gorceix, 'À propos de 47 cas de tentatives de suicides chez les adolescents', *Hygiène Mentale*, no. 6, 1961, 369.
9. Oeconomo, *op. cit.*, 816.

Part Two
The attitude of the adult and society to adolescent suicide

Introduction

The official statistics show figures that are notoriously lower, considerably so, than the real number of adolescent suicides. Even non-specialists are well aware of this, and in conversation and sometimes even in writing specialists are willing to acknowledge the fact. And yet these same figures continue to be used by national and international bodies; they are quoted in meetings and in scientific works, without the necessary reservations being made, as if they reflected a real situation, whereas, let me repeat, everyone knows that they are no more than a partial reflection of an unknown reality. This fact does not seem to be peculiar to France; it is to be found in many countries. Such persistence in presenting erroneous numerical data as accurate may not be without significance.

In Part III we shall see that this same attitude is to be found in the matter of causes and processes. If one cannot dismiss the problem in terms of insanity or a reassuring nosography, one might claim that adolescent suicide has the significance of an initiation rite, that the adolescent kills himself above all because he wants to live. This is not wholly untrue, of course; but to see it simply in those terms is surely, as in the case of the numerical data, to see only the partial reflection of the complex of factors that leads the young person to the suicide act. Again there seems to be a misunderstanding at work that merits our attention, and I shall return to it in Part III.

But to return for the moment to the numerical data, it is worth recalling that despite the inadequacy of the official figures, suicide appears as one of the principal causes of death. It is regularly among the first ten, and often among the first four causes of death among adults in industrialized countries, and one of the very first causes of death among adolescents

in many countries. Dr Aubenque of the I.N.S.E.E. has
expressed the concern of medical statisticians about suicide:
it is one of the few causes of death which, instead of decreasing, is increasing. Again, these facts are stated, and there the
matter rests. The other causes of death that are on the increase
are made the subject of research and special funds are set
aside for that purpose, but for suicide nothing is done. Such
an acceptance of erroneous data by otherwise rigorous minds,
such a facility for clinging to 'facts' whose clarity is illusory
and disappears as soon as one tries to make a realistic quantitative estimate of the number of suicide acts, such a lack of
concern for the importance of suicide among the causes of
death - such attitudes as these are intriguing in themselves.
But not everyone regards them in this light. Three main
objections can be made to my approach:

— The first would be that it is impossible, and therefore
useless to wish, to know the exact number of suicides. This is
true, but without wishing to have strictly accurate statistics
one could certainly wish for a more adjusted estimate. It is
not without interest to know whether suicide much exceeds
other non-accidental causes of death, or whether it is close to
death by accident, or perhaps exceeds death by accidents
other than road accidents. It is perhaps not unimportant to
know whether the suicide attempt is an exceptional act among
adolescents, or whether it should be counted not by the hundred, but by the tens of thousands.

— It might also be said that the fundamental problem where
adolescent suicide is concerned is not numerical, and that one's
main task should be to understand its significance, its mechanism, its causes, and its possible prevention, whatever its
frequency. This is also true, and I would subscribe wholeheartedly to such a view. But a knowledge of its frequency
may help us to understand its significance and its mechanism.
Otherwise, why continue to issue and to use false figures that
uphold a statistical pseudo-truth? They ought to be abandoned,
purely and simply.

— Lastly, it might be objected that even if the estimated
number of suicide deaths were to be doubled, it would still be
a very low figure - no more, per 1,000 inhabitants, than .32

for all ages and .12 for the 15-24 age group; and that so numerically unimportant a numerical fact does not justify long, difficult and costly research. But no funds have been devoted to research into suicide, and its relative numerical unimportance does not explain that absence. We have only to compare the problem of suicide with that of poliomyelitis, also a source of tragedy among children and adolescents. I shall take, not the figures for recent years, which are low thanks to the effect of vaccination, but those for the years preceding the introduction of vaccination. In 1957, in France, 292 deaths were declared to have been due to poliomyelitis among people of all ages, that is, a rate of .7 per 100,000 inhabitants, and 4,109 cases of the contraction of poliomyelitis were notified.[1] Thus deaths from poliomyelitis represent less than 1/20th of deaths from suicide, and the number of sufferers from poliomyelitis is less than 1/10th of the most modest estimates of the number of suicide attempts. Thus, even before effective measures were taken, poliomyelitis took a far smaller toll than suicide. And yet funds have been given for research into means of prevention and treatment. Preventative campaigns regularly take place and a national day is devoted each year to fund-raising.

If we compare suicide with road accidents, we see that in 1966, declared suicide deaths represented 62% of the figure for road deaths. Incidentally, this proportion is roughly the same in most industrialized countries. The State certainly makes a financially inadequate effort towards the prevention of road accidents, but an effort is made, which is more than we can say of suicide, to the study of which no public money has been devoted. Of course, deaths from road accidents are increasing only slightly. But we do not know whether suicide is or is not increasing because we are not in possession of valid statistics.

Of course, suicide is one of the chief causes of death among adolescents mainly because the other causes have declined. But if they have declined it is precisely because research has been undertaken and effective means established for their prevention. Again, I can only stress how astonishing it is that suicide is the only cause of death about which nothing has been done. It is equally astonishing that even from the admittedly incidental point of view of its economic repercussions, no one has thought to estimate the cost of suicide attempts to the community, that the Ministry of Social Security, usually so anxious to know where and how its money is being spent, has shown no desire to know the cost of suicide attempts in terms of hospital beds and work-days lost.

The persistent use of numerical data that takes no account of the real situation, and which do not even help one to estimate that situation, and our ignorance as to the causes and processes of adolescent suicide, cannot be explained only by the inadequacy of the statistics themselves, by the reticence of the suicides and their families, who wish to conceal the suicide act, or by the lack of scientific means of understanding the question better. It is as if we prefer to retain apparently accurate data that dispense us from exploring the question more deeply. As if, in a highly ambivalent way, at the same time interested in and disturbed by adolescent suicide, we try to compromise by confining our attention to data that keep us at a safe distance, and even prevent us from being led off in a direction that we are afraid to follow. To the question, how many human beings on the threshold of adult life commit a voluntary act of self-destruction, and why do they commit such an act?, we respond with a mixture of interest and suspicion. We are not indifferent to the question, but we are afraid of being caught up in an adventure about which we know so little. It is important to know whether these suppositions are true, or at least possible. If so, they would represent a fundamental *donnée* of the problem of adolescent suicide, or at least of our present knowledge of the question. The emphasis would shift from the attitude of those in immediate contact with the adolescent to that of all adults in general. It is this that I should now like to examine, taking in turn the adult's attitude to the adolescent, to death, and to the suicidal adolescent.

Notes

1. *Rapport épidémiologique et démographique*, O.M.S., Geneva, no. 19, 1966, 384-5.

7. The attitude of the adult to the adolescent

It is a commonplace, as I remarked earlier, that adolescence is the period of life about which we know the least, and about which research has made least progress. The adolescent is unknown to us for a variety of reasons, some of which, certainly, are to do with him - his changeability, and his refusal, his virtual inability, to communicate his experience. But there are other, perhaps equally important, reasons that are to do with us. The adult finds it difficult to get to know the adolescent because, above all, he is afraid of doing so. In this chapter I should like to examine the question of this fear. The way in which the adult speaks of the adolescent tells us as much about that fear, and about the defences that he sets up against it, as about his real knowledge of the adolescent. Never neutral, however much his compromise may look like neutrality, motivated by self-interest and fear, the adult defends himself from both, and reacts, as E.J. Anthony has shown,[1] by describing stereotypes. I need not go into the detail of Anthony's excellent work, but I should like to refer to a few aspects that are more directly related to my subject here. However, it should not be forgotten that each aspect must be seen in its context, and that its artificial isolation may give an exaggeratedly dramatic appearance to the adult-adolescent relationship that is belied by everyday observation. Anthony warns particularly, as also does Lebovici,[2] against the dangers of describing the adolescent as if he were always ill or maladjusted. By the same token, we must not see the adult simply and solely as defending himself against the adolescent. He also derives from his relationship with the adolescent considerable satisfaction, and, in fact, most of the time this relationship proceeds undramatically enough.

The adult's reactions are complex. They are similar, in certain respects, to those of the adolescent. Each serves as a mirror to the other, each is highly ambivalent in his attitude to the other, seeing in him both a dangerous object that is to be kept at a distance, and an object that attracts emotional investments of a more or less regressive kind, especially in the form of projective identification. The adult not only feels that he is regarded as a parental substitute by the adolescent, but that he is identified by other adults with the adolescent. This dual process is to be found in the attitude of the adult who represents society for the young. Since the reactions of every adult are, in certain respects, similar to those of parents, it is these I shall examine first.

A. The attitude of parents to the adolescent

The parental position - the most remarkable instance of human ambivalence - touches directly on the fundamental dualism. The parents/child relationship is constituted, like no other, by normally indissoluble links, and springs from the fact that before becoming another person the child is oneself, the issue of parental corporeity, a part of the mother's body. He is both a part of oneself that one must lose, a representative of castration and archaic elements, and a projection of oneself into the world, the bearer of parental phantasies. We also know the work of mourning that is involved in the repeated narcissistic loss of giving birth, the child's crisis of autonomy at the age of two, and the Oedipal period. This work of loss of the privileged object depends partly on the capacity of the parents for establishing an objectal relationship, and the possibility of compensating for the present loss by projecting into the future the postponed satisfactions promised by the developing child. The child is both the object of successive bereavements, evidence of the beginning of decline in the parents, which may arouse a fear of death, and also the fruit of Eros, the representative of the triumph of life over death. He is remarkable assurance against death. Through him, each parent hopes not to die completely, the line continues, the name or at least the

first name is passed on, the parent revenges himself on the
process of mortualization.

The child reactivates the claims of the ego ideal, even in its
most archaic aspects. He is another and yet not another, whom
one wishes to have the right and the power to manipulate at
will, in a phantasy of omnipotence, which the child sets out
to contradict in the course of the various phases of opposition.
He is also a factor in the revival of disappointed hopes, and in
the abandonment of the resignation operated by the reality
principle. The child, full of unknown possibilities, will embody
all the unbounded ambitions that one has indulged in phantasy.

It is on these archaic elements that the parents' counter-
Oedipal positions are based, with the ambivalence involved in
the child experienced as the other in the triangular relationship,
and identification with the child, reactivating as it does one's
own Oedipal experience.

The adolescent, in the grip of the reactivation of his internal
données, provokes the reactivation of the parents' genital and
pre-genital *données.*

The work of object loss is resumed, and must be completed.
The parents must undergo the mourning for the child on whom
they can act. His autonomy, which makes him definitively
another, is achieved at the same time as he is undergoing a
resumption of the Oedipal process and genital maturation.
This other, who has emerged into genital life, reactivates the
counter-Oedipal positions of the parents. The parents may
flee this anxiety-inducing situation by a return to projective
identification with the child, and a reactivation of the ego
ideal. This regressive movement on the part of the parents is
aided by the adolescent's awareness of his own impetuosity
and intense energy. So the parents' hope of seeing their unsatisfied phantasmic desires fulfilled is intensified; there is a
great temptation to manipulate the adolescent in such a way
that he will apparently fulfill all the possibilities that one
feels are in him, and to make of him all that one would like
to have been oneself. But the adolescent, in his desire for
autonomy, opposes this, attacks parental omnipotence, and,
resolving his Oedipal conflict, sets off in search of other love
objects in his own generation; he shows that it is all up with

his parents, that they are neither young enough (that is, they are on the wain) to be love objects, nor strong enough to hold the child. While the parents feel within them a growing fear of the conflict of the generations in which the adolescent represents the life to come and the parent one who is making his way slowly towards death.

The parents/adolescents relationship is in fact much more complex, more diverse, and develops with innumerable subtle variations. But it is not my intention here to delve further into this aspect of the question. I have simply mentioned a few of the main features, which, beyond the parents themselves constitute the factors operant in the basically ambivalent relationship that every society establishes with the adolescent, and which act as an obstacle to the understanding of the adolescent.

B. The attitude of the adult and society to the adolescent

The attitude of the adult to the adolescent is never a neutral one: the adolescent arouses in the adult contradictory feelings, conflicts of a more or less violent and anxiety-inducing kind. He tries to avoid anxiety in stereotyped reactions, which not only force the adolescent to play contradictory roles, but also impose stereotyped attitudes on the adult himself. This conflict makes him incapable of understanding the adolescent's experience, which is felt to be dangerous because it acts as a catalyst for a conflict that he does not really desire.

One of the sources of the conflict is to be found directly in the adolescent's behaviour. In his search for a model, the adolescent carries out massive attempts at identification on the adults that he meets. These adults are very flattered at being regarded as models, but the adolescent rejects them as rapidly, and as wholeheartedly, as he took them up, and this leaves its scars.

Another source of conflict is the danger that the mere presence of the adolescent will induce the adult to relive his own adolescence. Anna Freud[3] and Lampl de Groot[4] have described the difficulty in analysis in getting patients to relive their adolescent experiences, whereas they are quite willing to provide a historical account of their adolescence. This fact, which has been confirmed by many analysts, would seem to be of major importance for our subject; it has its counterpart in everyday life. Many adults remember their adolescence only in the form of incidents, which they accompany by stereotyped commentaries of the 'those-were-the-days' or 'what-fools-we-were-then' variety. But the memory of what it actually felt like to be an adolescent is generally lacking. It is as if the adult were saying: 'It's cost me enough pain and torment becoming an adult at all, without submerging myself once again in the turmoil of adolescence.' In this refusal, the adult reveals his fear of reliving the anxiety and the work of mourning that he has had to undergo. But it is also fear of reviving feelings of guilt for his youthful aggressivity, whether it had been expressed in action or merely in phantasy. It is also a fear of measuring the distance between his early hopes and his present, far more modest, achievements. In any case, the page has been turned, and he has no desire to go back and read it again. Looking back, he has a feeling that he had been playing with a bomb that didn't go off; he can see no point in running further risks.

For all these reasons, the adolescent disturbs the adult, who, at some cost, has achieved a measure of tranquillity. The adolescent stands before the adult as witness and prosecutor. 'Look at me,' he seems to say. 'See all the possibilities that you had in you. What have you done with them?' He is also an invitation to the adult to relive that adventure, at once so painful and so full of hope. As a sexual object, with his newly acquired genital life, attractive and attracting, the adolescent reminds the adult of the desirable being he once was, or of those who were the object of his amorous desires; at the same time, he also revives in the adult the memory of the Oedipal adventure. Thus the adolescent calls into question once more the whole system of defences that the adult has patiently and stubbornly built up. The adult must then strengthen his defences, reassure himself, stiffen his responses, refuse to see and to hear.

This is all the more necessary to him in that what the adolescent represents is not without its attractions for him. So much energy to be expended, so much passion, dynamism and hope, so much emphasis on truth, and on potentialities that seem about to be realized, place a seed of doubt in his mind, set him wondering whether his resignation is justified. He is tempted to try again, to try his luck at second-hand in the person of an adolescent. There is the risk that his ego ideal, which had bent itself to adult reality, will make itself heard again in its primal form. But sexual prohibition, his adult reality, which demonstrates the vanity of such hopes, his fear of losing the advantages that he has acquired as an adult, force him, in general, to refuse to relive his adolescent phantasies. Trapped between attraction and defence, he will be caught up in the subtle interplay of compromise, between his fear of reviving anxiety and guilt, and his interest in youth. Very probably, the compromise will be expressed in regressive ways, with reactions, either in action or in projective identification, that avoid the elaboration of terms of conflict. In various subtle combinations, the adult will identify in turn or simultaneously with the adolescent and his parents, will live as the accomplice of one against the other, and vice versa, and will try to safeguard his position as an adult who does not wish to be on the decline, while reliving the unfulfilled hopes of his youth. Though stereotyped, the reactions of the adult are too varied to be enumerated here. However, here are a few of them:[5]

— The attitude of the strong, experienced adult to the newcomer. In order to preserve the privileges of seniority, he places a low value on the productions of the adolescent, which he treats as childish.

— The moralizing attitude of someone who preaches to the adolescent the virtues of respect and submission, repressing his own revolt against his parents, yet trying at the same time to deflect away from himself, the adult representative of the parents, the adolescent's aggressivity.

— The more complex attitude of someone who wishes to understand and help the adolescent, presents himself as the good adult and suppresses his terrified hostility, identifying himself with both the ideal parents that he would like to have had and the aggressive adolescent.

— The attitude of the adult disguised as eternally young in order to dupe the adolescent all the more, to attach him to himself in an aggressive way, to manipulate him, and to try to realize, through him, his unsatisfied phantasies, hoping that the adolescent will not unmask the adult with the ideal of omnipotence that he really is. Again, though this is more than an attitude, there is the unusual, but not exceptional position of someone who renounces his reality as an adult in order to identify himself wholly and completely with the adolescent in a regressive fixation, and who continues to play the game of adolescence for the rest of his life.

The compromise is more subtle, but just as ambivalent, when the adult presents himself as the representative of society, whether confronted by a group of adolescents or as part of a group of adults confronting a single adolescent. The adolescent is on the side of society against the family, and Freud[6] has shown the importance of this interference. The adolescent, wishing to loosen the ties that bind him to his family, does not hesitate to use the support of society to defend himself against the refusal, real or imaginary, of his own family to grant him autonomy; society encourages him to break the bonds of family, satisfied that it will extract profit from a member of the narcissistic entity that a family is. But this newcomer must make his own contribution to society, without calling into question what has already been achieved, without destroying the work of those in authority, without wounding them by a systematic criticism of their work. Thus the adult who sees himself as a representative of society tends to vaunt the charms of the social life to the detriment of what the parent-adults are offering, but demand of the young respect for and submission to the adult members of society. This contradiction reproduces in many ways the contradiction that every adult feels in a relationship with an individual adolescent.

Not every adult/adolescent relationship is based on one or other of these stereotyped modes. The relationship is infinitely more rich, and contains highly positive factors, both on the individual and the social planes. I have placed these partial aspects to the fore in this artificial way simply because they present an obstacle to our knowledge and understanding of the adolescent. However one looks at it, the adolescent is disturbing for the adult. The adult may try to preserve himself in the strict position of an adult caught in present reality, outside the various stereotyped reactions outlined above. But then the adolescent shows him that he no longer has the attraction and energy of youth, and that he is moving towards death, whereas he, the adolescent, is the living representative of Eros, under whose aegis his personality is being formed. Thus he cannot but inflict narcissistic wounds on the adult, and reactivate the fundamental Eros/Thanatos conflict. The adult has a choice between reviving the anxiety of his youth, and assuming the anxiety of the new conflict that is taking place within him. Adolescence is certainly the awkward age, but it is so above all for the adult, since it disturbs his tranquillity and reassuring organization. Not knowing the adolescent, not understanding his experience, replacing the reality of this experience by a stereotype, is certainly a way of avoiding this anxiety.

C. The attitude of the specialist to the adolescent

In the preceding section, we dealt with the reactions of the 'average' adult. Those who, in one way or another, deal with adolescents from a professional point of view should be able, because of their greater knowledge and experience, to establish different positions. This is only partly the case, however, for the fundamental problem remains, if in a more subtle, more varied way, according to the training of the specialists. This partly explains the inadequacy of our knowledge of the adolescent, which I emphasized in Chapter 2, as compared with the abundance of description to be found in literature and in films. But the latter are always the work of adults, not of the adolescents themselves, and are therefore of little use, whether they are autobiographical memories made up of 'traces that have often been rearranged in the light of adult experience',[7] or whether, as in a 'psychological novel', they purport to be the sincere observations of adolescents themselves. They tell us more about the reactions of the adult author than about adolescents. The difficulty experienced by the specialist in gaining true knowledge of the adolescent, for reasons that concern him alone, can be observed in many different circumstances.

The educational field provides us with a good many examples.[8] The positions of teachers in permanent contact with adolescents often reveal a lack of perception of the needs of adolescents that would be astonishing if we did not know that it is part of the educator's defences against the young. The same problem is to be found at the level of those who work out the policy of the Education Ministry. The way in which the democratization of education was conceived illustrates this. In confining itself to the problem of increasing the number of schools and teachers - a very real and very important problem - and providing new names for the different kinds of school, or organizing changes in recruitment according to geography or age, the Ministry has misunderstood the problems of educational reform and the lives of the adolescents within the schools; this goes well beyond the question of programmes. It has also misunderstood the interference of processes of identification and of investment of intellectual and social success for the many young people who are pursuing studies at a level that is far higher than that of their parents, which is at the source of so many apparently inexplicable failures. Protesting against this refusal to know and hear them, the students and *lycéens* are demanding their right to speak. Adults and adolescents become afraid, a series of mutual reactions is set up, and the stereotypes of the dangerous and destructive adolescent or the deaf adult fixated in his defences take on an appearance of reality.

The same facts may be observed in the field of so-called leisure activities, whether at the level of the adults directly responsible for the young, or at the level of the Ministry of Youth. By advocating only an increase of sporting activities and the building of more sports stadiums, this Ministry is suggesting that the adolescent should overinvest his time and energies in physical recreation, which excludes language and communication. Here again, those responsible in the Ministry and those responsible for dealing directly with youth reveal their non-desire to know adolescents. They are astonished at the failure of their youth policy, whereas it could have been an opportunity of discovering what young people and their needs really are.

Psychological studies of adolescence certainly show that their authors have tried to avoid the more obvious reactions and projections of the adult, but ultimately they have failed. These studies, often in the form of opinion polls carried out among young people, avoid the use of pre-established hypotheses that are too imbued with the defensive reactions of the adult. Very often these opinion polls are restricted to the collection of young people's views on very specific facts or ideas. How can one hope to arrive at a knowledge of the deep movements and organisation of the adolescent personality through such rationalized material? One is inviting the adolescent to maintain his defences by intellectualization, to distance himself from his real experience and his well-founded fears. And so, in spite of all the precautions taken, and however well aware of the dangers he may be, the specialist expresses his own fear of the adolescent's emotions and drives.

The position of psychoanalysts in regard to adolescence is not without its problems either. Some years ago, Anna Freud[9] remarked on the lack of psychoanalytic studies of adolescence, which she nicknamed the poor relation of psychoanalysis. Such silence may be due to the Freudian discovery of infantile sexuality, which directed the attention of psychoanalysts to early childhood to the detriment of adolescence.[10] But this is an inadequate explanation. Other factors are probably involved. The lack may be due partly to the prudence of psychoanalysts, who are better placed than anyone to realize the difficulty involved in studying adolescence in view of the importance of the adult's reactions and projections. It may also be that psychoanalysts, like all other specialists, are subject to the same reactions, and adopt the same positions of distancing, of disinterestedness, and even of rejection.

As every author remarks, psychoanalysts often speak of the contra-indication of treatment in the case of adolescents, adding that psychotherapy is not possible at that age, or that it is difficult and the outcome unpredictable. It is certainly true that a great many of the difficulties relate to the adolescent himself, and that treatment cannot be carried out in the normal way; this poses technical problems, and may be a great source of perplexity for the analyst. But not all the objections concern the patient. Specialists in adolescence[11] insist on the importance of the counter-transferential problems. The counter-transference is more important, more intense, more profound, more difficult to overcome in the case of the adolescent than in that of any other patient. The vicissitudes involved in the treatment of the adolescent are partly related to the reactivation of the analyst's own difficulties. Anna Freud[12] and Lampl de Groot[13] have remarked that these difficulties also appear in the reliving of adolescent experience in the course of adult analyses, and that the analyst should be particularly sensitive to the workings of the counter-transference at such phases in the analysis. The counter-transferential resistance of the analyst would seem to reinforce the resistance of the analysand, which would explain why it is so difficult to achieve a reliving of adolescent experience in the course of adult analyses.

The reactions that arise from the personal difficulties of the specialist cannot be attributed only to the greater or lesser degree of co-operation offered by the adolescent patient, for these reactions do not only occur in the course of treatment, when one is actually confronted by an adolescent; they also appear as soon as the specialist has to confront the concept of adolescence, and make an effort to relive his own adolescent experience. I attach a great deal of value to the incident related by E.J. Anthony:[12] a team of researchers engaged on a longitudinal study were profoundly disturbed when they had to approach the adolescence of the subjects under study; the team was led to call its working methods into question, hesitated, and finally decided to leave adolescence to one side and to pass directly to the adult period. A similar event took place in a group of studies of adolescence with which I was connected. The group appeared to be sure of its approach where the methodical exposition of the established notions to be found in existing works was concerned; but as soon as we had to go beyond this pre-established framework, each member of the group launched into passionate and contradictory statements that reflected the emergence of memories of his own adolescence, and of his resistance to them. The attitude of each member, caught up as he was in his own conflict, made any collective exchange or scientific work impossible.

This brief outline of adult attitudes to the adolescent has stressed the personal resistances that every specialist has to overcome, the reasons why our knowledge of adolescence has made such little progress, and how little desire has been shown to undertake a thorough study of the subject. The specialist of adolescence knows better than most adults the obstacles that are presented by his own personality, and is better equipped perhaps to take the necessary precautions; but he cannot entirely escape them. No adult is neutral in his attitude to the adolescent. Each identifies with both the parents and the adolescent, and reproduces in himself the conflict and ambivalence that characterize the experience of the adolescent himself.

Adolescence represents both a lost paradise and a painful past, and together they prevent one wanting to reactivate in oneself what has made one suffer so much. The adult is afraid of the adolescent and so refuses to know him; he replaces the knowledge that he does not possess with stereotypes. But these stereotypes, which are formed by the adult's projections out of traces of his own adolescence, are also a source of fear. Thus the adult's reactions can be partly schematized by a chain of fears and defences, of reassurances, none of which is satisfactory.

Notes

1. E.J. Anthony, 'Les réactions des adults aux adolescents et à leur comportement', *L'abord psychiatrique de l'adolescence,* Excerpta Medica Foundation, 1966, 134-47.
2. S. Lebovici, 'Les modes d'adaptation des adolescents', in *Ibid.,* 149.
3. A. Freud, 'Adolescence', *The Psychoanalytic Study of the Child,* vol. XIII, New York, Int. Univ. Press, 1958, 259.
4. J. Lampl de Groot, 'Adolescence', *The Psychoanalytic Study of the Child,* vol. XV, New York, Int. Univ. Press, 1960, 95-8.
5. Cf. Anthony, *op. cit.*
6. S. Freud, *Civilization and its Discontents,* Stand. ed., vol. XXI, 99.
7. Lebovici, *op. cit.,* 149.

8.　This was written in April 1968. The events of May-June 1968 and the reforms now being undertaken might seem to make them obsolete. However, I have preferred to leave them unchanged, for they may be more relevant than might at first sight appear. The future of educational reforms does not only depend on the passing of legislation. It largely depends on a change of attitude on the part of the adults responsible for education towards *lycéens* and students, and of the kind of relationship that they establish with them. These lines also show that the events of 1968 were not as unexpected as many would have us believe.

9.　A. Freud, *op. cit.*, 259.

10.　*Ibid.*, 256.

11.　In particular A. Freud, E.J. Anthony, P. Male, S. Lebovici, E. Kestemberg.

12.　*Op. cit.*

13.　*Op. cit.*

14.　*Op. cit.*, 146.

8·The attitude of the adult to death

A. Man's attitude to death

Man does not know death; he has no representation of it, and he cannot achieve the paradox of going to the point of no return and then retaining the experience of it. But his attitudes and his behaviour towards death show that it is not something to which he is indifferent. Of course, his attitude differs according to whether he is confronting his own or someone else's death, the two being inextricably linked in the case of a loved one, who is both someone else and an invested object, part of oneself that one is losing.[1]

When confronted by the death of someone else, man's reaction is apparently clear: he feels guilt at seeing the fulfilment of his desire for the death of someone who is always to some extent an enemy. But this Oedipal-type guilt is underpinned by more archaic reactions: first, fear of the law of retaliation, which will, in turn, bring about his own death; and second, the struggle against his own aggressivity, expressed in the desire for the other's death, which reminds him that he bears death within himself since he is capable of desiring it. Lastly, by identification, the realization of the death of his fellow man makes him feel that he is mortal. So, in addition to the guilt that he feels through the interplay of archaic reactions, it is with his own death that man is confronted. The apparent diversity of his reactions, the multiplicity of the factors that motivate them, make man's attitude to death often difficult to interpret. But one fact is obvious: his attitude and his behaviour in the face of death are among those that change least with the passing of time, those that remain the most remarkably constant.

We have a good example of this in what remains of primitive thought. We know that man first regards himself as immortal, death being an avoidable accident; then, in a second stage, he regards himself as mortal because of evil spirits outside himself. 'Death wants him,' as he says paranoiacally. Man then believes that he bears death within himself, by cannibalistic introjection, death being a disease that the witch-doctor must cure.

At present, it is towards death that man has retained the most persistent primitive attitudes. Even now, he cannot reconcile himself to the idea of a natural death; he tries to situate death outside himself, to believe that it is coming to kill him, as when he says, 'Cancer is a big killer'.[2]

Of course, such attitudes, and their fixity, can be attributed to the fact that man does not know death because he has no means of feeling it within him, of integrating it, with the result that it is kept at a distance. But it can equally well be said that especially strong defences deprive him of all freedom of movement. In particular, one can compare his maintenance of death outside himself with the process of dichotomy and projection on to others of what is bad in itself in order to free himself of it magically.

More demonstrative still is the constancy and fixity of the prohibitions concerning death. Apart from the prohibition of suicide, which we shall return to later, the prohibition to kill others, which is bound up with the reasons mentioned above, is the oldest and still the strongest of the prohibitions. The 'thou shalt not kill', of which Freud said, 'such an imperative, formal prohibition can only be addressed to a particularly strong impulse',[3] shows at least that man is capable of perceiving the death of others.

The prohibition bears not only on the act of death, but also on the mention of death, and not merely when this involves threats of death or wishes for the death of someone. While in the last few years verbal expression has become, generally speaking, more free, more flexible, and its prohibitions more subtle, it is still just as difficult for man to speak about death. He manages to do so only in the abstract form of general philosophical considerations, or in a confiding tone, suggesting as much as he expresses, with the help of circum-

locutions that remain the most varied and widely used of any
in our time. To speak of it directly is regarded as indecent and
wounding. One does not speak of death to children, sheltering
behind the pretext that they would not understand (the same
pretext that used to be advanced as regards sex). The verbal
prohibition reflects the primitive view of the magical powers
of the word, the fear of killing with words. It is also the fear
of arousing in another the death that he bears within him, of
revealing to one's fellow man, and therefore to oneself, that
man bears death within himself. We can speak of death and of
the dead only if our discourse contains at the same time the
necessary reassurances, or if we imply that the dead are better
off dead than alive, and that those of us who remain alive
are safe.

The maximum intrication is observed in mourning and in
funeral rites. This is obvious in the traditional funeral ceremonial, which was until recently universally practised: imposing
rites that preserved the appearance of a sacrifice (in particular,
of a financial kind), attitudes specially adopted for the circumstances, obligations that the friends and relations of the dead
impose on themselves both to appease the dead and to reassure
the living (themselves above all), the tombstones to shut away
the dead and prevent them from coming back to fetch the
living. Widows' veils are also significant in a number of ways,
from their role as a warning to others that one has been in
close contact with death and therefore may be dangerous (a
role similar to that of the leper's bell), to the mark of triumph
of someone who has approached death, but has survived. They
are also a visible sign of the desire for sympathy and consola-
tion at having experienced a loss, and a demand to be left
outside the world with the dead man, from whom one cannot
yet be separated. They are the outward sign of anger directed
either against a reality that has suddenly confronted the
widow with death, or against the dead man himself; by depart-
ing, he has either shown himself to be unfaithful,[4] or, in dying,
he has become a link connecting the survivor with death and
thus placing her in danger. I shall not return here to the subject of the work of mourning, but it is worth remarking that
it is undertaken against the desire to annul the death of the

loved one and to deny reality, and is so meticulous, prolonged, painful, and costly that 'it is remarkable that this painful un-pleasure is taken as a matter of course by us'.[5]

The disappearance in recent years of the traditional funeral rites, as a result of American influence, is only an apparent change. The use of cosmetics so that the corpse will not look dead, the systematic suppression of the signs of mourning, the deliberately unruffled, smiling behaviour of the family are all expressive of a fear of death. The taste for displaying death in fiction and literature, which allows us to die at second-hand over and over again, and thus to reassure ourselves that death is not real,[6] is now replaced by a desire to turn real death into fiction, and the funeral ceremonial is replaced by a spectacle in which we are not personally involved. We must reassure our-selves and others by showing that one is not connected to death, that one is wholly on the side of the living, that one is not contagious. To show one's pain at the loss of the loved one becomes indecent; it is to unveil death, which must remain ignored because it might hurt others. This would not appear to be an improvement, for it is still based upon a primitive belief, on the notion that death is dangerous and contagious. It may even be worse, for how can the work of mourning be carried out if it must remain secret? It is to be feared that it can no longer be carried out in such circumstances, and that communication will be stifled. 'Real pain breeds upon itself when it is given no outlet . . . Between the crushing rites of the past and modern indifference, we have still to find the means of an effective solidarity.'[7]

The complexity of man's behaviour when he is directly con-fronted by death is obvious. But it is not confined to the special situations mentioned above; it is constantly present in the psychical life. The verbal material produced in the course of psychoanalysis shows this over and over again, but it is especially difficult to express and to disentangle, in which respect it is similar to the material concerned with adoles-cence; we know to what extent the progress of an analysis is influenced by the analysand's attitude to death, and the im-portant part played by the confrontation with death in the closing stage of analysis.[8] In everyday life, too, we can verify to what extent our 'tendency to exclude death from our calculations in life brings in its train many other renunciations and exclusions'.[9] Transposing what Freud said about the commandment 'thou shalt not kill', we can say that so much effort and so many renunciations can be motivated only by a feeling of the very grave danger that lies in not being able to keep death at a distance. So rigorous, so intense, so permanent a system of defence could only be motivated by a profound anxiety against which it is absolutely necessary to struggle.

Man's fear of death is so deeply felt that he is justified in mobilizing a considerable amount of energy to neutralize this anxiety, and to prevent it from invading his psyche. If we are to approach the question of the origins of this anxiety, we must abandon observable and comprehensible facts for hypotheses that must be interpreted with delicacy and accepted only with the greatest reserve.

At the first level we are confronted by the strange, irreducible paradox in which man is caught up in his attitude to death. Whereas he cannot claim to know what tomorrow will bring, he knows that he will die one day, that he is subjected ineluctably to the process of mortualization, that to live is to come closer to death. And yet he does not know when or how he will die. He lives in an ignorance that he cannot hope to overcome.[10] Death is a given fact that he cannot master; it is his only certitude. So man realizes that he is imperfect since he is not immortal, that he is evil because he can kill, and that he is weak because he cannot overcome his only unchallengeable certitude. In his desire for omnipotence, man cannot console himself for not being God, and the idea of death is the gravest wound to his narcissism. It is hardly surprising that it arouses the most acute, most unbearable anxiety. Although unable to master death, he tries at least to master the idea of death by an intense effort of intellectual transformation. In this context, it is easy to see that the fear of death lies at the origin of psychology and philosophy.[11]

But the wound to man's narcissism is probably not enough to account for the intensity of the fear of death. At a deeper level, we come back to the problem of the duality of the instincts and the existence of the death instinct. The absence of the representation of death in the psychical life in no way undermines the theory of the duality of instinct. As I mentioned in Chapter 1, this theory posits a connexion between the life instinct and the death instinct, the function of the first being to tie up the second and so prevent its irruption. As long as a man is capable of representation, he is alive, that is to say, within this connection the life instinct is dominant. If the death instinct became dominant death would come, and consequently, the subject would no longer be able to represent to himself. This, too, is a very wounding realization for man: to feel that he cannot know the death instinct that is within him directly without immediately becoming its victim, and that if he is to live he must accept his ignorance. Other theories of the instincts refer not to a death instinct, but to the notion of a regressive return to an absolute fusional communion. We find in such theories a search for the absolute that is close to the desire for omnipotence and identification with God. On the other hand, the concept of an absolute is antinomic with that of evolution, of dynamism, of movement that defines life; it is very close, therefore, to the concept of death and perhaps to the death instinct; although it does not directly express a return to the inanimate, it does express a desire for a return to definitive immobility that is very similar to it.

Whichever theory of the instincts one adheres to, it is clear that man expends a considerable amount of energy in his struggle against this internal tendency to return either to the inanimate or to absolute fusion. It is the supreme precondition for life. Whatever takes part in the defence against the danger is felt as a necessity, and not as a luxury. Man is afraid to call into question a system of defence the lack of which would be fatal.

An observation in favour of these hypotheses is provided by subjects who, without actually knowing death, have been near enough to it to have experienced within themselves what we might call 'the tendency to death'. R.G. Druss and D.S. Kornfeld[12] have studied the problem of resuscitation after heart failure in ten subjects. They have observed on the one hand defensive insomnia and the violence of dreams that indicate the mark left by the paramortal experience, and, on the other hand, behaviour involving the regression, suppression or displacement of anxiety. They confirm the importance of the defence mechanisms, and how resolute they are in preventing those subjects who have known the fear of death from being confronted with it again. They compare their observations with those that have been made about war neuroses. I have made similar observations among those who have survived the concentration camps: they prefer to be insomniac rather than dream, to work rather than not to have their minds directed outwards, and to maintain themselves in a compromise of endless activity that is intended to stifle their anxiety, which otherwise, they say, would become unbearable, and would kill them.

B. The attitude of the doctor to death

While the reactions of all men to death remain impregnated with primitive thought, it might be thought that the doctor, with the help of his scientific training, is in a position to work out another attitude to death. This is true, but he is still subject to ambivalence; confronted by his scientific training he is the locus of the fundamental anxiety of all men and of his own fear of death. It is hardly surprising that the doctor should be the locus for the projection of the fear of death and of the defences that it gives rise to. He whose task it is 'to cure death', who acts on life and death, is invested with the power of an omnipotent, mysterious, divining, curing magician. This solicitation evokes a response in the doctor, who often accepts the role. Many traces of this can be found in medical life: the persistence of a pseudo-scientific, cabalistic language that is incomprehensible to the public (and sometimes to doctors themselves), a refusal on the part of the doctor to admit ignorance by sheltering behind meaningless terms, and to rationalize his refusal in various ways - traditions that remain particularly entrenched in the medical profession. But man, in his ambivalence, also aggresses the doctor, for this is a way of aggressing death; many of the present-day attempts to put the medical profession 'in its place' are like a settling of accounts with death.

At the level of reality, of his social role, the doctor is invested with a precise role: to help men to live better and longer.
In choosing to become a doctor, he accepts this contract: 'like
the soldier, the doctor has tacitly abdicated part of his rights
as a man, he has a precise task: to cure, and he is no longer
free to obey his own feelings'.[13] But even if he can no longer
obey his own feelings, the doctor cannot help having them.
He has his own fear of death, follows the same path as other
men, and his anxiety is one of the sources of his medical
vocation. The role of magician that is offered him is experienced at the same level as his anxiety and its defences. Primitive thought is also present in the medical vocation. In concerning himself with the death of others, he hopes to make
himself forget death, and, above all, his own death. He operates
a dichotomy that is the opposite of that operated by others;
he projects his mortality on to others, and, in snatching others
from death, it is in fact himself that he is saving. But this first
system of defence cannot be maintained completely; it is a
hindrance to the practice of medicine, because it is denied by
everyday reality, it is too strongly in opposition to indispensable scientific thought.

Thus the doctor must find other attitudes. Among the means
of reassurance is that of denying that the patient is like himself.
The patient may then be reduced to the status of a partial
object: only a single organ is taken into consideration, or it is
transformed into an abstract entity, that is to say, a disease.
Or, again, his death is regarded as something incidental that
does not concern the doctor and leaves him indifferent.
Another means of defence is that death is rejected by science,
as if immortality were desirable and the medical profession
regarded the prolongation of life as a self-evident good.[14]

In addition to these methods of reassurance, the doctor can
always take the open way that leads to an acceptance of reality,
which makes it possible to practice medicine on a person, and
to establish an objectal relationship with the patient. This then
leads to a realization of the existence within the patient of the
ineluctable process of mortualization; the doctor must assume
the fact that neither he nor his patient will escape from that
process, and he must master, without repressing, his fear of

death in order to place himself at a safe distance from it.

Yet the attitude of the doctor is not a clear and simple one. It is worth noting how few studies have been made of the doctor's attitude to death. In one of these, Eissler[15] stresses the obstacles that are encountered in developing a thanatology, in view of the emotional charges and personal affectivities involved. The evidence of doctors who deal with patients suffering from fatal diseases is of great value here; they note the importance of the personal reactions of the medical team to the emotional reactions of the patients and of the patients' families, and any possible disturbances to scientific activity when the death rate becomes too high.[16] Quite obviously, a doctor can only deal with a certain number of dying patients at any one time.[17] We have an example of the reactions and emotions aroused by anything connected with death in my own field, and I have mentioned the problem of the death instinct several times already. The death instinct has aroused more reservations, more discussion, and more doubt, than any other psychoanalytic theory or hypothesis.[18] These reactions have spread well beyond psychoanalytic circles and have reached the whole of the psychiatric world; there is now hardly a single psychiatrist, whether he is a psychoanalyst or not, who has not taken up a position on the subject of the death instinct. This notion affects everyone. And yet little progress has been made on the subject. Such arguments as the lack of any representation of death in the psychical life, or the absence of imagination concerning death, are not entirely invalid; but they are not arguments against the existence of the death instinct. Indeed, it is obvious that 'a man's attitude to death imbues all his actions'.[19]

The fact that the scientist is beginning to approach the question is certainly an improvement on the attitude of people in general. But he is prevented from moving forward towards an answer by his own fear of death; this often forces him to seek reassurances that prevent him from arriving at the truth. The scientist, like everybody else, is afraid that if he approaches too close to death he will be contaminated by it. Theoretically, he should be able to overcome his anxiety to the extent that it does not interfere with his research. But practice shows that this is not easily done, and my own experience has taught me that it is always a difficult and sometimes painful task, and one that is not always crowned with the success that one might expect.

Notes

1. S. Freud, *Our Attitude towards Death*, stand. ed., vol. XIV, 289.
2. K.R. Eissler, *The Psychiatrist and the Dying Patient*, New York, International Universities Press, 1955.
3. *Op. cit.*, 286.
4. P.L. Landsberg, *Essai sur l'expérience de la mort*, Paris, Le Seuil, 1951, 39.
5. S. Freud, *Mourning and Melancholia*, stand. ed., vol. XIV, 245.
6. S. Freud, *Our Attitude towards Death*, 291.
7. A. Fabre-Luce, *La Mort a changé*, Paris, Gallimard, 1966, 81.
8. R. Barande, 'L'inachèvement de l'homme comme structure de son temps', *Revue Française de Psychanalyse*, no. 2-3, t. XXIX, March-June 1965, 283.
9. S. Freud, *Our Attitude towards Death*, 291.
10. Eissler, *op. cit.*, and Landsberg, *op. cit.*, 23.
11. S. Freud, *Our Attitude towards Death*, 293-4.
12. *Journal of the American Medical Association*, vol. 201, no. 5, 31 July 1967, 291.
13. A. Bayet, *Le suicide et la morale*, Paris, Alcan, 1922, 170.
14. Eissler, *op. cit.*
15. *Ibid.*
16. N. Alby, J.M. Alby and J. Chassigneux, 'Aspects psychologiques de l'évolution et du traitement des leucémiques enfants et jeunes adultes dans un centre spécialisé', *Nouvelle Revue d'hématologie*, t. 7, 1967, no. 5, 577-88.
17. Fabre-Luce, *op. cit.*, 74.
18. S. Freud, *Civilization and its Discontents*, stand. ed., vol. XXI, 119-20.
19. Eissler, *op. cit.*

9·The attitude of the adult to adolescent suicide

As we have seen, confrontation with the adolescent is one of the situations that arouse most resistance and defence in the adult. And although the reaction of the specialist (doctor, psychologist, teacher, sociologist) may be more subtle, it is basically no different - a fact that acts as an obstacle to an adequate knowledge and understanding of adolescence. Our ignorance in this area throws a good deal of light on our own attitude. We have also seen that man builds up a defence system against death that is archaic, rigid, and difficult to remove. Above all, he does not want to confront death, and his greatest concern is to reassure himself by placing himself at the greatest possible distance from it.

It is thus hardly surprising that the voluntary death of an adolescent arouses the maximum reaction of flight in the adult. Adolescent suicide has the sad privilege of arousing the most extreme intolerance; it would seem that no subject arouses more defences. As it is, people find it hard enough to bear the death of a young person by illness or accident. It is always felt as a profound error, as the monstrous coupling of two incompatible factors. It is also rejected by specialists, and M. and J.M. Alby and J. Chassigneux have emphasized how much more it disturbs medical staff than other deaths.[1] So it is easy to imagine what anxiety is aroused by the voluntary death of a young person.

A. The suicide act

Whatever the age of the subject, people find the suicide act unbearable in itself. It has everything necessary to shatter the defence system that man has built up at such cost. The hope of reducing death to an exogenic accident is brought to nothing by the individual who, by committing the act of voluntary death, shows that man bears the tendency to death within himself. Similarly, he causes a deep wound to man's narcissism, and impugns the image of the God-man, since in desiring death he renounces any hope of immortality. 'A man who makes an admission of his mortality goes in fear of being treated as an alien, as an outsider in the society of immortals that we form.'[2] Furthermore, by refusing himself the right to live, he denies his own value, and consequently that of his fellow-men. Durkheim[3] showed that he realized this when, speaking of sacrilege in human religion and of the sacredness of the human person, he remarked that suicide must be regarded as an immoral act and punished.

Bayet[4] stresses how the question of the licit or illicit character of the act has been presented in exactly the same terms for the past two thousand years, and that our moral view of suicide is unknown to us, as if powerful motives were preventing us from knowing what we think. He quotes A. Karr[5] who has never found anything more than a fear of death behind authors' declarations against suicide. The suicide is resented as a cheat, who, instead of respecting the rule of the game, that death should be kept in obscurity, brings it out into the full light of day, accepts it, and, what is more, summons it up among the living. He is felt to be dangerous, and is avoided as a monster. People speak of contagion (which has never been proved), as if the appeal to death might find an accomplice within others. The rule of silence (which is certainly a desirable one) is justified by the fear of seeing the number of suicides increase. Such an argument is highly ambiguous; if there really is a risk that suicide might increase by contagion, it is a quantitatively permanent, latent danger, like other contagious disorders, and therefore, as I have said, research should be carried out on it (none has been, of course). If, on the other hand, it is not contagious, then the rule of silence has no point.

When the suicide is a loved one, there is added to the ambivalence that attaches to any close person the feeling of a particularly wounding insult. By his act he cries out to those around him that they did not give him what could have made him happy, that he did not enjoy their company; he denies them the qualities of perfection and omnipotence that they hoped were theirs, and has put an end to them by crudely throwing death into the middle of a circle of loving friends.

Suicide arouses a more acute anxiety than any other kind of death, and triggers off even more intense reactions of defence and rejection. It is understandable, then, that the most entrenched attitude that man has found is to ignore it, and that he should show so little interest in research into the subject, and even fail to use the available statistics correctly.

B. Adolescent suicide

The voluntary death of the young person is the locus of the two most acute causes of human anxiety. All the projections, defences and rejections that operate in relation to adolescence, on the one hand, and to death in general and voluntary death in particular, on the other, converge in the suicidal adolescent. We cannot examine these in detail, for to do so would be to study all the degrees and forms of defence that man is capable of elaborating.

The attitude of the adult is further complicated by the fact that he uses the image of the adolescent to defend himself against death. To the different stereotypes (described in Chapter 7) that the adult adopts in order not to know the adolescent is added one that is especially related to death, the stereotype of the adolescent as representative of *joie de vivre*. The intensity of the adolescent's impulses makes him the symbol of the life instinct almost in its pure state. The adolescent is the image of happiness present and to come, the possessor of innumerable promised riches that will one day be realized, and one is expected to be happy all the time when one is twenty. In order to forget that death exists within every man, ugly, disintegrating, foetid, annihilating, the adult uses the image of the adolescent as a representative of beauty, freshness, love of life, full of energy that demands only to be expended, aspiring to innumerable intense and repeated pleasures (which, in actual fact, one denies him). The adult imposes this stereotype on the adolescent, thus forbidding him to express his difficulties, to give full vent to his suffering. At worst, the adolescent can express himself only in an archaic process of motor discharge, since he does not have the right to speak which further encourages his usual tendency to resort to action. Sometimes the adolescent reacts by rejecting this stereotype, by opposing it, which turns him towards the opposite stereotype of 'dark' youth, whether that of the *blouson noir* (Rockers, Hell's Angels, etc.), or that of gloomy romanticism. When this occurs the adult feels that the adolescent is in bad faith, that he is merely 'play acting', that he is not really 'dark'. The adult either denies him the right to have sufferings, troubles and disappointments, or refuses to take them seriously, regarding them as mere childish excrescences that have no right to tarnish the fresh image of youth. As Le Moal has pointed out, the adult reserves to himself the privilege of being the only victim of life, by virtue of his long experience. This attitude enables him to keep the adolescent in an irresponsible infantile position, while at the same time requiring him to be the antidote for his own fear of death. He wishes to enclose the adolescent in the stereotyped role of someone who has a song permanently in his heart. It is also a way for the adult to say: 'If I was twenty, I'd be happy at being so far from death.'

Sheltering behind this stereotype, the adult cannot bear that the adolescent should even think of death. The mere manipulation of the idea of death is condemned, and philosophical readings concerning the subject are treated either as intellectual snobbery, or as aggressive behaviour intended to annoy adults, or as a way of showing contempt for them. *A fortiori,* the suicidal adolescent is unbearable. How can someone whose mission is to personify *joie de vivre* seek death? The adult has the feeling that he has been duped, and it is easy for him to see the suicide act simply as a way of hurting and opposing him. If the adult tried to understand the motives that lie behind the suicide act, he would be calling into question his double system of defence against adolescence and death. He can re-establish his protection only by expressing his indignation, and by reproaching the adolescent for having played such a trick on him. If youth itself is unable to protect the adult against death, if those whose role it is to love life choose death, what is left to help the adult forget death? The double significance of adolescent suicide as evidence that the tendency to death exists even when one is at the peak of life's curve, and that the living have been unable to provide what the suicide expected, arouses in the adult an additional effort to redirect this criticism against its author, and a desire to punish him for committing suicide. One way of punishing him is un- doubtedly to ignore his suicide, and to behave as if it never took place.

The defence system of the adult is sustained by the fact that the adolescent, though unknown, is seldom for him a neutral being. He is always dear to him, if only because he represents the locus of the adult's projections. He is always invested by the adult, since he is the bearer of his stereotypes. The ambi- valence in one's feelings towards loved ones described by Freud is experienced about any adolescent who dies. To a greater or lesser degree, the adult feels both loss of the inves- ted object, loss, that is, of his projections, and aggressivity towards the other, and therefore guilt. In fact, the aggressivity and guilt concern this other person, this new competitor who has just won his place in the world, and who is a reminder that the older generation is growing old.

The unease that the adult feels in his relations with the adolescent is the basis of behaviour aimed at reassuring himself - and such behaviour further complicates the situation. The intrication is at its height when the suicide is an adolescent known to the adult. To reassure himself as to his acquired privileges, and in order not to fear this future equal, the adult needs to believe that the adolescent is not capable of running his own life, and that he must supervise his activities. Further- more, every adult feels morally responsible, and, indeed, is often legally responsible, especially if he has responsibility for the adolescent's education or lodging, even if only temporarily. But this feeling of responsibility, which, even if real, is used as a reassurance, becomes the cause of an important increase in guilt in the case of suicidal behaviour. By committing suicide, the adolescent automatically places the adult in a guilty position. This factor makes suicide more unbearable than ever, and partly explains the silence with which the question is received.

It is understandable that the adult, confronted by such a danger, should wish to keep himself at a safe distance, that he should be incapable of facing up to it squarely, even if, as a specialist, his function and training should help him to do so. It is understandable, too, that he should have no desire to know the exact number of persons in general, and adolescents in particular, who die voluntarily, and the number of those who try to do so. He is willing to believe any statistic so long as he is not asked to think about its implications, and above all if it minimizes the reality. And he does not hear when told repeatedly that suicide is one of the principal causes of death. He is not interested in the matter, which he no more wants to approach than he would a stick of dynamite. When he does seem to be interested it is to help him in the painful task of rebuilding his system of defences. He makes a last, feeble attempt to explain the voluntary death away as an accident, by attributing it to circumstantial factors: financial, professional or educational worries, depression, or disappointments. And, indeed, the official statistics for suicide are broken down according to such motives. Yet on closer examination one soon realizes that the causes advanced are mere banalities, the common lot of all men, whether or not they commit suicide; even if they do play a role, they are not enough to elucidate the significance of the suicide act.

The sociologists have also tried to provide reassurance by stating that a certain percentage of suicides is inevitable in any group. But what emerges from Durkheim's work[6] is that an increase in the suicide rate is a sign that the group is in a bad way. The exogenic causes would appear to lie, therefore, with the group, which is responsible for its members, thus making the other members guilty for the suicide of one of their number. In which case the members of the group have a choice between a position of guilt, punishment for which might well be death, or that of the individual subjected to pressure who might also run the risk of wanting to commit

suicide. The comfortable means of studying suicide are therefore quite inadequate. Willing to accept anything rather than
the profound motives of suicide, whether it is the possible
existence of a tendency to death in all of us, or the hypothesis
that suicide is caused by a serious inadequacy on the part of
the group, man prefers to keep at a safe distance from the
question in order not to feel concerned, in order not to have
to admit that the explanations offered seem very improbable.

At this point I should like to take up again the comparison
with road accidents. I said that in 1966 the figure for suicide
deaths was 62% that for road accidents, without taking into
account the suicidal pseudo-accidents that should be added
to the first and subtracted from the second. Of course, the
number of accidents increases each year, and the amount of
money spent on accident prevention is not only fully justified,
but inadequate. Thus when a particular road intersection is
responsible for several deaths, a great deal of money is spent
on altering it. But it was not until 300 people had thrown
themselves off the Eiffel Tower that preventive measures
costing about £1,000 were taken. Naturally, such measures are
relatively very small in scope, and do little to alter the intentions of those who will carry out their act elsewhere. But the
doubtful value of preventive measures compared with the cost
of their implementation is no justification for their not being
implemented. Taking up the suggestions made by Daumezon
(in an unpublished paper), one notes that everyone feels concerned about road accidents. It is the ideal death from the
point of view of the defence system outlined earlier, because
one is killed and the dead are victims. It is the ideal type of
the apparently exogenic death, one that in no way compro-
mises man's phantasy of immortality, and which does not
require the existence of an internal tendency to death. Men
are unanimous in their concern for 'death on our roads'; they
demand that steps be taken, and treat the whole question as
a problem common to us all. In this way, the hope of over-
coming death, conceived as an exogenic, avoidable accident,
finds satisfaction. On the other hand, to be interested in the
risk of suicide is to feel concerned by a death that everyone
bears within himself, and to demand that research into

suicide should be carried out is to arouse an anxiety that people find very difficult to contain. By being indifferent to the problem, one hopes to remain foreign to it.

In Part III we shall see how little is known as to the causes and mechanisms of adolescent suicide, and how dubious are the explanations that are often advanced. Such silence, such a lack of understanding, allow us to accept as scientific fact hypotheses which, to say the least, are uncertain. It might be thought that our knowledge cannot be more advanced than it is by virtue of the very inaccessible nature of the question. But one can equally well wonder whether the opposite mechanism does not operate. Perhaps, only too relieved at having found an explanation that frees us from the obligation of going any further, we have no desire to approach the truth, to get to know the problem of adolescent suicide more intimately. It does not seem to worry us that this explanation is inaccurate, or accurate to the extent that it does have a part to play in the determination of the act, but is in fact only one element, sometimes a minor one, in the total complex of the suicide situation. Concentration on a partial aspect transforms truth into error, prevents us from understanding suicide, and reassures us. Thus it is often said that when an adolescent commits suicide it is simply and solely that he wishes to live. This is not untrue, since we know that the life instinct is never totally absent from any human behaviour. But to concentrate on those elements in the suicide situation that express the life instinct to the exclusion of others is, again, to take the part for the whole. If the adolescent who commits suicide wishes to live, it is also possible, probable even, that he also wishes to die.

In actual fact, the reason why I have devoted a good deal of space to numerical estimates and to the errors that they contain is not because I am particularly concerned with statistical rigour. I believe that knowledge of the exact number of suicide deaths is only of relative interest. To attach too much importance to it would even have serious drawbacks; it could be a means of reconstructing resistance to knowledge of the why of the suicide of certain young people. The mere abstract manipulation of the figures would be reassuring. There is the saying that one death is a tragedy, five deaths an event, and a hundred deaths a statistic. The fundamental question is not how many adolescents commit suicide, but why they do so. Nevertheless, a critical study of the numerical data is not without interest. Beginning with the figures, we have been able to examine the deeper causes that have prevented these figures from being more accurate. We have also seen that these deeper reasons find expression in a silence that extends not only to the statistics, but to an understanding of the motives for the suicide act among young people. Since the study of these motives is even more complex and more hypothetical than the numerical study, it was essential, before approaching it, to be aware of this silence. In this way, we will not be surprised by our ignorance and our inability to reply to the fundamental, the only really important question: why do the adolescents choose to die? I shall deal with this question in Part III.

Notes

1. 'Aspects psychologiques de l'evolution et du traitement des leucémiques enfants et jeunes adultes dans un centre spécialisé', *Nouvelle Revue d'hématologie,* t.7, 1967, no. 5, 577.
2. A. Fabre-Luce, *La Mort a changé,* Paris, Gallimard, 1966, 203.
3. E. Durkheim, *Le suicide,* Paris, P.U.F., 1960, 370.
4. A. Bayet, *Le suicide et la morale,* Paris, Alcan, 1922, 5.
5. *Ibid.,* 764.
6. *Op. cit.,* 420 ff.

Part Three
Suicidogenic factors

Introduction

As we have seen, the question 'how many adolescents commit suicide?' remains unanswered. To suggest an answer would certainly be of practical and theoretical interest, and it would be a mistake to abandon it. But we cannot hope to arrive at an exact number of suicide deaths, let alone suicide attempts. And even if, at an enormous expense of effort, such a thing did become possible, would it be necessary, or even desirable, to make it one of our main concerns? To emphasize a static fact, divorced from total reality, would be to encourage a dangerous attitude, and to assist in the formation of the very resistances examined in Part II. There would be a danger that the study of suicide would become confined to the improvement of statistics, and that the essential question, that of the why and how of the adolescent suicide act, would be evaded. Even if this act was extremely rare, we would still have to answer the question of its signification. We cannot hide behind the practical problems that arise from its relative frequency or rarity, and fail to ask ourselves by what process certain adolescents arrive at such an apparently aberrant act.

As things are at present, it is absolutely necessary to try to answer this question before embarking on further work; an initial period of reflexion is indispensable to any re-examination of other modes of approach, in particular the numerical one. The fact that at present we are in no position to give an answer does not alter the situation. What do we know of what are known as the 'causes'? As I remarked in the introduction to Part II, we are as lacking in our knowledge of the why and the how as we are of the how many. We come up against the same obstacles, the same unverified 'facts' circulate, the same statements, which are more traditional than scientific, continue to be made in a way that closes the question instead of opening it up.

I have repeatedly stressed the inaccuracy of all statistics on suicide in general, and adolescent suicide in particular. Similarly, I have expressed reservations about the methods used, and about the hypothesis according to which, if the inaccuracy is taken as being constant, it is possible to make comparisons between inaccurate figures. The factors responsible for these errors are variable and invalidate such an argument. I also have similar reservations about the causes. To a varying degree, they may encourage the concealment of the suicide, either by the subject himself, his relations and friends, or society in general. These elements may therefore increase or decrease a particular cause in the statistics.

Furthermore, qualitatively certain causes have been traditionally emphasized - psychiatric, sociological, or circumstantial causes - to the detriment of other possible causes. And above all, the question why was answered with a juxtaposition of the figures for possible causes, without going into either their interrelations or the suicidal process itself.

In recent years, an important development has begun to take place. The work of teams of researchers into the question of suicide, and of adolescence, has introduced new elements into the situation. These researchers stress their dissatisfaction with classical theories. Their efforts are directed more towards grasping the actual experience of the adolescent, and the anxiety that he feels, over and above theoretical rationalizations. Even if the answer to this multi-faceted problem has not been found, it is necessary, as a first stage, to ask the question, if new perspectives are to be opened up.

The theoretical positions

Our knowledge of the causes of adolescent suicide is very shaky. The main difficulty lies in the critical evaluation of the various notions available to us. As things are at present, no one explanation can be accepted as authoritative, but neither can we afford to reject any hypothesis. The theoretical positions may be based either on those concerning suicide, or on those concerning adolescence.

The various theories concerning the causes of suicide (see Chapter 1) may be divided roughly into two groups. The first - the traditional group - presupposes a single cause, with the sociological thesis at one extreme and the psychiatric thesis at the other, taking into account, of course, the recent modifications and increased precision that have made such approaches more fruitful. The other group is based on the notion of associated multiple causes. What we have to do, then, is to try to determine the part played by the various possible causes and their interaction.

If we refer to the explanatory theories of adolescent behaviour, we may ask ourselves whether they are applicable to the particular form of behaviour that is the suicide act. The same theoretical development is to be seen on the subject of adolescence as on that of suicide (see Chapter 2). The search for a single explanation has been followed by the search for a number of associated factors. In view of the fact that adolescence is the period of life in which the influence of many different factors is most apparent, do specialists in the subject tend to view adolescent behaviour and disorders in terms of the interaction of many different factors?

The two ways of approaching the question - that is, from the point of view of suicide, and from the point of view of adolescence - are therefore less opposed to one another than at first seemed the case, since the theoretical positions in each case have followed a similar course. At this stage, it would be wiser to adopt the notion of associated factors in the determination of adolescent suicide as a working hypothesis. A return to the single-cause theory would be to go against the present current of theoretical work on both suicide and on adolescence. In such a situation, the very term cause becomes inadequate; it would be better to speak of suicidogenic factors. This would avoid placing undue stress on particular factors, thus suggesting *a priori* that it is they that determine the act.

Outline of the study of suicidogenic factors

The most fruitful approach would be a dynamic study of the conjunction of factors and of the suicidal process in the adolescent, the role of the different factors being indicated as we go along. But our knowledge is too inadequate to adopt such a procedure at once, for we would end up with an account that was both incomplete and confused.

We must avoid the trap of the hierarchization of factors, which would lead us to yet another impasse, but it is certainly true that all the factors involved do not exert the same influence or operate in the same way. In particular, we must ask ourselves whether some of these factors are necessary and specific, and whether others are interchangeable without being specific. In short, do certain of the factors usually mentioned really have any influence at all, and should they be excluded?

In order to present these questions in the correct way, we must first know more about each of the supposedly suicidogenic factors. But this division, necessary as it is to facilitate our approach, must not make us forget that the isolated study of each factor is artificial, and does not in itself justify us either in refuting it, or in confirming its importance. We must also avoid enclosing ourselves in a reassuring system, which, by fragmenting the question, would separate us from the experience of the young suicide.

The factors referred to as suicidogenic are so numerous and so varied that it is not possible to study all of them. I shall deliberately leave to one side those that quite obviously have no more than a negligible effect, and those that have no special connection with adolescence. In the next three chapters, I shall examine in turn the circumstantial, sociological, and psychiatric factors. But I shall not develop any general notions, preferring to emphasize above all what seems particularly relevant to adolescence. I shall then devote five chapters to those factors proper to adolescence: the tendency to resort to action, the manipulation of the idea of death, and the tendency to so-called depression. The fact that I pay more attention to these factors does not mean that I regard them as playing a more determining role. But they do constitute the original part of my subject, and seem to have received less attention than others. Finally, in Chapter 18, after mentioning a few factors that I have not studied, I shall examine the question of the association of all the different factors in the suicidal process.

10. Circumstantial factors

A. The role attributed to circumstantial factors

The cause most often cited for the suicide act is of a circumstantial kind. This is confirmed by the suicide himself, either
in the messages that he leaves behind him or in what he says
when he survives the attempt, by those around him, and by
the general public. This frequency is reflected in the press,
and the role of such a cause is regarded as so self-evident that
its possible absence is a cause for special comment. Thus, one
might read in a newspaper: 'X, aged 17, committed suicide;
the boy's action remains unexplained, for he appears to have
had no problems either at school or at home.' And when the
attempt fails, the suicide himself might insist on the lack of
any event that could explain his action: 'and yet I had no
reason to do it, no worries . . .' But recourse to circumstances
by way of explanation, which is frequent enough among
suicides of all ages, is just as common, perhaps more so, among
adolescents than among adults. Furthermore, even if the
event mentioned has in fact played no part in the suicidal
process, it is still worth noting that the suicide is often attributed to such events. Such a constant may be significant in
itself, and may help us to gain a greater understanding of our
subject.

The suicide, those around him, and the general public are
not alone in stressing the importance of circumstantial causes.
In the official statistics, in the heterogeneous list of the
probable causes of suicide, we find personal problems side by
side with mental disorders, drunkenness, incurable diseases,
etc.[1] The same kind of list is sometimes found in scientific
publications. It is true that they are both concerned with

suicides of all ages, and do not relate the proportions according to cause to the age groups.

On the other hand, the traditional theories of suicide tended to reject the role of circumstances. Durkheim[2] and
Delmas[3] were in agreement on this point at least. This rejection would seem to be justified. But in our attempt to
examine anew all the various notions advanced about adolescent suicide, we could hardly ignore circumstantial factors
entirely. Of course, I do not intend to include them among
the *real* causes of suicide. But perhaps between their complete rejection and their promotion to the status of a cause,
their place as a contributory factor in the suicidal situation
is worth discussing.

Circumstantial factors are cited as the real cause of suicide
in very few works on adolescent suicide. They are referred to
variously as motives, attributed motives, factors, or subsidiary
causes, and are either mentioned without further comment as
to their possible role, or regarded as secondary rationalizations
intended to conceal the true causes, or regarded as factors
that help to trigger off the act.

An interesting way of approaching a critical study of the
role of circumstantial factors would be to calculate the frequency with which each type of event is used to explain the
suicide act. Two sets of figures would be necessary: the
frequency with which each event is cited, and the frequency
of this same event in a sample of the same age group. Unfor-
tunately, there are hardly any documents of this kind, and
we are particularly lacking in statistical data. There are no
official statistics on the probable causes of suicide among
adolescents, and there are very few works indeed which, like
that of Gaultier *et al.,*[4] publish the frequency of the 'triggering
-off' factors.

However, even with these authors, we must bear in mind
the influence of the way in which the questions about motives
were presented. We must also bear in mind that the sample
was taken entirely from adolescents who had used various
kinds of toxic substances, and was therefore not representative
of all adolescent suicides. Yet a study of the frequency of
circumstantial causes, whatever their true role, would not be

Circumstantial factors mentioned in a group of adolescents who had attempted suicide by poisoning (Gaultier, Fournier, Gorceix and Zimbacca).

	Boys	*Girls*	*Total*
Educational problem	3	3	6
Conflict with a parent	3	5	8
Exhaustion	6	20	26
Social or family problem		3	3
Emotional/sexual problems	8	10	18
No precise cause	3	8	11
Other reasons		2	2
Death of a parent		3	3

without interest. In the absence of any such study we are reduced to approximations.

The most varied events are cited, from an ordinary argument to some serious event that led the subject to believe that his whole future was in jeopardy. In different works, one finds such events as a refusal on the part of parents to allow the adolescent to go out, or to buy a particular article of clothing or some other object, or the choice imposed by the parents at the time of the purchase, a row with friends, lack of success at school, disappointment in love, being sent away to boarding school, upheaval in the family on the socio-economic plane, or the combination of such an upheaval with the sudden changes in the intra-family affective relations that it involves, the loss of some loved person, in particular the father or a friend, and sometimes a more distant relation or a friend of the family. In my own experience, I have found the same diversity, but with a particularly high frequency of lack of success at school, disappointment in love, and loss of some loved person, especially the father. On the other hand, I have noted that certain events, such as long-distance moving of house and intercurrent somatic illness, are rarely mentioned.

All these circumstances are put forward by the suicide or those who knew him. There is another type of event that is sometimes mentioned by those concerned, but much more often by the general public, namely, the example of other suicides, either of friends, or of persons, either well known or unknown, mentioned in the press, in the cinema, and on radio and television. The notion of contagion recurs constantly, and is worth emphasizing since it gives rise to such attitudes as that the mass media wields influence.

B. Estimation of the possible role of circumstantial factors

The notion of the circumstantial factor

Apparently, the circumstantial factor is difficult to define. It includes any chance event that occurs during the adolescence of the subject, and which, by its very existence, may be supposed to have played a direct role in the determination of the suicide. It should therefore be quite easy to distinguish it from the sociological and psychological factors, and from ancient factors that act upon the subject through the medium of the traces that they leave in the social environment, or in the individual's psychical organization.

In fact, this distinction is a very delicate one, and in many cases remains rather arbitrary. The true circumstantial event would seem to be that which occurs by chance, without being the consequence of a peculiarity of the biological, psychological or social organization. It may include a purely somatic intercurrent illness, failure in an examination due to the inevitable imponderables of this type of situation, disappointment in love due to the impulsive over-optimism normal in adolescence, and the loss of a loved person. It might also be said to include a sudden, unexpected change in the situation of the family in its socio-economic or psycho-affective organization, thus involving an upheaval in parent/child relations.

But these and other events may be less fortuitous than they seem, and may in fact be the more or less inevitable culmination of particular psychological and social processes. Thus, in many cases, failure in examinations is the result of an error in educational orientation, an inadequate educational level in the school, or a particular form of behaviour on the part of the pupil; generally speaking, it is a result of parent/child conflicts, or of a particular psycho-social-economic situation. Similarly, in many cases, disappointment in love may be the result of pressure exerted on the partner, or of inadequate relational behaviour, both of which lead to failure in love. It may also be the result of pressure exerted by the family or social group, in application of moral principles, in which case it then takes on the significance of a sociological rather than a circumstantial factor.

On the other hand, there are events that are not in themselves suicidogenic, but which may have consequences that do act as circumstantial factors in suicide. Thus, in the case of somatic intercurrent illness, we must distinguish between its direct effects, such as the rupture in the rhythm of life, changes in one's awareness of one's own body, worry over one's health, and its indirect consequences, such as aesthetic sequelae or consequences on educational progress, which may involve the loss of a school year, and even abandonment of certain projects. Similarly, a change of residence inevitably brings in its train a whole series of changes and uncertainties, but the local conditions of the new place of residence may encourage or discourage educational and socio-affective reintegration.

Thus although there are events that are really fortuitous, there are others which, under the appearance of fortuitousness, are merely the result, either of earlier fortuitous events that are no longer active, or of psycho-pathological or social factors that are the only factors really involved. It is therefore as the latter that they should be studied, and they do not belong to the factors being studied in this chapter.

Value of the true circumstantial factor

Among all the really fortuitous circumstantial factors, one is of particular importance, namely, the loss of a loved person during adolescence. It must be emphasized both because it is found with surprising frequency, and because it is not some everyday event that occurs in the lives of most adolescents. But probable as this point may appear, it is nevertheless no more than a hypothesis. In order to confirm it, it would be necessary to make a statistical study of the correlation between this loss, especially of the father, and suicide, by establishing a comparison with the frequency of the loss of the father in the non-suicidal adolescent population.

Although it is not mentioned in the publications, I believe that we must also attach some importance to the death of a grandparent when this occurs in a particular context. It seems to me that such a death may have an indirect effect in cases where a particularly close relationship existed between the grandparent and his or her child, that is, the father or mother of the adolescent. This relationship is evidence of the persistence of a strong Oedipal link that has been highly infiltrated by pregenital motions. It seems to me that the effects on the adolescent take place at the time of the death of the maternal grandfather in particular, and to a lesser extent of the paternal grandmother.

Similarly, it seems to me to be useful to attach some importance to the sudden, unexpected character of the reputedly suicidogenic event. The shock that results and the psychological upheavals that it gives rise to play at least as important a role as the nature of the event itself.

The other most commonly mentioned events - a row with one's parents about going out or about clothes, failure in examinations, disappointment in love, have this in common: they are ordinary, everyday events that occur constantly in the non-suicidal adolescent population. In fact, it would be difficult to find in the present adolescent population a young person who has not experienced one of these three events, and in most cases all three together. It would be difficult to treat as a cause of suicide, or even as an associated suicidogenic factor, events that are fundamental characteristics of the lives of all young people, which are even an integral part of the process of adolescence, and which do not appear to have any great detrimental effect on the majority of these young people. They cannot seriously be regarded as responsible for the suicide of a very small minority. Common sense tells us that we can regard as a suicidogenic factor only events which, occurring throughout a random sample, would cause suicide among a majority of that sample, or at least among a sizeable minority. This is obviously not the case with the events usually mentioned.

Confronted by this elementary observation, one is tempted to reject the whole notion of events as suicidogenic factors. But clinical observation forbids me to do this. One is bound to remark that however common such events may be they do occur with particular frequency in the period leading up to the suicide act, and are, quite obviously, the starting point in time, if not in aetiology, of changes in behaviour and psychical life that culminate in the suicide act. In this context, they cannot be rejected *en bloc,* and one must continue to regard them as possible suicidogenic factors.

Significance of possible suicidogenic circumstantial factors

Quite obviously, not all the events mentioned as causes of suicide, or at least as factors that trigger it off, have the same significance. It does not depend on the type of event, but on the context in which it occurs.

Some of these events are obviously cited after the suicide act as a justification, and are used, consciously or unconsciously, as a secondary defence rationalization to avoid uncovering the true suicidogenic factors. This type of rationalization is mentioned by most authors, and has long been known. Durkheim[5] understood its importance, and used this argument to reject circumstances as suicidogenic factors. Despite the everyday nature of the process, whose function is easy to understand, the use of the fortuitous event as a secondary rationalization is worth investigating from the point of view of the motives involved in the use of such a type of defence.

The most obvious motive is the conscious concealment of the true cause. This may be concealment by the suicide himself, who, by enabling those around him to avail themselves of the first pretext to come to hand, keeps to himself the real motives of his act. It may also be a conscious concealment on the part of the family, which is anxious to keep the deeper causes secret. More profound, but better known, is the secondary rationalization that conceals and maintains a process of repression. This may involve a rationalization by the suicide, who keeps from himself, in the unconscious, the true motives for his act, or it may be a rationalization by the family, who wish to repress the shame or guilt that a knowledge of the deeper motives of adolescent suicide would arouse in them. The mention of a fortuitous event gives the suicide act the appearance of an accident, and absolves the suicide himself from all suspicion of being psychically abnormal, and the family and friends from all responsibility for that abnormality.

But these mechanisms do not seem to take into account all the motives that lead people to use the event as a secondary justification of the suicide act. If the fortuitous event is used in preference to any other explanation, it may have something to do with the deeper attitudes to death referred to earlier.[6] To cite a fortuitous event is to cite a factor that is both external and accidental. This means that the adolescent has not committed suicide, but has been killed by an unexpected, external event. This is strongly reminiscent of residual primitive thought, according to which man does not die, but is killed accidentally. The use of the fortuitous event is related, partly at least, to an attempt to negate death, and *a fortiori* voluntary death.

Although the use of the fortuitous event as the rationalization of a factor that in fact plays no part in the process of suicide is frequent, it cannot be said to be the only mechanism. We lack too many of the links in the chain of the process to be able to deny that it is a true suicidogenic factor. In particular, we do not know how this external factor is connected to the adolescent's internal experience, and are therefore unable to say whether it has or has not played a part in the process of voluntary death.

One remark should be made here. I said earlier that the fortuitous events are ordinary, everyday occurrences in the lives of most adolescents. This would seem to be the case, and objectively they are the same events that occur in the course of every human life. But is this so from a subjective point of view? We do not know whether the failure in an examination experienced by the suicide is the same as that experienced by another pupil. We do not know whether disappointment in love, however ordinary and fortuitous the event may appear from the outside, as experienced by the suicide is the same as that experienced by any other young man or woman. It may be that what seems identical in terms of visible phenomena is profoundly different in a minority of subjects.

Indeed, many authors have stressed to what extent the events referred to varied in their objective importance, from events similar to those cited by adults, to the most childish and apparently futile events, similar to those cited by young children who commit suicide. But certain authors, such as Le Moal, and Launay and Col,[7] have also emphasized how carefully we must judge the futile character of the motives cited by the child and adolescent. Le Moal has also emphasized the tendency of adults to regard systematically as futile and unimportant the motives of children and adolescents, as if only adults enjoyed the privilege of having serious reasons for wishing to die. This shows how precarious is the pseudo-objectivity involved in judging the seriousness of ostensible motives. However common and normal these motives may be, we must still discover whether their representation in the psychical life of suicidal adolescents is the same as in that of other adolescents. And as we pursue this hypothesis, we obviously come up against the notion of personality disorders, or, at least, of peculiarities existing prior to the event. This then refers us to the psycho-pathological factors of the suicide act, which, once again, would lead us to believe that the event did not act as a suicidogenic factor.

Before reaching such a conclusion, however, we must ask ourselves one question. If the fortuitous event had not occurred, would the suicide act have been triggered off? Two hypotheses present themselves. According to the first, the fortuitous event played the role of a non-specific factor. This implies that some event would inevitably have occurred that would have triggered off the suicide act, though perhaps at a different time and in different circumstances.

According to the second hypothesis, the event may have played a specific triggering-off role. Because of certain elements peculiar to the suicidal personality, the event in question is able, in a quite special way, to trigger off the process that culminates in the suicide act. In this context, one can see that if the event in question had not taken place, the risk of suicide would not have become a reality.

These are, of course, no more than hypotheses whose validity cannot be verified at present. In any case, they appeal to the notion of a pre-existing psychological peculiarity, and they show that although the events may be regarded as factors that trigger off the suicide act, or which are favourable to it, they cannot be regarded as actual causes of suicide. Moreover, if, as I have said, one remembers that most, apparently fortuitous, events are in fact merely the expression of psychological or social processes, of a long-standing or overall kind, the study of circumstantial factors refers us necessarily to the sociological and psychological factors.

Notes

1. Cf. the *Annuaire statistique de la Ville de Paris et de la Seine*, Paris, Imprimerie Municipale.
2. E. Durkheim, *Le Suicide*, Paris, P.U.F., 1960, 334.
3. A. Delmas, *Psychologie pathologique du suicide*, Paris, Alcan, 1932, 165.
4. M. Gaultier, E. Fournier, A. Gorceix and N. Zimbacca, 'Étude clinique et statistique d'un groupe de mineurs suicidants', *Semaine des Hôpitaux*, no. 50, 8 November 1963, Paris, 2379.
5. *Op. cit.*, 334.
6. Chapter 8.
7. C. Launay and C. Col, 'Suicide et tentative de suicide chez l'enfant et l'adolescent', *Revue de Praticien*, t. xiv, no. 6, 21 February 1964, 620.

11·The sociological factors

Either to emphasize or to challenge their importance, the sociological factors are regularly mentioned in relation both to suicide
and to adolescence. It is absolutely necessary, therefore, in any
study of adolescent suicide, to examine their nature and function. Their importance seems to be confirmed by everyday
experience. This does not make their study any easier, however,
and a number of obstacles soon present themselves.

The first obstacle is of both a theoretical and practical
nature. Whereas the sociologist bases his work primarily on
statistics, we are, paradoxically, particularly ill-equipped in
this field. There is no need here to repeat the errors that de-
tract from the value of all statistics on suicide, and I have
already shown that the persistence of these errors could in
turn become the object of a psycho-sociological study.[1]
Furthermore, the official statistics are of little help to us
because they are very inadequate and often, indeed, silent on
just those points that are of most interest to us.

Clinical work provides a good deal more information about
these factors. But it is often concerned with particular groups
that are unrepresentative of the average suicide. Furthermore,
the lack of any standardization of research means that the
disparity in the data collected and their classification makes
comparison difficult. Similar difficulties are encountered in
dealing with the psychiatric factors.

The result of this lack of numerical data on the collective
facts is that those that seem most likely to be important can
only lead to hypotheses and comments based on clinical
observation.

The second obstacle concerns the diversity of the sociological factors cited. This diversity facilitates the tendency to

confine one's study of them to a juxtaposition by descriptive enumeration, to the detriment of the crucial problem of their mechanism of action. So it seems to me that if we are to avoid this kind of dispersal it would be better to deal with only a small number of factors, and to develop those that seem best able to illustrate the matter. While calling in question unverifiable, but commonly accepted views, I shall concentrate mainly on three questions:

1) Do the sociological factors really play a role in adolescent suicide?

2) If they do, are they the same factors that operate in adult suicide, or are they peculiar to adolescent suicide? In order to answer this question we must re-examine all the sociological factors usually regarded as suicidogenic in the case of adults; but this would take us outside the scope of this book.

3) Lastly, and perhaps most importantly, to what extent are the sociological facts suicidogenic in the course of adolescence? Of course, this question goes well beyond our subject, and touches on the whole question of the relations between sociology and the medico-psychological disciplines.

On this basis, we shall examine first the small group of the family, then the wider social structures that the adolescent has to confront, bearing in mind, of course, the problem of the interrelation of the two. We shall then examine the value and mechanism of action of the factors cited.

A. Familial factors

The familial situation of young suicides includes a number of factors, only some of which have been studied.

— It is perhaps worth mentioning the *marital situation* of the individual concerned. Although the question does not arise for younger suicides, it does arise in the case of older ones. Durkheim[2] pointed out the detrimental influence that early marriage, under the age of twenty, can have, especially on the male. But this point is hardly mentioned in most works, no doubt because there were far too few subjects for whom this was the case for any conclusions to be drawn. It is a fact that although the average age of marriage has lowered, early marriages have become much more rare. On the other hand, marriage has become much more frequent among students, and it would be interesting to bear this in mind.

In fact, familial factors concern above all those of the young suicide's family, and it is these that we shall now examine.

—*Relations with brothers and sisters* have been studied by a good many authors. Contrary to one widespread notion, the proportion of only children would not appear to be higher among young suicides.

Opinion is divided in the case of eldest children. Many authors attribute to them a higher proportion, while Duché[3] sees no evidence for this. I, personally, have found no evidence for this.

Rank in the family does not appear to play any role. But it must be admitted that this point has seldom been studied. In my opinion it should be, providing one specifies the modalities of the rank, in particular concerning age gaps and the sex of the children. Similarly, it might be interesting to investigate the possibility of a dead brother or sister, especially one who died before the suicide was born. Without wishing to exaggerate its importance, this factor has seemed to me to be relatively frequent.

—*Anomalies in the familial structure* are the principal factor. They are both frequent and diverse - opinion is not divided on this point. Among adolescent suicides, those with a normal familial situation are relatively few, and are even in a minority. The same anomalies recur over and over again: firstly, the absence of one of the parents, and with relative frequency of both parents, for the most diverse reasons - death, prolonged illness, abandonment, an unmarried mother, etc. And it may occur in a context of separation, divorce, remarriage, one of the parents living with another partner, etc.

One point that is seldom specified seems to me to occur with a certain frequency: habitual and long-standing co-habitation with other members of the family (aside from the need to take in a single, elderly parent). Here, too, the most diverse situations occur, but they may be reduced schematically to the cohabitation of several generations, that is, with the grandparents, one or both, or with a more distant relation (an old aunt, etc.). It may occur in the home of the grandparents, or the parents, or the two adult generations might only live in close proximity, in the same building for example, with a *de facto* community life of the two homes. All these types of situation give rise to changes, of varying degrees of importance, in the familial constellation, culminating, in extreme cases, to a *de facto* absence of the atomic family of father/mother/children.

In addition to these anomalies in the overt structure of the family, there can also be, within an apparently normal atomic family, important disturbances in intra-familial relations. Their effect is obviously more difficult to assess, on account of their subjective character, and of the nature of the criteria, but they may range from the incompatibility of the parents to the mental illness of one (or both) of them.

— *The absence of the father* deserves particular mention. It has been found by all authors to occur with remarkable frequency. This absence always goes back to childhood, and may be the result of the most diverse causes: the real absence of the father by abandonment, death, or some fortuitous event, or the *de facto* absence of a father who is 'physically' present, but who establishes no relationship with his child. On the other hand, the parental lack is attenuated when another man in the immediate environment is able to establish a satisfactory relationship. And it is a strange fact that the absence of the father may have an effect not only on a son, but also on a daughter.

B. Social factors

Beyond the family, the young person has to confront the structures of society as a whole.

Socio-economic factors

I have little to say about the socio-economic and cultural level of the family, other than that I am in agreement with the almost unanimous opinions of the authors. Again, contrary to a widely held belief, this factor does not appear to have any effect. Young suicides are to be found in all levels, and have parents belonging to every professional group. They are not more numerous in families at the more extreme levels; indeed, they might even be proportionately less numerous among the economically more deprived.

These observations on the family are especially valid when the socio-economic level of the young person is the same as that of his family. This is so in the case of the younger adolescents, who, because they stay longer at school, do not have economic independence. But what of the older adolescents? There are the students, for whom, according to several publications, there is a greater tendency to suicide. But no large-scale numerical research has been done to justify such an assertion, and we are bound to fall back on a reference sample.

Among those who earn their own living, their socio-economic and professional distribution does not appear to have any influence. In particular, those with satisfactory professional qualifications, and those who earn a normal living, appear in normal proportion. This leaves those without qualifications, above all those who show a lack of professional stability. But this group does not appear to be very large and should be assessed with great care: 'professional instability does not have the same significance at this age as later; one cannot say that an extremely mobile social situation is a permanent state'.[4]

Nevertheless, the specialized study of certain professions can provide us with valuable information. The work of Castets[5] on young female domestic servants and assistants in food stores shows to what extent a network of facts concerning social status and interpersonal relations is built up on the basis of one's work.

On the other hand, it seems to me that the notion of socio-economic and cultural 'shift' is worth examining, though it has received little attention so far.

One might mention in passing the case of adolescents sent out to work at an unusually early age. This category does not usually appear in the figures. This may mean that they are rarely to be found among the suicides, but they are also becoming increasingly rare in the general population, owing to the higher school-leaving age, at least in the great urban centres; they form, therefore, a special social group.

What seems to me to be of particular importance is the socio-economic gap between the familial environment and the social environment (school, leisure activities, etc.). This sometimes has an effect when the young person belongs to a social environment that is lower than that of the familial environment but it seems to have an effect above all in the opposite case, when the young person belongs to a social environment that is economically or socially higher than that of his family.

— *The cultural level* also seems to present problems of gap. At the family level, the gap may be in either direction: the family may have attained a comfortable economic level without possessing the corresponding socio-cultural level, or it may have a high cultural level, yet lack the corresponding degree of social success.

Again, a cultural gap between the adolescent and his family may have its effect. It occurs in cases of failure at school, when the adolescent does not reach the level usual in the family. But it is more likely to have an effect when it works in the opposite direction. I have already stressed the importance of this problem,[6] which has considerable affective implications, but which also touches on fundamental sociological problems concerning the cultural development of society, the democratization of the educational system, etc. It also leads us to a consideration of a structure that plays a role of the utmost importance:

The organization of the educational system

This may be examined from the limited point of view of teaching methods, which is already indicative of a certain sociological option. But the school is also the place where the adolescent forms relationships both with individuals of the same age group as himself and with adults who possess knowledge and disciplinary power.

I have no wish to draw up the case against the traditional school - this has already been done several times. But one cannot fail to notice the obstacles that any attempt at genuine reform continues to face. Opposition is either overt, or is hidden beneath minor concessions and successive peripheral reforms that elude the main problems. Such resistance tells us a great deal about the basis of the relations between pupil and school, and about the desire for the school to retain its repressive role.

However, the fundamental problem has not attained the same degree of acuteness everywhere. The quality of the relations and the genuinely educative concern of the teachers vary from one school to another. In order to discover whether the harm done by the traditional educational system has any influence on suicide, it would be useful to make an analysis of both in different schools.

By the same token, it would be interesting to study the correlation between the tendency to suicide and the type of teaching. I mentioned in an earlier work[7] the hypothesis that suicide might be less frequent in technical schools than in secondary schools of an 'academic' kind. It would be important to verify this, and, having done so, to understand the reasons for it.

I will not deal in detail with the problem of boarding schools, which I mentioned earlier in relation to circumstantial factors. In many ways, it is typical of the complexity of this type of problem, since, in France at present, the fact of being in a boarding school at all is more and more often the consequence of other psychological or social difficulties, and it is difficult to assess the possible role of either in the suicidal process.

Adolescent groups

This question is one of the chief areas of activity in the sociology of youth. It has received more attention than other aspects of adolescence, especially in relation to delinquency. But, even here, a good many of the assertions made must be invalidated. A large number of works have been published on the subject - far too many to be summarized here - and I would refer the reader to these. In any case, the relations between group membership and suicide have hardly been studied at all. I have made a few observations on this subject, but they are too partial and too summary to have any other value than that of hypotheses.

On the whole, it seems to me that young suicides do not belong to any group more frequently than is the case among the young population as a whole. Sometimes, they belong to a micro-group of three to five adolescents, but this micro-group is characterized by its isolation from the life of young people as a whole. Their situation is more one of group solitude, with close interpersonal relations but without the structure proper to a larger group. In the case of young suicides who do apparently belong to a group, it often turns out that they did not really belong. They have made an attempt, and sometimes a great effort, to become integrated, but have not succeeded. They feel different from the rest, either because they feel rejected by them, or because they do not feel within themselves a deep need to take part in group life. It would seem that there is a connection between group membership and protection against suicide, but we do not know exactly how this protection may operate.

The above remarks seem to me to be valid for all kinds of groups, whether groups of an official nature (youth clubs and youth movements, all characterized by a strong collective super-ego), or those unofficial, but closed and highly structured groups referred to all too readily as adolescent gangs, or, again, those flexible, ever-changing groups that are formed by most adolescents on the basis of the technical, cultural or social activities that happen to interest them. When integration in one of these groups is a reality, there appears to be no difference in the proportion of suicides from one kind of group to another.

The attitude of society to adolescent suicide

In Part II I tried to analyse how our attitude motivated our ignorance of adolescent suicide. We can now take up the question again, but from a different point of view, and ask ourselves whether this collective resistance to knowledge, this connivance in ignorance, combined, curiously enough, with acceptance of its transposition into fictional or journalistic terms, encourages or discourages the suicide act among adolescents.

The question is not new, and different answers have been given. Apart from those who deny the role of imitation altogether, and consider that it is quite useless to keep silent on the matter, there are those who believe that silence is necessary and cite in defence of their position whole series of suicides that have occurred when the details of one have been published. There are also those who believe that silence is dangerous, for by placing a prohibition on the subject, one tends to dramatize it and lend it a certain spurious glamour. Napoleon forbade the publication of suicides. Durkheim,[8] on the other hand, denies the role of imitation, and can see no disadvantage in speaking of the subject. However, he does attach importance to the way one speaks of suicide, and believes that if one does not condemn it as immoral one is virtually encouraging it.

In fact, it is quite wrong to present the question in these terms. There is a confusion here between three factors that may exist in isolation, or may combine in various ways: publicity, moral judgment, and one's deeper attitude to the experience of the potential suicide. Publicity is useful in that it provides a means of assessing the attitude of society, as Bayet[9] has shown so well; but, at the level of the possible role of imitation, it seems to belong, not to the sociological factors as such, but to the circumstantial factors. Like them, it is a commonplace, and cannot therefore be regarded as a cause of suicide.

Moral judgment may be more effective as a defence mechanism for keeping the problem at a distance than as a means of increasing awareness. In any case, one only has to remember the failure of the religious factor to influence suicide.

On the other hand, the deeper attitude that one may have towards the question may influence the suicide act, though we cannot say in which direction. Adolescent suicide, as I have said, arouses the maximum collective fear. Society is afraid of death and its taboos are very strong; it is difficult to speak of death other than in abstract terms. Adults are afraid of the adolescent, and defend themselves by erecting the stereotypes of the adolescent-in-love-with-life and the adolescent-who-resorts-to-action-and-destroys-everything. Adolescents know that, with suicide, they arouse the maximum fear in adults. It might be thought that the collective prohibition would help the adolescent to suppress any temptation to suicide. But one might equally well presume the opposite. The impossibility of speaking of death and suicide prevents the process of development from taking place and encourages regressive forms of expression in action, which are added to the natural tendency of adolescents to resort to action, and to the temptation to live up to the stereotype of the adolescent-who-resorts-to-action. Furthermore, the stereotype of the adolescent-in-love-with-life may arouse in the adolescent a desire to oppose it and to draw attention to his fascination with death.

C. Critique of the sociological factors

To deny the existence of sociological factors in the suicidal process in adolescents would be a systematic rejection of apparently obvious facts. But what do we know of these sociological factors, and how can we understand their role?

From the statistical point of view, we have on the one hand numerical data that are easy to assess, such as rank in the family or socio-professional rank, and on the other purely clinical data that have not been subjected to numerical control, such as membership of a group or relations with grandparents. In any case, we usually lack more detailed numerical data, such as, for example, the way in which the different possibilities of structural anomalies within the same family fit together. We also lack, for all these data, the double reference to a sample of adolescents with other psychological or social difficulties.

Furthermore, the sociological data that I have cited are of very different kinds. Some, such as participation in the organization of a school, are an integral part of the social life of all adolescents, while others, such as a broken family, are to be found more frequently among young suicides.

Despite these handicaps, I shall attempt to make a comparison with the suicidogenic factors present in the adult. Traditionally, these factors are seen to converge in the notion of a relation between suicide on the one hand, and social structure and degree of integration in a group on the other, whether the anomaly is due to peculiarities in the conditions of the individual's social life or in the structure of the group. The most frequent result is a feeling, or a real state, of isolation. The evidence that I have been able to collect concerning the adolescent corroborates this view: isolation, and peculiarities in the subject's integration in the group, due either to the group or to the subject himself. But it is difficult to carry the comparison further, for although the consequences are of the same order, the factors responsible for them differ according to age. It is obvious that the conditions of social life are not the same for the adult and for the adolescent, either at the level of collective structure or at that of social rules: school life and leisure are peculiar to the adolescent. But the suicidal adult and adolescent do have one thing in common: an anomalous familial situation, not in the present, but in the past, in childhood.

If we try to go deeper into the question, the main obstacle lies in the very nature of sociological information. Specialists in the medico-psychological disciplines are reluctant to subscribe to the practice of enumerating facts seen only from the outside; they see such an approach as unhelpful in an attempt to grasp the nature of the combat between life and death that takes place in the ego of the adolescent. It is unsatisfactory to regard the family from the point of view of enumerating its members, when one knows how complex are the ties that bind them together, and their profound influence on the development of the child's personality. It seems all too easy to enumerate the collective facts, correlate these with suicide, and derive a relation of cause and effect, without considering whether it might be a case of mere concomitance. There is the risk of ending up with a collection of abstractions that throw no light at all on how the collective facts influence such an individual act as suicide.

It is not a question of denying the importance of sociological factors, but of understanding the link that exists between them and the individual internal process. The relation of cause and effect cannot be established so long as one is content with mere juxtaposition. We must ask ourselves how each individual feels and experiences the collective fact, what he does with it, and what it does with him. If we are to deepen our understanding of the question, we must subjectify the sociological facts, separate the links that constitute the individuation of collective facts and the collectivization of individual facts.

In fact, for several years now, researchers have been doing just this. For a long time now, sociologists have been confronting their data with the individual Unconscious, and Freud devoted a considerable part of his work to collective psychology. The recent work of G. Mendel[10] makes an interesting contribution to this research. We have only to examine his proposition of the dual process of the transmission of unconscious acquisitions by socio-cultural institutions and of the sociogenesis of the unconscious, to elucidate the relations between certain sociological facts and suicide.

Thus the role of various institutions and situations whose influence is apparently obscure now becomes comprehensible. For example, the school, the representative of social repression and of the obligation of affective regression, acts identically on all pupils. But whereas the majority reacts in various ways, this action may have a particular impact on the ego of young suicidal adolescents.

The same may be said of the Father in his role as a link between social Power and the developing ego of the child. His real absence creates a rupture. But his presence is also frustrating if, too bound by the 'technological Ideal',[11] he is no more than the representative of that Ideal and is absent *qua* Father.

The same may be said of society's attitude to adolescent suicide, which I have mentioned several times already. Funeral rites or prohibitions concerning the mention of death and suicide are representations of unconscious acquisition and collective fear; and, participating in the sociogenesis of the unconscious, they affect individual behaviour towards death and suicide.

It is also possible to elucidate the relations between circumstantial and sociological factors. Disappointment in love is a good illustration of this. Of course, it depends essentially on individual development. But the social rules concerning the sexual life of adolescents intervene by aiming, at least in part, at helping the young person not to overcome the Oedipal conflict, but to regress towards pregenital positions. And the depression, accompanied sometimes by the idea of suicide, that ensues is comparable with that which occurs after disappointment with collective events - political events for example - that have been experienced as failures in the struggle against the Father.

Lastly, one can examine the relations between society and the family, who act sometimes as accomplices, sometimes as competitors, in the exercise of repressive power over the adolescent.

Notes

1. Introduction to Part II.
2. E. Durkheim, *Le suicide,* Paris, P.U.F., 1960, 282.
3. D.J. Duché, Les tentatives de suicide chez l'enfant et l'adolescent', *Psychiatrie de l'enfant,* Paris, P.U.F., 1964, vol. VII, fasc. 1, 51.
4. M. Gaultier *et al.,* 'Étude clinique et statistique d'un groupe de mineurs suicidants', *Semaine des Hôpitaux,* no. 50, 8 November 1963, Paris, 2377.
5. B. Castets, 'Note sur 350 observations de tentatives du suicide', *Recherches sur les Maladies Mentales,* vol. II, Paris, Imprimerie Municipale, 1963, 274.
6. Chapter 7.
7. 'Le suicide chez les mineurs', *L'Hygiène mentale,* no. 2, 1964, 56.
8. *Op. cit.,* 136.
9. A. Bayet, *Le suicide et la morale,* Paris, Alcan, 1922.
10. *La Révolte contre le Père,* Paris, Payot, 1968.
11. *Ibid.,* 17 ff.

12·The psychiatric factors

There are several ways of looking at the relations between suicide and mental illness. One consists in studying suicide in isolation, from a psychopathological point of view. One sets out to discover in what sense it is pathological, and to what particular disorder it belongs. It may be regarded as a pathological entity of suicidal insanity or suicidal-monomania, or as belonging to a more complex context. I have already mentioned the history of this point of view,[1] and I shall return to it later.

Another way is to seek the relations that may exist between suicide on the one hand, without defining its nature, and mental illness on the other. One tries to establish a correlation between them, though without prejudging that correlation in terms of cause and effect.

In this chapter I should like to speak of the psychiatric factors and of mental illnesses in the traditional, more limited meaning of the term. I shall keep to the traditional nosography, but this must not be taken to mean that I am prejudging my position concerning either this nosography or the place that suicide may occupy in it. Despite this relatively precise frame of reference, the question still presents problems. There is still a good deal of lively nosological discussion in psychiatry; the terms used and their content vary from one set of statistics to another, thus making any comparison extremely difficult. However, despite these variants, one can find rough agreement on the more important syndromes and the more marked mental illnesses. But this is not the case in borderline areas. This question raises the difficult and inexhaustible problem of the boundary between the normal and the pathological. Taking traditional psychiatric concepts as our frame of reference, to what extent and from what point do certain personalities enter the psychiatric nosographical framework? This point is of particular interest for us because it is during adolescence that a relatively large number of mental illnesses make their appearance; but it is also at this period that diagnoses are most difficult to make, for a considerable proportion of adolescents with disorders remain borderline cases.

I have no wish to go over the whole field of relations between suicide and psychiatry. The question at issue, for the psychiatric as for the other factors, is whether adolescent suicide is bound up with psychiatric factors similar to those operating in adult suicide, or whether there are specific psychiatric factors. So, before going any further, I shall outline briefly the psychiatric factors operating in the case of adult suicide.

A. Psychiatric factors and adult suicide

As far as the 'psychiatric promotion of suicides'[2] is concerned, that is to say, the proportion of suicides suffering from mental disorders, I provide in Table 34 a summary of percentages drawn from various authors.

The proportion varies widely from one author to another on account of the highly variable conditions of research. On the one hand, the diagnostic possibilities differ, in particular according to whether we are dealing with a suicide death, when the psychiatric diagnosis is often retrospective and indirect, or a suicide attempt, when the diagnosis may be either retrospective or present, indirect or direct. Similarly, it is important to know whether it is based solely on evident facts, generally dating from an earlier period, such as internment or at least consultation or specialized treatment, or whether it is based on a recent clinical examination, with no account being taken of an earlier history. On the other hand, it is important to know whether one includes in mental illnesses only the more generally recognized disorders, that is to say, the broad categories of psychosis in their overt forms, or whether one also includes mental unbalance, neurosis, the various character disorders, etc.

Table 34. Proportion of psychiatric and parapsychiatric disorders in suicides of all ages, according to various authors.

Authors	2 sexes		Men		Women	
	Psych.	Parapsych.	Psych.	Parapsych.	Psych.	Parapsych.
Deshaies	60				18	
Legoyt (in Deshaies)			14			
Brière de B (")	50					
Serin	33	28				
Piker	7					
Weichbredt	36		79		65.5	
Vedrinne			38	46	38	63
Castets	9.80	5.82				
Doignon	100					
Schneider		4.2				
Problèmes	17.3					
Van Mayer (in Ey)			30		50	

Table 35. Proportion of suicides among mental patients according to various authors.

Authors	Manic-depressive	Epilepsy	Schizophrenia	Disequilibrium	Confusion	Chronic alcoholism	Chronic delirium
Cor	30	17.2	8	35		12.1	8
Lemperière	30		10	35			
Esquirol (in Ey)	10						
Brière de B. (")	25						
Viallon (")	16						
Gucci (")	32						
Deshaies	28		7	30	10	11	6
Quidu	2.3			patients in general			

— For *the frequency of suicide among mental patients,* I have indicated in Table 35 the principal nosographical categories, together with the proportions drawn from various authors.

The most important suicidogenic categories are, of course, manic-depressive psychosis, characteral unbalance, and, to a lesser extent, chronic alcoholism, schizophrenia, epilepsy, and chronic delirium. On the whole, between 10% and 25%, according to the author, of mental patients commit suicide or make a suicide attempt, to which, according to Deshaies, we must add 9% who have an active propensity to suicide, that is to say, who have definite ideas of committing suicide.

Taking the principal mental illnesses observed among mentally ill suicides, one finds in the same order manic-depressive psychosis, characteral unbalance, then alcoholism, schizophrenia, epilepsy, neuroses, etc. But, as Schneider[3] reminds us, these figures have no value in themselves; they have to be compared with the figures for the total intake of the establishments in which they were collected.

B. Porportion between suicide and mental illness among adolescents

As in the case of the adult, we have two ways of studying the relation between suicide and mental illness among adolescents: we can begin with suicide or we can begin with mental illness.

— *The proportion of suicides among mentally ill adolescents.* We have little information on this question. For such an estimate, we would need to know the number of adolescent suicides admitted to a hospital psychiatric department in relation to the total number of adolescents admitted. But most of the publications of the specialized departments show only the number of suicides. In an earlier work,[4] I showed the results of a poll carried out at the student clinic of the Hôpital Sainte-Anne in Paris over a period of five years (1958-1962). Out of a total of 120 girls under the age of 21, admitted for various reasons, we found 32, that is, 26.66%, who had made one or several suicide attempts before admission into hospital; out of 61 boys under the age of 21, 9 had made an attempt, that is, 14.75%, before admission. This makes a proportion of 22.65% for both sexes together. Danon-Boileau and his colleagues[5] show the results collected over six years at the Maison Universitaire Médico-Psychologique at Sceaux. Out of 377 students admitted, 66 had made at least one attempt before, during, or after their admission, that is, 17.5%. Of the 66, 38 were psychotics, that is, approximately 60%, of which 22, or 33%, were schizophrenics, 22 suffered from neurotic depression, 4 were psychopaths, and 2 had mental disorders as a result of organic illnesses (diabetes, tuberculosis, epilepsy). The high proportion of psychotics, as the authors point out, is hardly surprising, since it corresponds to the general ratio of the number of psychotics in the establishment.

I know of no other estimates of the number of suicide attempts in relation to a group of mentally ill adolescents. It is hardly possible to draw any statistically valid conclusions from these figures alone. All we can do is to compare them with those provided for adults, which, according to Janine Cor,[6] yield a proportion of 13%, and according to Deshaies[7] a proportion of 11%. The figures quoted seem to indicate, then, a higher overall proportion of suicide attempts among adolescents. In addition to the lack of statistics, there are the nosographical difficulties, which I shall examine later.

— We have more information about *the number of the mentally ill among suicidal adolescents,* but it is still relatively small in relation to similar information about adults. By way of example, here are the figures published by:

Fau, Château, and Machu:[8] out of 23 subjects, 1 psychosis plus 3 doubtful cases, 5 cases with neurotic symptoms, and 4 with character disorders;

Zimbacca, Gorceix, and Lejeune:[9] out of 71 subjects, 16% were psychotic, especially of a schizophrenic type, 15% neurotic or with neurotic features, 37% psychopathically unbalanced, 5% suffering from severe juvenile crises, 8% with atypical personalities, and 17% normal.

Szymanska and Zelazowska:[10] out of 100 cases, 8 psychoses, 11 severe neuroses and 48 slight neuroses, 8 cases of character disorders, 4 cases of epilepsy, and 17 psychopathies.

Launay and Col:[11] 10% were cases of schizophrenia.

I have not been able to draw up a comparative table of the figures produced by these authors. The variability of the nosographical terms of reference used is such as to make it extremely difficult to assess the different figures correctly. This nosographical difference may of course be due to differences in the schools, but it would seem to be due more to the difficulty of categorizing accurately the disorders observed among adolescents.

We can distinguish two kinds of disorder and two kinds of figures: the typical, overt disorders that correspond to 'authentic' mental illnesses, and a whole series of more or less accurate diagnoses that merely record unusual psychological characteristics, and to which one cannot apply nosographical categories. Thus most authors agree in stating that the proportion of psychotics among suicidal adolescents is between 10% and 20%. But the figures become much less defined when one approaches the other pathological categories with a view to dividing the subjects into those with neurotic features, slight neuroses, character disorders, psychopathic disorders, severe juvenile crises, isolated symptoms, reactional disorders, etc. Such a variety of diagnoses betrays the uncertainty of the authors, and the feeling that in fact most subjects cannot be slotted into the usual psycho-pathological categories.

Roughly speaking, for many of the authors, the overt, characterized disorders, psychoses and overt neuroses, represent between 10% to 30% of cases, various disorders - that is, isolated, or poorly defined pathological features and cases of psychopathic unbalance - represent 20% to 40%, and subjects who do not appear to have any overt pathological features, and who may be regarded as normal, or as atypical, or as presenting a severe juvenile crisis, or, again, as suffering from a light neurosis, represent at least 1/3 and may even be in excess of 1/2.

In fact, if one does not keep solely to the figures, one finds that the authors admit that, generally speaking, they have found only one pathological feature, and that they are unable to posit any particular structure from it. Thus, for Szymanska, those cases known as slight neuroses are, in fact, basically healthy children and adolescents who 'found themselves plunged into a pubertal crisis . . . and, in many cases, this was the first and only pathological manifestation'.[12] Similarly, for Fau, 'I can only stress the rarity of a really developed and defined neurotic syndrome, whether in the sense of conversion or in that of character . . . Among adolescents suicide is seldom a psychotic symptom'.[13] Again, Gorceix remarks that 'a number of subjects have fairly minor pathological features . . . Apart from the suicide attempt, most psychoanalysts would have regarded them as normal and simply as bearers of an accentuated characteral feature. In fact, few of them are overtly psychotic . . . Most adolescent suicides are psychopaths, but many of these have only minor features of instability. Most of them belong to a population of borderline cases'.[14]

Personally, I share the feeling expressed by these authors, and I have found a similar opinion among my colleagues, whether psychoanalysts who happen to have examined a relatively large number of adolescents, or psychoanalysts in charge of emergency services that admit suicides of all kinds; all agree that the traditional nosographical framework is unsuited to a classification of suicidal adolescents.

The majority of them are regarded as 'normal'; they may possess isolated or ill-defined, relatively unstructured pathological features, but these are not enough to put them in any kind of nosographical category. So, if we wish to keep within the criteria of mental pathology proper, we can say, at most, that between 20% and 30% of suicidal adolescents are mentally ill according to the various estimates that have been made.

Among these 20% or 30%, what are the most common types of disorder encountered? Among the subjects regarded as psychotic, all the authors agree that a majority of them are schizophrenics, and that the others are subject to delirious attacks or to psychotic depressions. For many authors, adolescent suicides of a psychiatric nature are almost entirely cases of schizophrenia.

If one compares the figures for adolescents with those for adults, one sees that the proportions of suicides who were schizophrenic are either similar, or slightly higher in the case of adolescents. The difference in the total number of psychiatric suicides is due, on the one hand, to the high number of non-classifiable, doubtful cases; among adults the overt neuroses are more important, and the cases of characteral instability are more clear-cut and may be regarded as a nosographical entity, in contrast to the mass of doubtful and borderline cases among the adolescents. On the other hand, while manic-depressive psychosis represents an appreciable proportion of adult suicides, and in particular an appreciable proportion of the psychotics, this category is very poorly represented, or virtually not at all, in most statistics concerned with adolescents. Traditionally, there are no adolescent suicides due to manic-depressive psychosis because this psychosis hardly ever begins before the age of twenty.[15]

The rarity of psychotic or overt psycho-neurotic states among suicidal adolescents, and the frequency of doubtful, borderline, undefinable states are, however, subject to considerable doubt; one may well wonder whether, among all the undefined cases, there are not pathological states that have not yet established all their usual manifestations. A number of authors have suggested this. Thus Bergouignan[16] insists that frequent atypical depression may be the beginnings of a schizophrenia that might be expressed in a suicide attempt. Le Moal recalls that for Laignel-Lavastine, Barbe, and Delmas suicide is particularly frequent at the beginning of dementia praecox, and that many apparently inexplicable child or adolescent suicides were really the first manifestation of it. Similarly, Lemperière and des Lauriers[17] emphasize the difficulties involved in the diagnosis of the psychotic suicide, particularly in view of the lack of symptoms in the earliest stages of the illness - the suicide attempt being perhaps the first overtly pathological sign. On the other hand, although melancholia is traditionally absent from adolescent suicides, the first depressive phase of melancholia often occurs during adolescence, but the discreet symptoms of this initial phase 'are attributed to puberty . . . since the first discreet attacks of melancholia appear above all at puberty'. Lastly, for Lemperière[18] and Kielholz,[19] reactional depressions are particularly frequent among young people between the ages of 16 and 30, and this observation is not without importance when we remember, as we shall see later, that reactional depression occurs above all in a personality that is pathological for some other reason.

C. Significance of the psychiatric factors

To conclude, then, we are confronted by three types of suicidal adolescent from the traditional psychiatric point of view:

1) Normal subjects, representing between 20% and 50%, taking all the estimates into account.

2) Subjects with minor disorders, representing, according to the estimates, the majority of subjects that can be regarded as normal, or even the majority of all subjects.

3) Mentally ill subjects, representing between 15% and 30% of all subjects.

— But this classification does not throw light on the question of *the relations between suicide and mental illness*.

For both groups, as we have seen, there is doubt as to the normality or really minor character of the disorders. In cases where the disorders may be the beginnings of more severe mental illness, there is still the problem of the suicide act as the initiator of the clinical phase.

For the group of overtly mentally ill subjects, the problem is just as complex. Can we be satisfied with the explanation of suicide in terms of mental illness alone? Such a hypothesis is surely unacceptable and would evade the question, since it seems, according to the few estimates that have been carried out, that only about 20% of adolescents admitted into hospital for psychiatric reasons are suicidal. And, again, it is easy enough to see that suicide is one of the principal reasons for hospitalization, and that this proportion would be lower in a sample of mentally ill adolescents receiving treatment as outpatients or from a mobile psychiatric unit. This is especially true of the psychopathically unstable.

Apart from manic-depressive psychosis, which may be regarded as the model of the suicidogenic illness, for all other categories the suicides are in a minority. It might be useful, then, to take up this point, and, since most of these subjects are schizophrenics, I shall examine in greater detail suicide among schizophrenics.

Suicide among schizophrenics

It seems to be the general opinion that about 10% of all schizophrenics make suicide attempts, and that 2% actually kill themselves. But this proportion is not distributed equally at all stages of the illness. It is unanimously agreed that the suicide occurs above all at the beginning, in the first few years, of the illness. It is a classic symptom of the prodromic phase, and we know how necessary it is to identify the signs of incipient schizophrenia in an atypical attack of depression in a young subject. This fact is worth emphasizing, since 2/3 of all schizophrenics enter the evolutive phase of their disorders during adolescence. It may be assumed therefore that many of the 10% of suicidal schizophrenics are young subjects, and that the proportion of suicidal subjects among adolescent schizophrenics is well above 10%.

However, apart from suicides in the phase of full development, a new type of schizophrenic suicide has appeared in the past few years. Recent developments in therapeutics have transformed the traditional chronicization table into a disease with acute phases and remissions; suicide may occur either during a period of improvement and attempted readaptation to ordinary life, or during a new acute phase.

Broadly speaking, then, although schizophrenic suicides vary considerably in form and clinical context, they may be divided into two main types:

1) Suicides that occur at the beginning, either during remissions or during new acute phases. They occur in a context of depression, which some specialists regard as 'reactional' in some sense to an awareness of the gravity of the illness, or in a context of 'acute anxiety caused by a psychotic disorganization of thought'.[20]

2) Suicides that occur in a period of full development, such as those of the hebephrenic, the severe catatonic, and the subject suffering from paranoid delirium. Generally speaking, they are impulsive in origin, and traditionally regarded as unexplained, inexplicable, and unforeseeable. In other cases, those of delirious subjects in particular, suicide is said to be an absurd act because it seems to correspond to the unmotivated character of delirious behaviour. Thus, the suicides of the period of full development are explained either as a result of impulsivity, which might be a cause in itself, or as a direct consequence of delirium, which is itself reduced to an error of judgment. Obviously, to regard delirium solely from the point of view of rational judgment and as a cause of suicide throws no more light on the schizophrenic's motives for suicide than does the notion of impulsivity.

To sum up, then, mental illness is an obvious factor in only a minority of suicidal adolescents, and among mentally ill adolescents the suicidal are in a minority. Although mental illness may have a part to play, it cannot be regarded as the sole explanatory cause of suicide. Otherwise, how can we explain that the majority of the mentally ill do not commit suicide? Must we conclude, then, that the majority of suicidal adolescents do not suffer from psychiatric disorders, or that we must revise our notions of what constitutes a psychiatric disorder?

Notes

1. Chapter 1.
2. G. Deshaies, *Psychologie de suicide*, Paris, P.U.F., 1947, 78ff.
3. P.B. Schneider, *La tentative de suicide*, Neuchâtel, Delachaux et Niestlé, 1954, 124.
4. 'Le suicide chez les mineurs', *L'Hygiène mentale*, no. 2, 1964, 57.
5. H. Danon-Boileau, F. Lévy and A. Rousseau, *Le suicide chez l'adolescent universitaire*, 11th European Congress on Pedopsychiatry, Rome, June 1963.
6. *Tentative de suicide et alcoholisme chronique*, thesis, Paris, 1956, no. 1013.
7. *Psychologie de suicide*, Paris, P.U.F., 1947, 80.
8. 'Le suicide chez l'adolescent, á propos de 23 observations médico-psychologiques', *Annales Médico-psychologiques*, t.I, no. 1, January 1965, 10-12.
9. 'Étude psychométrique', *Semaine des Hôpitaux*, no. 50, 8 November 1963, 2390.
10. 'Suicides et tentatives de suicide des enfants et des adolescents', *Revue de Neuropsychiatrie infantile*, no. 12, December 1964, 734.
11. 'Suicide et tentative de suicide chez l'enfant et l'adolescent', *Revue du Praticien*, t. XIV, no. 6, 21 February 1964, 623.
12. Szymanska and Zelazowska, *op. cit.*, 735.
13. Fau, Château and Machu, *op. cit.*, 11 and 13.
14. *Op. cit.*, 2390.
15. T. Lemperière and A. des Lauriers, 'Le risque de suicide dans les psychoses', *Revue du Praticien*, 1 December 1962, 3253.
16. 'Les dépressions symptomatiques', *Revue du Praticien*, 1 October 1963, 3040.
17. *Op. cit.*, 3254.
18. T. Lemperière, 'Les dépressions psychogènes réactionelles, d'épuisement, neurotiques', *Revue du Praticien*, 1 October 1963, 3022.
19. P. Kielholz, 'Clinique, diagnostic différentiel et traitement des états dépressifs', *Acta Psychosomatica Geigy*, Basle, 1959, 2814.
20. Lemperière and des Lauriers, *op. cit.*, 3260.

13 · Factors peculiar to adolescence: the resort to action

We must now approach the question as to whether adolescence contains in itself a desire for voluntary death and a natural tendency to realize that desire. Does the human being, at the moment when he becomes capable of leading his own life and of transmitting life, have a tendency to leave life, to put a premature end to his personal drama just when it is really only beginning? If this were so, the concept of the autonomy of adolescent suicide in relation to adult suicide would be justified. The possibility of its autonomy would open up new questions. In particular, it would present the notions of normal and pathological suicide in a new light.

A. Is adolescence suicidogenic?

In Chapter 2 I defined this period of life as the work of adolescence: the calling in question of oneself and the world, accelerated integration of many different acquisitions in an intense confrontation that will turn the adolescent into an adult like no other and yet one who can recognize himself as belonging to the human community. It is in this intense reorganization that we must seek the elements that may relate to suicide.

The answer is apparently obvious: the adolescent readily resorts to action, he is frequently and acutely preoccupied with death in general, his own death, and suicide. Furthermore, he is often depicted and readily depicts himself as being depressed. We thus might be quite happy to conclude, without investigating the matter any further, that adolescence is a suicidogenic factor. The next step would be to state that the suicidal adolescent is suicidal because he is adolescent. But such a position is too reminiscent of those schematic views that we have of him and which he gives us of himself. To accept without further discussion the tripartite movement depression/idea of suicide/resort to action as being characteristic of the adolescent would be to run the risk of hiding once again behind a stereotype, that is to say, of refusing to understand or even merely to state that we do ñot understand what the adolescent is trying to say to us or conceal from us.

The difficulties of approaching the question

We must try to grasp the texture of these three phases of adolescent behaviour. But this will not be possible if we study them in artificial isolation. If we are to try to understand their significance, we must restore them to the overall context of adolescent development. Then, perhaps, we will begin to see what it is in that development that reinforces the tendency to voluntary death.

In trying to approach, even in a relatively superficial way, the multifarious aspects of adolescence, I have come up against the same obstacle as all the other authors, namely, the confused and inadequate state of our knowledge of the adolescent.

One of the main difficulties is our inability to express in communicable terms the conflict that rages within the adolescent between his contradictions, his ambivalences, and his apparently irreducible paradoxes. This conflict on all fronts, in which allies and adversaries are forever changing sides, eludes all description. At adolescence, more than at any other time, everything is contained in everything else, each manifestation is charged with a multiplicity of meanings. One cannot distinguish between behaviour that is the result of impulse and behaviour that is the result of some defence mechanism, for the same action may represent either. The same behaviour may be both regressive and progressive, what may seem impoverishing may have a structuring effect. The only approach that does not distort what is taking place too much is to grasp the movement that concerns, at one and the same time, impulses and defences, regressions and progressions, destructuration and structuration.

But any account requires clarification, simplification, classification, which distorts description, and removes us further and further away from the adolescent's living, dynamic experience. This is even more the case for death and suicide than for any other factor, and we are faced with a highly unsatisfactory choice. Either we can attempt - supposing that such a thing is possible, which is doubtful to say the least - to give a faithful account of the adolescent's experience of the notions of death and suicide - in which case, we reproduce the tangled mass of conflicts in which he is caught up, and abandon any attempt at understanding anything whatsoever. Or we can attempt to describe it, while at the same time trying to clarify our material, even if this involves distortion by the very fact of classifying it. I have opted for the second alternative, bearing in mind, however, that each notion, incorrect in itself on account of the diversity of its simultaneous meanings, is of value only in its context. We must be satisfied with partial truths, that is, errors that can be corrected only by successive rectifications, retracings of one's steps, and repetitions. While fully aware of its inconveniences, it is this method that I shall adopt.

One way of reducing the difficulty is to speak of the adolescent in terms of mental pathology,[1] and say that every adolescent is psychotic, obsessional, hysteric, delinquent, melancholic, etc. But this amounts to saying that the adolescent is psychotic, for example, except when he is not, or, to be more precise, that we see him and speak of him 'as if' he was psychotic, neurotic, or delinquent. This is merely a convenient way of putting it, and certainly does not mean that every adolescent suffers from one or other of these illnesses. We lack the words to describe adolescent behaviour without distorting, willingly or not, its pathological significance.

Even if we retain this terminology, it is important that we should see it as a whole,[2] and not isolate individual aspects: 'it would be . . . a very great mistake to reduce the crisis of adolescence, even temporarily, to one of these symptomatic elements. The crisis is a unity, and we must approach it as such, in all its diversity and complexity'.[3] This is particularly the case with those aspects that directly concern suicide.

However, I have no wish to give undue emphasis to these aspects, to add the stereotype of the consistently depressed, suicidal adolescent or that of the adolescent with a morbid and obsessive preoccupation with death to the already lengthy list of schemata of the normal, but psychotic, neurotic, or the delinquent adolescent.

Taking up, in turn, the three traditional notions of the resort to action, the idea of death and suicide, and the tendency to depression, I hope to examine the subject of suicide as it occurs in adolescence.

B. The tendency of the adolescent to resort to action

Suicide is an act. It is not mere artifice to trace a theoretical and practical frontier between the suicide act and what is called the idea of suicide. This distinction illustrates the difference in the processes of thinking and acting. But there is also the question of the boundary between the suicide act and other acts. This question gives suicide its medico-legal and criminological dimension, and contains hypotheses of its possible kinship with or differences from delinquency.

Furthermore, the adolescent readily resorts to action. All specialists in the psychopathology of the adolescent know to what extent this frequency affects the diagnostic, prognostic, and therapeutic problems. It is of special importance as regards the indications and practice of psychotherapy. It is no accident that so much research on the tendency to resort to action should have been done by specialists in adolescence.[4] But this tendency is not the only fact about adolescents with psychical difficulties. It is a constant characteristic of this period of life, and all those concerned with the education of adolescents know this and are concerned with it.

Is the adolescent's tendency to act in itself a suicidogenic factor? Such a question is lacking in precision: we must first investigate the nature and significance of the act in the case of the adolescent. But this is not as simple as it seems; in particular, we must avoid seeing it in terms of an adult mode of resorting to action, thus ignoring its own specific qualities, or of referring to the stereotype of the active, disruptive adoles-

cent. Any form of simplification is to be avoided. The adolescent act is a remarkable illustration of the complexity of
adolescent behaviour in general, on account of the multiplicity
of factors that determine it and the diversity of their significance. The importance and scope of this question go well
beyond the bounds of suicide. This is not the place to go into
it in detail, and I shall be content to summarize it by referring
to the report made by J. Rouart.[5] This report makes good
use of the most important psychoanalytic work on the subject.

Conditions favourable to action in the adolescent

In so far as certain social conditions encourage a resort to
action, those that concern the adolescent directly do so to a
far greater degree. I dealt with these latter conditions in
Chapter 11, so there is no point in repeating myself here. But
it might be worth remembering to what extent the adult,
because of his fear, has a repressive attitude that encourages
regressive attitudes in the adolescent - verbal non-commun-
ication, the impossibility of expressing one's real experience,
with a consequent falling back on various stereotyped modes
of behaviour which the adult then describes as typically
adolescent.

But it is above all in himself that the adolescent finds conditions favourable to action. There is produced within him
an alliance between factors from the past and factors from the
present, each accentuating the other to form a whole that is
very favourable to action. As we shall see in greater detail in
the next few chapters, adolescence simultaneously reorganizes
all conflicts, all levels of organization, in particular the old
pregenital factors. In its unifying role within the ego, genitalization has an apparently disorganizing effect that is expressed
in dysharmonic behaviour. Genetic studies on the resort to
action have shown how considerable an influence the first
years of life, that is, the pregenital factors, and the oral factors
in particular, can have on any constitutional factor. All these
archaic factors are reactivated, as is the tendency to resort to
action, with all the characteristics proper to these types of
organization of the ego.

Among the factors deriving from the present, the physical factors play an undoubtedly important part, as is shown in the difficulty the adolescent has in mastering his motility. The important pubertal biological changes, and the important and sudden variations in hormonal production are instrumental in creating the rapid changes of mood and of available physical energy. But I should like to stress above all the general physical changes that puberty involves, and the many different effects that these changes have on the adolescent.

The adolescent's experience of his own body is concentrated above all, of course, on the appearance of genitality. The anatomical and physiological changes that result form the background to that experience. The unease that he feels in relation to his own body is largely due to the anxiety that he feels about his sexuality. Sometimes, this anxiety is experienced directly, but in other cases it is expressed indirectly by a displacement over the body as a whole.

This unease also has other causes, which are not properly genital, and there is a constant intrication and interaction between the various causes of anxiety. The other causes are related to the pregenital factors, and concern awareness of one's own body. They are due to the intensity of the physical transformations taking place, and concern overall measurements, the relations between the segments of the body, the general forms, and the visible signs of the visible aspect (beard, voice, etc.). The awareness that the child had of his body has become outgrown. The adolescent has to get to know his body all over again: this new body is a stranger to him, both because of the new sensations that it gives him, in particular genital sensations, and because of the alteration in the relationship between the osteo-articulatory system and his physical dimensions. As a result, he has to face not only unknown genital factors, but he has lost his former familiarity with the pregenital factors.

In a sense, the adolescent suffers from a disturbance in his body image. This also implies a disturbance in the perception of the environment. Having lost his measuring instrument, his own body, his vision (in the physiological sense) of space is also outgrown. He has to relearn distances and volumes, resitu-

ate the material and human world, and resituate his body in
that space. The system of reference that has served him for
several years has now broken down. The changes occur at an
accelerating rate; hardly has he become aware of his body and
of the surrounding space than the data change once again. He
is constantly trying to keep up with his own body.

To this are added an intense instinctual drive and a sudden
increase of energy. The rapidity and intensity of the transformations have not given him time to learn to control either.
He has little control over his impulses, especially his sexual
impulses, or over his suddenly increased muscular strength. He
feels like a kind of sorcerer's apprentice in relation to his body,
which merely increases his unease, his feeling of being a stranger to himself.

We can compare the physical difficulties that the adolescent
experiences with those that he has to face in the verbal field.
As we saw in Chapter 2, he is faced with a gap between his
child's language and a whole new world of experience: this
language is quite incapable of expressing what he feels.
Suddenly, words no longer have the same meaning, and he
does not have at his disposal the words that could express
what he feels and thinks in a more or less confused way.
Again, he is betrayed over and over again by the rapidity of
change. He no sooner succeeds in forging an adequate vocabulary, than what he has to express has changed; once again,
words fail him. He is dysphasic, and there is a constant gap
between the intensity of his emotions and the poverty of his
verbal expression. We know that his liking for complicated words
is, among other things, an attempt to remedy this inadequacy.

Generally speaking, the adolescent finds himself in the
grips of a powerful instinctual drive, strong emotions, increased muscular strength, and, on the other hand, a psycho-
motor and verbal equipment quite inadequate to control the
whole and to communicate it to others. Without equating this
state with any real instrumental inadequacy, we can say that
there is a certain analogy, and that the adolescent suffers from
a temporary deficit in instrumental equipment. They are the
conditions that are usually met with in cases of disturbances
to ideo-verbal development.

To this temporary inadequacy are added inhibition factors. The adolescent is afraid of his body, and does not dare to use it. Above all, of course, he is afraid of using his genital equipment, and of having the satisfactions that he desires, of sinning against prohibitions. But he is also afraid of using his body in a general way, caught as he is between fear that he will not use it properly, because of his lack of control and co-ordination, and desire to use it properly, which is an overt expression of his newly acquired strength. Fear to show that he is as strong as an adult, and a desire, sometimes repressed, sometimes satisfied in fits and starts, which merely accentuates his feelings of lack of control.

The same fear is to be found at the verbal level. The adolescent does not want to tell us what he feels. He is afraid of not being able to control his phantasies; he does not want his emotions to rise to the surface, or find words to express them, for fear that they would get completely out of control. To this is added guilt at expressing his new experience, since he does not know how that experience would be accepted or tolerated by others. He prefers to leave it all in unverbalized, preconscious uncertainty. But there is also the ambivalence that, at certain moments, drives him to pour forth all that he has to say with a suddenness that does not leave him time to give it adequate expression, thus merely increasing his feeling of inadequate control.

Thus the adolescent presents at the same time an inadequate psycho-motor and verbal organization, and an ideo-verbal development, associated with an ambivalent attitude towards his body and his affects, composed of a refusal and a desire to use his body and to express what he feels that results in an inadequacy in the expression of his affects. This ambivalence forces him to undergo phases of inhibition and phases of impulsive expression. We have here, in combination, the conditions that are usually favourable to a resort to action.

The function of the adolescent's tendency to act

The notions referred to above are no more than favourable conditions for the tendency to express oneself in action; they cannot be offered as explanations for it. Our attention must still be concentrated on the multiple significances and functions that action represents in the adolescent process. One of the main functions of action is a regressive defensive function against the anxiety aroused by a confrontation with an inadequately perceived reality, amounting to a process of avoiding that reality. A defence by denial, which 'denies by the magic of action and gesture', a defence in the struggle against dependence on the parents, and on the mother in particular.[5] But, like all resort to action, it is also, perhaps above all, a defence against the revival of painful memories: the adolescent acts in order not to know.

But in addition to constituting in the adolescent an obstacle to further development, self-expression in action also has a 'progressive', a 'maturing' function.[6] As the adolescent work of disinvestment and reinvestment is taking place, it helps to provide continuity and unity in the ego, and constitutes a mode of experiment necessary to the adolescent process. Action enables the adolescent to try out his newly acquired strength, to confront it with reality, and to test his power over that reality. It also enables him to try out his autonomy in relation to others, especially to his parents. It is a reactivation of archaic factors, carried out with a view to mastering them and integrating them in a personality that has not yet acquired a definitive organization. It is 'experiment that makes the adolescent, before thought about action gives him the possibility of doing otherwise'.[6]

Adolescent action has similarities with other types of self-expression through action, but it cannot be assimilated to any one type. I agree with those authors who believe that the term 'acting out' should be applied only to the passing over into action that occurs in psychoanalytic treatment, that is to say, 'transferential acting out', and I do not think that adolescent action, which is behavioural action, can be assimilated to such 'acting out'. However, there are certain similarities. But because adolescent action takes place outside a transference situation, and because of its non-specificity and its disordered, impulsive appearance, it is much closer to what has been called 'direct acting out'.[7] Similarly, it is closer to the adult's expression in action of behavioural disorders, by virtue of its urgent character, its need for immediate satisfaction, and its inability to defer satisfaction, which reflects a non-mastery of temporality. Since adolescent action has similarities with both 'acting out' and behavioural resort to action, we may regard it, as does Rouart,[8] as the meeting-point between the two.

But it is not only an expression of archaic factors. It is also a 'progressive' factor, action in its own right rather than simply a resort to action, a stage in the adolescent's developmental process. So, because of its diffuse and all-embracing character, and because of its multiplicity of causes and functions, I prefer to speak of a tendency to act, which covers what in the adolescent is close to acting out, the resort to action, and action itself.

Intensity, forms of action, and the suicide act in the adolescent

The multiplicity of favourable factors, and the diversity of significance and functions, explain the frequency of action in the adolescent. Motor participation is a constant factor in all his behaviour. It affects all forms of his action, and is expressed at all levels, from simple, elementary, automatic actions, resembling tics or rites, to sudden, explosive motor discharges, expressed in impulsive actions, and on to complex forms of behaviour that constitute an intermediate stage in the developmental process. All these forms are the mark of impulsivity due to non-mastery of motility, and to the tendency to rapid discharge of the impulses.

But whatever its type and modality may be, the main characteristic of the adolescent act is that it remains 'transitory, harmless',[9] as variable and mobile as the adolescent ego. All authors agree that when it becomes fixed and takes on a more serious form, its true cause lies in factors anterior to adolescence. The most classic case is delinquency. The adolescent's behaviour is punctuated by individual and collective resorts to action, but these are rarely anti-social; although he often goes fairly close to delinquency, and sometimes commits minor infractions to the law, he rarely becomes truly delinquent, despite the all too widespread stereotype of delinquent youth. And specialists in the matter would never dream of associating delinquency with adolescence alone. They emphasize the multiplicity of biological, psychological, and social factors that determine it, and the early pre-pubertal origin of the individual factors involved.

This leads us to the classic comparison between delinquency and suicide. The analogy rests on two factors common to both: both are serious, possibly dangerous acts, and both are the result of associated psychological and social factors. Since Durkheim,[10] the relation between the two types of act has often been made. Some authors believe that they develop quantitatively *pari passu,* while others believe that they develop in inverse proportion, both being aggressive behaviour, whether directed outwards upon the world or inwards upon onself. The comparison has often been made in relation to adolescents too. Le Moal, in particular, stresses the frequency with which impulsive subjects are to be found in both cases, and Launay and Col[11] examine the correlative increase of both phenomena.

Whatever relation may exist between the two phenomena, one can say that delinquency is not only inconstant, but relatively infrequent in adolescence, and that suicide is still more rare. Two notions, then, emerge from this brief study of the adolescent's tendency to act: although all adolescents have a tendency to resort to action, few commit serious or dangerous acts, and of these only a small proportion commit suicide.

When the act becomes persistent or serious, it is essentially an expression of disorders originating in an earlier, prepubertal stage, and cannot be explained simply in terms of the adolescent's tendency to act. Still less can the fact that the destructive act is turned towards the subject himself be explained in terms of adolescence.

It seems obvious enough that the tendency to act cannot be regarded as a cause of suicide. It does not explain why only a small number of young people commit suicide. But this does not mean that it plays no role in the suicidal process. It is possible, even probable, that it determines, or at least influences, two types of situation:

1) As we saw in Chapter 5, the impulsivity proper to youth partly explains the choice of suicide method. It favours the use of methods that lie ready to hand, that are immediately usable; it also leads to suicidal acts that are more desired than well prepared and carried out, which accounts for the proportionately smaller proportion of deaths. Thus, the fact that the young subject commits as many suicide acts as the adult, but kills himself less often, is related to the tendency to act.

2) The young often commit dangerous acts. Some of these acts express a desire for suicide, while others are related more to an overwhelming, uncontrollable need to act. What, then, is the relation between these two types of act, and what intermediaries exist between them?

It emerges, then, that the adolescent's tendency to act may favour the determination of the suicide act, but is not its cause - that the suicide act itself originates at a deeper level. The tendency to act cannot therefore explain the adolescent suicide act, but it does affect the way in which it is carried out, and therefore gives the question a certain specificity.

Notes

1. K. Eissler, 'Notes on problems of technique in the psychoanalytic treatment of adolescents', *The Psychoanalytic Study of the Child*, vol. XIII, New York, Int. Univ. Press, 1958, 226.

2. P. Male, 'Étude psychanalytique de l'adolescent', *La Psychanalyse d'aujourd'hui*, Paris, P.U.F., 1956, 226.

3. K. Kestemberg, 'La psychanalyse des adolescents', *Psychiatrie de l'enfant*, vol. III, fasc. 1, Paris, P.U.F., 1961, 303.

4. J. Rouart, ' "Agir" et processus psychanalytique', *Revue Française de Psychanalyse*, no. 5, May 1968, 927-82.

5. *Ibid.*, 976.

6. *Ibid.*, 977.

7. M. de M'Uzan, 'Acting out "direct" and acting out "indirect" ', in *ibid.*, 996.

8. *Op. cit.*, 980.

9. *Ibid.*, 977.

10. *Le suicide*, Paris, P.U.F., 1960, 384.

11. 'Suicide et tentative de suicide chez l'enfant et l'adolescent', *Revue du Praticien*, t. XIV, no. 6, 21 February 1964, 625.

14 · The idea of death and the idea of suicide in the adolescent

In youth, the theme of death is basically a philosophical pre-occupation. Adolescents often speak of death, even of suicide, in a more or less abstract way. Almost all adolescents think about death in general, and many think about their own death, often about their own voluntary death. Of course, it is easy to disprove the widespread notion that those who speak of suicide do not commit it; on the other hand, we must not conclude that every adolescent who thinks about suicide is himself a potential suicide. Very few adolescents commit suicide compared with those who think about it, and still fewer compared with the overwhelming proportion of those who think about death in general. What is the significance, the function, the origin, and the consequences of such speculation? What is the link between the idea of death and the idea of suicide?

Before continuing further, we must tackle the first obstacle that confronts us, namely, the very concept of the idea of death and of suicide. The traditional formulation of 'idea of suicide', and the philosophical form of speculation that the adolescent gives it, tend to lend it an intellectual appearance, and to suggest that it is the result of cognitive activity. I must admit that I have doubts about this, and would prefer to speak of a 'tendency to suicide',[1] rather than an idea of suicide. Similarly, in the case of death, the term 'idea' closes the way to further research. The term 'knowledge' is more satisfactory, but is only acceptable if it is made clear that the term implies psychical activity as a whole. I prefer the term 'notion' of death, as being intentionally more vague, or even 'feeling' of death.

But we must not exclude the cognitive aspect; there is still the question of the relations between the adolescent's intellectual development and his attempt to know death. Is it his new capacity for generalization and abstraction, the source of philosophical reflexion on death, that first introduces the adolescent to the concept of death and of being mortal, or is it his fear of death (or tendency to death) that forces him to philosophize by way of compromise? In other words, what is the nature and function of the adolescent's search for knowledge about death?

A. Origin and consequences of the idea of death and of the idea of suicide

The intellectualist view whereby the idea of death emerges at adolescence, the period of speculation, encloses us in an insoluble misunderstanding. At the level of intellectual representations alone, whatever our age or our cultural level we do not know what death is. No human being can represent to himself in advance a state towards which he is moving, but about which no other human being has been able to provide a first-hand account. So we are forced either to deny any possibility that the human being can bear within himself anything relating to death, or to disintellectualize the question, to place it on another plane, and to return to the feeling about death; we must go back to its origins, and try to understand what form it takes in the child. If we do this, the hypothesis according to which the idea of death emerges at adolescence is invalidated. We must distinguish, as carefully as possible, between the true origins of the feeling about death, its evolution, and the elaboration of it that enables one at adolescence to attain verbal and conceptual representations of it.

The notion of death in the child

The intellectualist misunderstanding has led to a denial of its existence. Four stages are usually described:
1) a denial that life can exist;
2) death seen as a temporary disappearance, a long illness; it concerns only the elderly and is reversible;

3) at about nine, death is understood better, but remains reversible, and children are exempt from it;

4) the final stage is reached later, at an age that varies from child to child.

Such a description maintains the confusion between the feeling about death, an integral part of the instinctual life whose general development it follows, and its conceptualization. And because the idea of death results from a convergence of an increased capacity for cognitive elaboration and the feeling about death, such a description takes account only of the first aspect, and the apparent result of this association, to the detriment of the instinctual elements. This way of amputating the problem already existed in the nineteenth century; Le Moal has located it in particular in Brière de Boismont and Durant-Fondel. In fact, this problem of death is experienced at another level than the conceptual and ideo-verbal. I have myself observed on several occasions the existence among children under the age of six of a diffuse, but solidly based, notion of death and a certain fear of death.[2]

However, the young child usually says very little about death and seldom expresses his fear. There would appear to be three main reasons for this. The first is the powerful, overwhelming prohibition laid down by the adult about the mention of death. The second is the inadequacy of the child's ideo-verbal elaboration. The third, and perhaps most important, is the child's capacity to relegate the problem of death to a more distant level of consciousness. The denial of death, of the irreparable loss that it involves, seems, partly at least, to be bound up with the capacity of the infantile ego to deny reality and to replace it with opposed imaginary productions.[3] 'Intellectually, they were very well able to distinguish between phantasy and fact. But in the sphere of the affect they cancelled the objective painful facts and performed a hyper-cathexis of the phantasy in which these were reversed, so that the pleasure which they derived from imagination triumphed over the objective "pain" '.[4] So there intervenes not only the moment when the child becomes intellectually capable of having an idea of death, but also the moment when his ego loses the ability of repressing this real displeasure.

The adult's denial that a child feels death reappears in the case of child suicide, which though rare, does exist. But because children are supposed to be incapable of seeking death, it is often interpreted as an accident, the argument being based on the apparent inadequacy of the motives.

To sum up, this overwhelming adult denial plays an essential role in the apparent absence in the child of a preoccupation with death. But the importance of the defence implies the existence of a fear of death; according to the type of defence used to neutralize it, it indicates the nature and level of its elaboration. We can say that the fear of death is considerably anterior to the idea of death, and that it exists from early infancy.

During the latency period, academic knowledge[5] usually encourages the maintenance of the dissociation of affect and concept, especially where death is concerned. The child keeps to the concrete aspects of death, without communicating any personal reflexions on the matter,[6] thus avoiding an irruption of anxiety within himself. This loss of distance, together with the acquisition of academic knowledge, allow the child to express himself more clearly and more precisely. It is probably for this reason that the adult situates the emergence of the idea of death at this period.

The notion of death in adolescence

With puberty, the feeling for death and the idea of death are subjected to the same process as the personality as a whole. The unifying action of genitalization completes the effacement of the dissociation of affect and concept as the intellectual capacities increase. Feeling for death, fear of death, and idea of death fuse together to form a knowledge of death. At the same time, the reactivation of the most archaic impulses provokes a resurgence of the fear of death.

The manipulation of the idea of death is both a structuring activity and a defence against impulses that the adolescent fears he is unable to control. By rationalization, he hopes to achieve a knowledge of death without arousing overmuch his fear of (or tendency to) death. It is a compromise between anxiety and a need for knowledge. But this overall process cannot be applied indiscriminately to any phase of adolescence. The manipulation of the idea of death would not appear to operate according to the same modalities at every phase of adolescence.

We know very little about what takes place at the onset of adolescence - about the adolescent's attitude to death or to anything else. The narcissistic withdrawal of the young adolescent leaves us in ignorance of his actual experience of things. Replies to questionnaires are impersonal: they fall all too readily into a conformist stance, and seldom give anything away. 'Young people of 14, 15, and even 16 reflect above all as to what happens after death, whether or not there is a heaven, etc. . . Some say that they refuse to think about death, or that they are very afraid of it, or, again, that they are not afraid of it because they know that it must come.'[7] In my own experience, I have found that adolescents seldom express any concern with death, but that occasionally they give vent to sudden outbursts on the subject.

Several hypotheses might be mentioned. Either the young adolescent is already manipulating the idea of death in an emergent intellectualization that will become dominant in the course of adolescence, but, in accordance with his general position of narcissistic withdrawal, he does not communicate his reflexions on the matter. Or there is a reactivation of the fear of death under the effect of the general process of impulsional reactivation; because the young person has not yet acquired the new intellectual equipment that he needs if he is to struggle against his anxieties and impulses, he borrows the ideas of death of the adult environment in order to maintain a defensive distance. Or again, the very young adolescent, dominated as he essentially is by genital activation, is generally very little concerned with death, but, as a result of the reactivation of the impulses, experiences occasional quite sudden attacks of anxiety about death. Since the beginning of puberty represents the triumph of Eros, it leaves little room, according to this theory, for Thanatos, which is pushed into the background most of the time. If we are to avoid the danger of making statements that reveal more about our adult rational-

izations than about the true experience of these young adolescents, we cannot go much beyond the level of hypothesis.
But, on the whole, it would seem that one can scarcely speak
of the idea of death and its manipulation at this period. What
we are dealing with are premisses, with borrowings from parental ideas made according to an infantile mode, and perhaps
even a withdrawal from the latency period, as a result of
genitalization, with occasional sudden moments of anxiety.

Intellectualization is at its maximum intensity during the
second period of adolescence. The young person tries to relearn the world in a compromise between theoretical views and
a pregnant anxiety that suddenly invades him, in a unification
that is necessary to his structuration. A juxtaposition then
takes place between his fear of death, whether verbalized or
not, and theoretical ideas about death - the second being more
readily expressed than the first. With time, the ideas that he
expresses about death become less and less general, and more
directly relevant to himself. This does not necessarily indicate
a greater fear of death, but may be the effect of greater facility
in verbalization and an attempt to control his fear through
verbalization. It is therefore the period that most enables us
to understand the adolescent's growing knowledge of death,
and the function of the manipulation of the idea of death.

B. Functions of the manipulation of the idea of death

The manipulation of the idea of death is a fundamental need
for the adolescent, which is why it recurs with such constancy.
The idea of death, which is one of the major themes of adolescent intellectualization and one of its best representatives,
is a perfect demonstration of the functions that are performed
by this rationalization.[8] On the one hand, it has a structuring
function in the cognitive activity, which is undergoing enrichment and organization; it is also a means of increasing one's
knowledge of the world, of others, and of oneself. The idea
of death fulfils this role remarkably well. To attain to this
idea is to attain to man's most important preoccupation, the
preoccupation that is the foundation of philosophical thought.
It is also to attain to a knowledge of the life/death opposition

that governs the animate. It is not simply a question of having
more knowledge, it is knowledge itself, the possibility of
penetrating nature's secret. This attempt at knowledge culminates in a failure, in a recognition of the impenetrability
of death, of the impossibility of representing it to oneself,
and hence a realization of the harsh reality of man's limitations.
At the same time, it leads to a recognition of the death of
those close to him, and of himself.

On the other hand, intellectualization acts as a defence
against the impulses, or rather as an arrangement that makes
it possible, by distancing them, to express them without
danger. Thanks to the idea of death, the adolescent is able
to manipulate hetero- and auto-aggressivity with relative control. Various representations of the impulses can now be expressed. Of course, the death impulse remains in the fore-
ground, but so does the will to power, in the form of a desire
to possess the world through understanding its fundamental
secret. We also know with what sexual overinvestment all
intellectual activity is charged, becoming as it does a privileged
symbol of strength, power, and virility.

The manipulation of the idea of death is not devoid of
pleasure. The adolescent must derive quite considerable
pleasure from it to indulge in it so willingly. It has something
of the ambiguous pleasure of playing with fire with the
attendant risk of burning oneself, a pleasure not without an
element of masochism. But it is the tribute paid that helps us
to guess how great the pleasure is. It has a number of different,
sometimes contradictory, sources, like all adolescent pleasures,
and it is the important counterpart of the anxiety that accompanies the idea of death.

The cognitive benefit derived from manipulating the idea of
death, the benefit derived from controlling reactivated drives
and impulses, both of which contribute to the structuring of
the ego, and the pleasure derived from these activities, are
all inseparable. It is artificial to try and describe them
separately, but there is no other way of describing them.
Together they form a movement that may be expressed in
terms of a series of successive stages, starting from the two
poles, the feeling for death and the idea of death, which are

dissociated at the outset, culminating in the unity of the problem of our knowledge of death. These stages follow one another as one moves towards the anxiety and so gains control over it. They operate according to a concentric model, in a gradual approach from the world in general, through relational objects, to oneself.

The function of knowledge of the world

Reflexions on death in the world constitute the first, the most reassuring approach - one by which the anxiety can be kept at a distance. This intellectual exercise makes it possible to establish the fundamental categorical distinction between the inanimate and the animate world, which, in the first instance, is defined as mortal. By both scientific and metaphysical reflexion the adolescent experiences a hope, highly charged with pleasure, for it will make him equal to God, of perceiving the trajectory followed by living beings from birth to death; he hopes to penetrate the mystery of the process of death, and, extrapolating beyond that trajectory, to penetrate the mystery of the 'after-death'. He thus hopes to know the secrets not only of the internal process of the visible world, but also of its invisible extension.

Such an abstract approach has two advantages. On the one hand, it would prove, if possible, the excellence of the intellectual instrument that is capable of elucidating all mysteries. On the other hand, it would make it possible to acquire mastery over the world, over life and over death, thus avoiding the fear of death. (This probably accounts for the interest shown by young people in biology, medicine, and surgery, and it may be that certain medical vocations are bound up with this.) But by reasoning about death, the adolescent is inevitably confronted by the death of those close to him.

The function of knowledge of his objects and his object relations

Reflexions on the death of those he loves place the adolescent in a very different position. The intellectual pleasure is still present of course. By recognizing that those he loves are mortal, and therefore living, he gains knowledge of the intimate process that is taking place within them and which will lead them to death. But the manipulation of the idea of death, in relation to those close to him, confronts him more directly with his own ambivalence, with the intrication of pleasure and anxiety, and the more or less forbidden impulses emerge more clearly.

In the first place, it enables him to manipulate his aggressivity in a reassuring way. His reflexion on the death of the Other, a rationalized representation of his unconscious desire for the death of the Other, help him to form a compromise. By associating it with the scientific or metaphysical process, he can think about it without feeling guilt. At this point, of course, we approach the Oedipal situation.[9]

Secondly, it is a way of approaching reality. In his ambivalent parental relationship, the adolescent wants both protection and autonomy. The desire for protection, an infantile residue, is activated at a time when he is confronting the obstacles of adult life. He has to accept the fact that sooner or later he will be alone and will have to face life on his own. He has a work of mourning to carry out. By manipulating the idea that those close to him, in particular his parents, can and will die, he takes up once more, only to abandon them with the help of cognitive modifications, the magical positions of childhood that first enabled him to believe that his parents were immortal, then, when he no longer believed this, to continue hoping that perhaps they might be after all. Thus with one blow he annulled both his aggressivity and his anxiety at the loss of protection. He now integrates this unavoidable reality in a philosophical form. In learning that those he loves are mortal, he is learning to accept their death, to undergo object loss, which is an important stage in the preparation for the work of mourning.

The integration of his feeling of autonomy is bound up above all with the feeling of his own death. But the integration of the reality of the future death of those close to him helps the adolescent in this work. He desires, while at the same time fearing, this autonomy that the death of his parents will most certainly bring about. The anxiety that accompanies this aggressive desire makes him express it in a more or less modified form. 'I don't want them to die, but I do wish they'd leave me alone and behave as if they weren't there' is a common assertion. One finds a similar compromise when the adolescent indulges in certain forms of 'wild behaviour', or suddenly breaks off his studies to take up some paid job: both are attempts to live as if the parents were not there. But the most frequent compromise is still an abstract approach to death; to reason on the fact that parents are mortal may be a way of expressing the hope and the fear that they will disappear.

The function of self-knowledge

Reflexions on the mortality of others are also, indeed above all, a means whereby the adolescent can approach the problem of his own death. It is perhaps about his own death that he experiences most pleasure in manipulating the idea of death: the pleasure of defining and knowing himself, pleasure at mastering his own death impulses, pleasure at sounding out his own freedom.

The adolescent needs to know that he is mortal to know that he is alive. I should like to stress the fact that the period of genital capacity makes its appearance with the preoccupation with death. At one and the same time, the adolescent has accepted the reality of his death and his birth, that is to say, the sexual union of his parents, which is rooted at the level of the primitive stage, and his capacity to procreate, to give life to another being. To be born of the sexual act, to give life by the sexual act, and to be mortal, are the fundamental terms that enable the adolescent to know that he is a living being; it is the first stage of the reply to the question 'Who am I?'. In his desire for intellectual power, he hopes to penetrate the mystery of his own life.

But he must experience the limitations of that power, and recognize his own powerlessness: like others, he does not know when he will die, nor what he will be after death. Here, too, there is a similarity with birth; he knows when he was born, but he does not know where he came from, and he thinks at great length about the origins of life and the mysteries of the transformation of living matter. He has to accept this uncertainty, which is a basic element of the notion of death, that he does not know when he will die, but that he will die, that it could be the next minute or several decades later. 'Not only do I possess evidence that I am immediately faced by the real possibility of death, at every moment of my life, today and always. Death is near me. Human uncertainty in face of death corresponds not only to a gap in the science of biology, but to ignorance of my fate.'[10] The adolescent has to defend himself against the anxiety that accompanies this uncertainty, and against the anxiety that he feels about what he will be after death.

Uncertainty about when his own death will take place enables the adolescent to approach the concept of time. The death/time relation has often been stressed.[11] Giabicani discovered from his researches that the appearance of the notion of passing time makes its appearance between the ages of 10 and 14, the age at which the idea of death also makes its appearance. Its manipulation helps in the integration of the notion of time; the knowledge of one's own death and the uncertainty of when it will occur help in the integration of the notion of relativity and in the abandonment of the vestiges of magical attitudes.

The manipulation of the idea of death also plays a part in the adolescent's growing awareness of becoming an adult, by helping him to become aware of his autonomy and freedom. I have already broached the question from a number of angles: the pleasure involved in manipulating the idea of death despite the prohibitions laid on one in childhood about manipulating one of the topics usually reserved to adults, and the pleasure of thinking about the death of others at the same time as one's own death, thus feeling oneself to be like other men: and, of course, thinking about the death of those around one, one's parents in particular, implies autonomy in relation to them.

Conversely, one's own death does not depend on them and may result from external facts beyond their control. The adolescent may, of course, fear the aggressivity of those around him, but he is also aware of his growing muscular and psychical strength, and feels that he is becoming increasingly capable of resisting any act of aggression, real or imaginary. Thus, not only does he learn that he can live without others, but he also learns that he need not die on account of others. His death is no longer dependent on those on whom until recently he was utterly dependent; he becomes independent as far as the maintenance of his own life is concerned. But this observation is counter-balanced by the realization that his death does not depend on himself either.

It is around his ignorance as to when and how his natural death will occur that the gap between the idea of death and the idea of suicide is formed. Manipulating the idea of his voluntary death enables him to push back the boundaries of his power, and to confirm his idea of freedom and his awareness of being alive.

By thinking that he may voluntarily bring death upon himself, he is reassuring himself against the fear of uncertainty as to the when and the how. He throws down a challenge to the mystery of nature's actions. He may also brave the mysterious natural elements that are preparing his death by going ahead, believing that he can cut the ground from under their feet if he so wishes and die when and how he will. This re-establishes his power over himself, the feeling of being his own free arbiter, possessing an autonomy that annuls the mystery on which he remains dependent.

He also braves those close to him in thinking that he can bring death upon himself, and confirms himself in his independence of them. However much they may wish to see him go on living, he can deprive them forever of his presence without their consent. His death depends solely on himself and if he goes on living it is because he wishes to. Being free to die, he is free to live. The manipulation of the idea of suicide, the idea that one is free to go on living or not, is the most important, the most fundamental form that awareness of one's freedom can take. 'The temptation to measure the ultimate limits of one's freedom is one of the most profound that can occur to the human soul. . . The problem of free death is one of the fundamental problems of all the great moral philosophies. . .'[12]

Lastly, the thought that he can die of his own free will gives the adolescent the certainty that he is alive and helps him to define himself as a living being. The fact that he can abandon life is proof that he possesses it (like the man who imagines that he is poor in order to feel all the more strongly that he is rich). Knowledge helps him to give at least a negative defini-tion of life: it is that which he can suppress by killing himself.

In this period of calling into question, of movement, of constantly renewed uncertainty, in which nothing is either true or false from one moment to the next, the idea of suicide introduces the notion of permanence into his life and guaran-tees his stability. At the same time, it is a reassuring, almost palpable proof that he is alive and free, and therefore no longer a child.

C. The value of the conceptual factor in adolescent suicide

The fact that manipulation of the idea of death plays an important part in the work performed by the adolescent in defining himself as a living being and as an adult-to-be does not mean that this is the sole origin or the sole function of the idea of death. To believe this would be to subscribe to an outworn dichotomy between the cognitive life and the instinctual life. It is obvious that the idea of death (in the intellectualist sense) is part of the defensive system set up against anxiety in general, a fear of death in particular, and that it is bound up with the instinctual organization. In par-ticular, it represents a compromise between hetero- and auto-aggressivity on the one hand, and guilt and fear of death on the other, between the desire to see and the fear of seeing others, and himself, die. It represents a discharge of the anxiety that facilitates the development of 'the feeling of death'. Various hypotheses can be made about this. It might be supposed that the defining cognitive activity must involve the elaboration and manipulation of the idea of death and that the adolescent ego, building up its defences with what it has, uses it in the adolescent's attempt to master his fear of death. Or it might be that the idea of death is merely a defen-sive rationalization and is only instinctual in origin. But it might also be supposed, in terms of a more unitary view, that the feeling and fear of death on the one hand, and the idea of death on the other, are the simultaneous expression of the activation of the various spheres of the psychical apparatus, and that their intrication merely reflects the intrication of that apparatus. In any case, whatever its origin, this defining function of the idea of death exists, and plays a crucial role in the formation of the adult ego.

The same is obviously true of the idea of suicide. Its structuring function does not exclude its defensive function as a mediator between, for example, the tendency to suicide and the defence against this tendency. It would be unwise, therefore, to affirm that the existence of the idea of suicide, and above all its expression, excludes the desire for suicide. But it would be equally unwise to affirm that the idea of suicide always expresses such a desire. It would seem that the idea of suicide can exist in the adolescent's mind without being accompanied by any real desire for it, and independently of the defensive role of intellectualization. That the adolescent should need to know that he can kill himself does not necessarily imply that he wishes to, for, on the contrary, it may be confirmation of his pleasure in living.

However, it is often said that manipulation of the idea of death and suicide is dangerous; that by dwelling on it over much, by looking at it too closely, by juggling with it, the adolescent may be so fascinated by it that he is tempted to taste it and so bridge the gap that separates him from it. But in so far as this intellectual activity is not primarily a defence against the desire for death, can it produce such a desire that is then carried over into action? Of course, rationalization is not always far removed from action; many speculations and their verbal expression are the result of the tendency to act, a verbal form of resorting to action. But, in this case, we are no longer dealing with the manipulation of the idea of death and of suicide as such.

Carrying such a hypothesis further, we are brought to that of philosophical suicide. The possibility of a purely abstract reflexion as the source of self-destructive behaviour has given rise to a good deal of controversy. Philosophical suicide has been posited as the prototype of normal suicide, especially by suicides themselves and by some writers. But we know what value to place on secondary rationalizations intended to justify and to 'normalize' an action. It is often the most intellectual constructions that are closest to the resort to action, with its implied disturbance to the process of elaboration, and the philosophical suicide is rightly regarded as one of the most pathological. If we accepted the rationalization of the philosophical suicide at face value, we would fall into the defensive trap that the adolescent holds out to himself and to us. We would confirm the intellectualist explanations that participate in the adolescent's defence system - the adolescent wishing to hide from himself and from us his most deeply felt experience - and we would be abandoning any attempt to understand why the adolescent does sometimes kill himself. For one fact remains: the manipulation of the idea of death and suicide is a valuable structuring and progressive activity in adolescence. It is a constant, whereas very few adolescents commit suicide. However this does not mean that it plays no role in the suicidal process. That an activity in the service of life should sometimes place itself at the service of death is a paradox that should come as no surprise. It may, then, be a factor, but in any case it is not in the cognitive sphere that we can hope to find the suicidogenic factors proper to adolescence, if such exist, factors that participate in an act that is above all an instinctual manifestation.

Notes

1. H. Ey, 'Le suicide pathologique', *Études Psychiatriques*, t. II, Paris, Desclée de Brouwer, 1948, 341.
2. *Ibid.*; and A. Giabicani, *Étude sur le sens de la mort chez l'enfant*, thesis no. 109, Paris, 1955, 110.
3. A. Freud, *The Ego and the Mechanisms of Defence*, London, Hogarth Press, 1942, 85.
4. *Ibid.*, 86.
5. Giabicani, *op. cit.*, 111.
6. A. Gesell, *L'adolescent de 10 à 16 ans*, Paris, P.U.F., 1959, 526.
7. *Ibid.*, 536-7.
8. Cf. Chapter 2.
9. Cf. Chapter 15.
10. P.L. Landsberg, *Essai sur l'expérience de la mort*, Paris, Le Seuil, 1951, 23.
11. Giabicani, *op. cit.*, 27; R. Barande, 'L'inachévement de l'homme comme structure de son temps', *Revue Française de Psychanalyse*, no. 2-3, t. XXIX, March-June 1965, 283.
12. Landsberg, *op. cit.*, 119-20.

15 · Adolescence: depression or mourning? 1 · Adolescence and the Oedipus Complex

A. The depressive aspects of adolescence

'A profound crisis of despair . . . need for movement, a state of agitation, a defensive attitude, persistent burstings into tears and revolts against one's fate, a squandering of emotion and movement . . . The subject is constantly rising up against the person responsible for his ills and against his fate . . . Inclined to contradiction, insolent and haughty to those around him, he seeks solitude and rejects all help. . .'

'Expression of a conflict accompanied by emotional and intellectual disorders . . . often struggles long and desperately against these painful conflicts. A sharpened sensitivity, instability, stronger emotional reactions. . . Unjustified outbursts of anger against others, irritability, impatience and growing internal and external agitation. If conflicts with those around him are added to emotional pressure, his anxiety and feelings of uselessness may reach such a pitch that they become unbearable. . .'

'The cyclothymic constitution . . . shows analogies with the variations in self-assertiveness to be observed in adolescents, that is to say, moments of excitation followed by moments of depression. . . Young people undergo this constant shift of mood . . . suddenly they feel weak, self-critical, uninteresting, all their wishes seem to come up against a brick wall. . . During the periods of melancholia, the subject reduces his activity to a minimum, isolates himself, and experiences moods of great pessimism.'

'Melancholia is one of those ambivalent emotions typical of the fifteenth year. It is composed of motiveless sadness, slight lassitude, expectancy tinged with anxiety, all of which are not without their attraction for the adolescent, and which seem to correspond to a lowering of psychological tension.'

These quotations take us at once to the heart of the problem, for they could all be taken from the same book on adolescence. But although the last two are from a book on adolescence,[1] the first two are taken from studies on depression.[2] The similarity of the descriptions explains the frequency with which adolescence is associated with depression.

It is obvious that at an ordinary, superficial level of observation, many of the features of adolescent behaviour and thinking are reminiscent of depression. A host of other quotations could be offered from works describing the adolescent in terms that could be equally suitable for describing the minor forms of melancholia and other forms of depression such as traditional neurasthenia, depressive pseudo-asthenia, or, still better, the various neurotic depressions. The latter, in particular, on account of the diversity of the clinical tables in relation to the underlying neurosis, provide us with a whole range of psychological features characteristic of adolescence.

By the same token, there is no literary work on adolescence that does not speak of sadness, pessimism, the feeling of uselessness, etc. Direct observation of everyday life also provides us with innumerable examples of sad adolescents who seem to be permanently sunk in despairing lassitude, or inhibited, listless, easily immobilized in morose rumination, the face visibly marked by the signs of the depressive series. Others, like those suffering from slight depression, manage to a greater or lesser degree to avoid showing their true depression in agitation, irritability, anger, opposition - forms of behaviour that are often intended to divert attention from the tears that they feel are coming. And when an adolescent (any adolescent, not just those who consult a specialist) agrees to confide in us, we recognize either someone who feels imprisoned in painful, silent isolation, or someone who expatiates at length on his unhappiness at being isolated and misunderstood, or one who expresses his pessimism in romantic terms, or one who expresses nothing but doubt about himself and the world, denies all value, internal or external, and expresses a feeling of irremediability, or, again, someone who is caught up in shame-ridden, guilt-ridden anxiety because whatever he does he makes a mess of it.

I should now like to turn from the external manifestations of depression to their signification. As we saw with the manipulation of the idea of death, appearances hide complex phenomena that are often very difficult to elucidate in their various aspects.

In the gigantic struggle that occurs in adolescence, it would seem that there are a great many situations that open the way to depression. In the immense contradiction that afflicts the adolescent, in the fundamental ambivalence that marks each of his objectal and narcissistic investments, he has constantly to make choices, in which, whatever he does, he stands to lose. As a result of pubertal maturation, he must at the same time take up the reactivation of Oedipal links and his independent desire to earn a place for himself in the adult world, abandon his childhood pleasures just when his pregenital impulses are returning in a more powerful form than ever, and assert himself as a being of dialogue just when he no longer knows who he is, when he feels that he has lost himself. He must take up the struggle against the reactivated impulses just when his desire for power makes him deny his fears, when he is deprived of both super-ego and ego ideal. He is reorganizing and enriching himself narcissistically just when narcissistic losses and wounds shower upon him. Whatever he does with his investments and disinvestments, he both gains and loses. He loses his objects and himself at the same time as he finds others and a new self.

All increase in impulse is accompanied by its own defence, and in the adolescent is manifested essentially in its defensive opposite.[3] Whichever wins, the adolescent 'sticks' to it. To disinvest is to lose an object, to maintain an investment is to abandon one's dynamism, to experience a narcissistic loss. In this confused adventure, object loss and narcissistic loss lie constantly in wait for the adolescent, alternatively or simultaneously.

The profound reshaping of the objectal and narcissistic investments, the struggle between the increased impulses and the correspondingly increased defences, have been studied in particular in recent years by Anna Freud[3] and, in France, by Male[4] and Kestemberg.[5] I have borrowed extensively from these works. But I must stress once more how difficult it is to separate the representatives of the impulses from those of the defences. What, for adolescents, may represent the counter-investment of an impulse may also represent an impulse. The same behaviour may appear to be progressive and regressive at the same time, what may seem like an impoverishment may have a structuring effect. It does not seem to me to be possible, if one wishes to remain faithful to the facts, to describe impulses on the one hand and the defences against these impulses on the other. In my view, the only approach that does not traduce what actually occurs is to perceive the situation in terms of the objects of the adolescent, to try to grasp the infinite complexity of these objectal and narcissistic investments and disinvestments, taking into account both impulse and defence, regression and progress, destructuration and maturation.

It is this tangle of appearance and risk of depression, this ambivalence of impulse and defence, of objectal and narcissistic investment and disinvestment, that I shall try to describe, incompletely, perhaps even confusedly - like the object of my study, the adolescent confronting what he is losing. For convenience, I shall examine in turn the various manifestations of these objectal investments, then the narcissistic investments, but such a distinction is of course a purely artificial one. As we shall see, we cannot deal with the former without referring to the latter. In fact, the adolescent is always being referred back from others to himself and vice versa.

B. The manifestations of the investments of the Oedipal objects

At the centre of adolescence is the resumption of genital development, with its line of force linking the Oedipal situation and the castration anxiety. The excessive energy at the adolescent's disposal drives him to win his independence, to free himself from parental control, and to resolve the Oedipal situation. But he has a long way to go before he can achieve this. He first has to face the reactivation of his Oedipal links, and his correspondingly increased sense of guilt, and at the same time he has to ensure the protection of his narcissistic integrity. Caught up as he is in such a potent ambivalence, he tries out various solutions in turn. But whatever solution he chooses, it involves the risk of an objectal or narcissistic loss. The Oedipal objectal loss, the Oedipal disappointment, which is inevitable until a free renunciation of the direct Oedipal object can take place, revives pregenital conflicts, which in turn bring with them a tendency to depression and suicide.[6] The adolescent, then, must try out a number of different methods before finding a way out of the labyrinth. I shall now try to describe some of these.

—*The resumption of the Oedipal situation* involves danger for the adolescent. The young person finds himself in the grips of contradictory motions. The representatives of the impulses peculiar to the triangular situation appear reactivated in the dual dimension of the direct and inverted Oedipus complex, with attachment to and aggressivity towards each of the parents. But also, and more often than the adolescent is willing to admit, he is beset by conscious images of Oedipal love relationships that assume the intensity almost of reality at the time when the maturation of the genital organs is taking place. The frequency of these conscious images gives a particular colouring to the situation. They cause a considerable narcissistic wound, for the young man feels not only guilty, but profoundly unworthy, and loses his self-esteem. Moreover, they force him to feel the Oedipal situation as really dangerous, not to say untenable. And both the guilt and the fear of punishment are all the greater. We know to what extent the fear of castration, when experienced not as a phantasy but as a real danger, as a result of this 'realistic' context, can open the way to depression.

Thus the adolescent fears that he can live through the Oedipal situation only at excessive cost, and feels hemmed in by his own contradictory demands. A violent struggle takes place between his impulses, which he feels unable to control, and the demands, real or imagined, of those around him. He builds up a system of defence,[7] lays down stern prohibitions, and uses other impulses as an Oedipal counter-investment. In this way, he can hope to avoid depression, but he cannot be sure that each attempt does not bring with it new conflicts and frustrations.

— *Of the many defensive methods,* regression is particularly tempting. It has the advantage of reviving memories of the lost paradise of childhood and of reactivating pregenital impulses. It is also solicited by the still powerful figure of the mother, who wishes to keep her child for herself, and who may, at the same time, be re-experiencing her own Oedipal complex, in a situation that dare not speak its name. But satisfying as regression may sometimes be, it also brings bitterness. Childhood pleasure cannot efface the wound of genital amputation that it presupposes and the loss of the Oedipal object. And how can someone have respect for himself when he retreats before the prospect of genitality, renounces the force that drives him towards new, unknown, but already discerned satisfactions, and sacrifices his objects and himself on the altar of parental love.

The young man is tempted to repair the wound that he has thus sustained by adopting a narcissistic withdrawal into himself - a solution that is encouraged by the reactivation of the narcissistic attitudes characteristic of early adolescence. This withdrawal appears to avoid danger, and is valuable to the process of healing, but in fact it merely serves to aggravate the losses and wounds. It confirms the loss of the Oedipal object and the renunciation of genitality. It forces the young man who wishes to remain enclosed within his narcissistic boundaries to struggle against an excess of energy that is driving him to go out towards the world. A renunciation on such a scale is impossible without involving psychosis. The only possible compromise for the adolescent, if he is not to renounce his genital maturation entirely, is masturbation. But then he must either see himself as the sullied, imperfect, unworthy masturbator, or give up masturbation too and deprive himself of all sexual pleasure. Thus the narcissistic withdrawal, which was intended to heal the wound, creates others and is yet another cause of depression. The haughty attitude of the adolescent wishing to seem self-sufficient is a way of trying to avoid the danger of depression.

When all these cures prove worse than the disease, the adolescent may try to preserve, at one and the same time, his Oedipal link, his dynamism, and his narcissistic integrity, by maintaining a certain distance between his parents and himself, thus protecting himself from the effects of any impulsive outbursts on his part. He readily adopts a hostile attitude - a less compromising way of loving. But since this hostility is an attempt to struggle against Oedipal love, it soon reinforces the aggressivity that it over-invests, thus bringing about an inversion of the affects. This interplay, sustained by reactivated pregenital impulses, opens the way to destructive impulses and depressive attitudes. Such a process is often merely incipient or intermittent, and is deflected by other influences. But if, as a result of various factors, it does develop and continue, the adolescent is faced by a dramatic dilemma: either he gives vent to his phantasy of destructive aggressivity and imagines himself to be a murderer whom he will himself despise, or he turns that destructive aggressivity against himself. Feeling their own aggressivity aroused by that of their child, the parents fail to hear the anguished cry that it conceals. In extreme cases, the circle may contract and the adolescent is faced by an alternative that is depressing however one looks at it. This is one of the culminating points of the dramatic secret of the adolescent, and forms a particularly favourable background for depression.[8]

The adolescent comes to the painful conclusion that his various attempts at counter-Oedipal defence are as dangerous and costly as the Oedipal situation itself, and that in the last resort they are not very effective. The impulse is still there, however it is represented. The only way remaining to him by which he can try to attenuate his painful conflicts, to obviate losses and demeaning behaviour, is to sharpen the struggle against the impulses. He begins to adopt an ascetic mode of behaviour - a reaction that is too common to require description. This mode, too, is generally no more than incipient and temporary, but asceticism is from the outset a depressive position, since it is a choice of self-castration, an incipient form of suicide, pure frustration, repudiation of the instinctual impulse and pleasure *in toto,* whereas regression, for example, involves the secondary benefit of archaic pleasures.

Beginning with the Oedipal genital movement, there is a repression of all the instinctual impulses that may even be carried to the point of refusing to take the steps necessary to the preservation of life.[9] Thus, paradoxically, the asceticism that aims at preserving the parental relationship causes the destruction of the parental image even in its most archaic pre-genital aspects, going so far beyond its intention as to create a solely frustrating image. We are then no longer faced by the risk of depression, but by depression itself, an equivalent of suicidal behaviour. Fortunately, it seldom goes so far and, generally speaking, asceticism is only one attempt among others to find a compromise and is soon outgrown.

The renunciation of the Oedipal situation

With time, the adolescent's aggressiveness dies down, and he works out an approach that will take him out of the bi-polar situation in which he finds himself, caught between his narcissistic position and the Oedipal situation. He is then trapped between his inner world, inhabited by one, two, or three characters, and the external world that he is beginning to see more clearly, as he emerges from the pubertal 'vertigo' that prevented him from seeing anything other than himself. He is still caught up in the Oedipal relationship, but he will try out new arrangements which, this time, will not be confined to his parents and himself; he introduces others, or, at least, the image that he has of them.

These arrangements are centred on the now half-glimpsed possibility of a renunciation of the Oedipal situation. It involves, at least, a loss of the Oedipal object, a recognition that he is unfitted for the Oedipal situation. He sees this as acceptance of defeat, as a lesson in humility. But is he willing to accept this? He cannot do so without sacrificing something, without a certain amount of hesitation, without a feeling of losing an indispensable object, and without a feeling of his own unworthiness: so here, too, there is a risk of depression. Sometimes he accepts, even desires this renunciation, sensing the benefits to be gained from it; at other times, he is no more than resigned to it, experiencing it as a loss.

Often at this period, as also during the infantile Oedipal phase, the attachment to the parent of the same sex is strengthened, both because the infantile homosexual Oedipal element is reactivated, and because it makes it easier to bear the loss of the other parent. For the boy, the attachment to the father as partner in the Oedipal triangle is doubled by the attachment to the father as representative of reality, each reinforcing the other. What we have here is ambivalence, together with all the causes of difficulty and depression that occur in the early stages of the juvenile Oedipal situation. In the case of the girl, she is divided between a strengthening of the Oedipal situation with the mother, who is also the all-powerful, dangerous mother-nurse, and the link with the father as representative of reality, which runs the risk of keeping alive the direct Oedipal link with all the conflicts and anxieties that this involves. In trying to free himself from this dual Oedipal link, the adolescent will use new defensive methods that show that he is beginning to perceive the world.

He tries to disinvest the parental object to the advantage of other objects. But this parental disinvestment is felt by him as a matter of urgency, and he does not always have a substitute object at his disposal. He then finds himself without an object. He feels this lack of an object quite simply as a loss. Confronted by his need, he throws himself into what can easily look like a compulsive quest for an object. Meanwhile, he replaces the lost parental object by an image of the perfect ideal object, and lives in a state of hope that is doomed to disappointment.[10]

However, his growing appreciation of the world enables him to try out various displacements. He begins to perceive other objects; these may be adults occupying a privileged position as friends of the family, teachers, youth club organizers, or another adolescent, either a friend or a girl with whom he establishes a love relationship. It may also be a group: a gang, a youth organization, or some movement based on a political, philosophical or religious ideal then becomes the substitute object. But does this displacement succeed in investing one of these new objects? Very often, the attempt ends in failure. Various authors[11] believe that the adolescent is not capable of establishing an object relationship, but that instead he sets up a projective, over-invested identificatory relationship. He projects on to the chosen object the image of the ideal, perfect being that I spoke of earlier. He is soon disappointed and is doubly wounded, in his Oedipal investment and in his idealized narcissistic identification. He then suddenly withdraws his investment, and finds himself once again lacking an object. The attachments and detachments occur one after the other, and are therefore followed by an alternating sequence of vacuity and projective identificatory over-investment, thus producing cyclothymic variations. The displacement, which offers certain definite advantages, also involves difficult periods, occurring at irregular intervals, when the subject is in a position very reminiscent of the depressive position. To a far greater degree than the adult, who brings about changes in his investments in a quite natural way, the adolescent resembles a trapeze-artist who, letting go of one piece of equipment, remains unsupported for a brief instant in the void, before taking up his position on another.

We have already discussed at some length the functions of the intellectualization process: the investment of the new cognitive functions of the ego and the defence against impulses that are felt to be dangerous by virtue of their new charge of energy. Fearing that he will be unable to control his impulses, the adolescent places a protective barrier of abstraction between his objects and himself. This also serves as a defence against the tendency to resort to action, and it is reinforced when the impulses and the tendency to motor reaction increase. When heavily reinforced, it can then lead to a veritable paralysis of action, but even when only moderately reinforced it leads inevitably to a diminution in or complete absence of pleasure. It protects the object to such a degree that the object becomes invisible, virtually absent. Trapped between a paralysing inhibition that completes the loss of the object and the narcissistic over-investment of intellectualization, any weakening of which is felt as a narcissistic wound with consequent loss of self-esteem, the adolescent finds himself in a depressive dilemma whatever the outcome. It is this type of defence that is to be found in the adolescent who cannot tolerate compromise.[12] Any object that presents itself as it really is, with all its flexibility and sense of compromise, is seen as a bad, wounding object that must not be invested. Any object worthy of being invested is a frustrating object.

Thus, in all the various modes of defence against his libidinal impulses and his object investment, the adolescent meets one disappointment after another; he sets up defences to protect himself against depression, but these defences bring with them their own depressive factors. Whatever he tries to do, he is soon confronted by his own inadequacy, and he constantly feels a lack, the lack of an object or the lack of an effective defence that would give him a sense of his own value.

Notes.

1. M. Debesse, *La crise d'originalité juvénile*, Paris, P.U.F., 1948, 180-1.
2. P. Kielholz, 'Clinique, diagnostic différentiel et traitement des états dépressifs', *Acta Psychosomatica Geigy*, Basle, 1959, 16-17 and 20-21.
3. A. Freud, *The Ego and the Mechanisms of Defence*, London, Hogarth Press, 2nd ed. 1942, 270.
4. *Psychothérapic de l'adolescent*, Paris, P.U.F., 1964.
5. *Op. cit.*
6. Cf. K. Abraham and E. Jacobson.
7. A. Freud, *op cit.*, 267 ff.
8. *Ibid.*, 270-2.
9. *Ibid.*, 274.
10. Cf. Chapter 16.
11. A. Freud, *op. cit.*, 263.
12. *Ibid.*, 274.

16. Adolescence: depression or mourning?
2. The manifestations of narcissism in the adolescent

The narcissistic displacements, withdrawals, and over-investments serve, through a process of regression, as Oedipal counter-investments, thus producing an important reshaping of narcissism in the course of adolescence. This narcissistic reshaping is above all an enrichment of the ego, a source of important pleasures, and is necessarily invested by the subject. I have no wish to labour the point that this enrichment and pleasure are also accompanied by anxiety and by wounds caused by the reawakening and reshaping of infantile positions, a situation that involves a good many renunciations and losses. The narcissistic satisfactions of the adolescent must not be underestimated, but they are obtained at a price, and in a situation of extreme ambivalence. If the resolution of the Oedipal conflict is not a painless operation, the pains that accompany this reshaping are deep, intense, and are particularly important elements from the point of view of depression and suicide. I shall not try to present an overall study of this vast question,[1] but shall select those aspects that are relevant to my approach.

A. Loss of identity

The question 'Who am I?', which really means 'Who am I becoming?', lies at the centre of the problem.[3] The search for an answer, the discovery of 'I', is a fundamental part of the work of adolescence, and is accompanied by mixed feelings. The adolescent derives intoxicating satisfactions as well as particularly painful narcissistic wounds from this process of discovery.

Loss of physical identity

The adolescent has to confront himself with his physical identity - a fact that I discussed in Chapter 13. Of course, he derives intense satisfactions from his body. But he is also made well aware of it by the trouble it causes him. The genital impulse, by driving him to 'enforced pleasure', causes anxiety and guilt, which lead him at times to curse his body. He tries to defend himself by regressing to earlier physical preoccupations and satisfactions; but even at this level, his body lets him down. Temporary instrumental deficit, due to sudden physical changes, results in brutal and clumsy behaviour, involving material damage and sometimes injury to people, that brings with it a flood of reproach from others and from himself. To this is often added the (correct) feeling that his errors of motility are facilitating the emergence of his aggressivity. He then sees his body as something to be ashamed of; this leads to attempts at physical negation, and even to classic 'angelism'. Disturbance in his consciousness of his body and a feeling of its unworthiness combine to give him the feeling of not knowing who he is, and when he sees the image of his body he receives a painful feeling of narcissistic dissatisfaction. Effects on his general bearing and various forms of exhibitionism are often merely a reassurance against these painful wounds.

Loss of psychical identity

Just as he no longer recognizes his body, the adolescent no longer recognizes his ego, which is undergoing just as many changes. The fundamental lines of his ego are being displaced, reshaped, they disappear only to reappear transformed; although his ego is being enriched and strengthened, it is curiously weak, the adolescent does not recognize it, and sometimes quite genuinely feels that he has lost it. This reshaping affects the pregenital and genital infantile motions, which are being reactivated and, after a process of transformation, will eventually find their definitive form; but it also affects the appearance of new representatives and new functions. All this is made possible by the excessive energy that appears at puberty and which drives the adolescent to new re-orderings, the rapidity of which is the visible expression and the essential factor of the loss of psychical identity.

In Chapter 15 I discussed the new representatives of impulses and interests that appear in the Oedipal relationship. Generally speaking, the new functions, the new appetencies, are both a source of narcissistic satisfaction and a cause of unease; they are not always recognized at first, and can be felt as dangerous, unknown intrusions. The adolescent feels a stranger to himself, astonished at his own behaviour, and often feels that he is outside his ego, even to the point of denying its existence.

But it is above all the dizzy speed of the changes that he is undergoing that gives him most satisfaction and most unease. Because of this speed, the adolescent feels absent, is ceaselessly running after himself without ever catching up, without ever having time to recognize himself. One adolescent described this feeling of 'I don't recognize myself any more' as being like a shipwrecked man in a storm at sea who clings to his raft, expecting at any moment to be swept away by a wave. The adolescent is afraid of being submerged by the tumultuous forces that well up from within him. He has lost his unity; a part of himself, but never the same part, is always missing. Although, at times, he may have a vague feeling that all these changes are ushering in an increase in his own value, at others he is afraid that he will never be able to recapture what he has lost; he feels an acute narcissistic loss, he feels less intelligent, less gifted, and he seems to have lost all self-esteem. The mobility of his investments expresses this loss of ego elements. His old interests disappear, new ones take their place, only to disappear in turn; investments and disinvestments appear and disappear with equal suddenness. Between two sequences, he may feel profoundly empty, inert, incapable of being interested in anything, which merely enhances the feeling of no longer recognizing himself, of having lost his way, of having changed and not for the better.

When he feels too lost inside himself, the adolescent has two opposite methods at his disposal to find guide lines and reassurance. Either he can cling to the feeling of 'becoming', to his growing awareness of the new features of his personality, or he can be helped by counter-Oedipal, defensive regression, and by the reactivation of pregenital motions that enables him to rediscover within himself a fund of familiar infantile experience. This latter method seems satisfactory when he is feeling particularly disorientated in the storm of adolescence, but he soon realizes that it brings with it a good deal of confusion and danger.

The pre-genital impulses take on a new reality. But they place the young person in a dilemma, in which either alternative is wounding and disorientating. If his reactivated pregenital demands are felt by himself and by others to be unreal, satisfaction is refused and he undergoes just as many frustrations and wounds. If he does gain satisfaction from them, even at the price of regression, he feels that he is renouncing all the benefits of genital maturation. Caught up in this conflict, he may swing from one to the other, feeling in either case a lack, or he may try to keep both, in which case he is afraid, quite rightly, that he will lose both, and thus destroy himself.

Of the pregenital motions, oral and anal aggressivity is particularly reactivated, and we know to what effect it diminishes the adolescent's self-esteem, to what extent, in his guilt, he feels it too strongly, turns it against himself, torturing himself like a melancholic.

Lastly, and perhaps above all, his object relation is imbued with pregenitality: phantasies of fusion, of incorporation, of introjection reappear, with all the disturbances that accompany this type of object relation; any loss of love, any removal of the object from sight, is felt as an object loss, which, through introjection, encourages auto-aggressivity. Furthermore, the archaic pregenital motion that interests us most here is reactivated - the motion which, for want of a better term, I have called the tendency to death. If this tendency is linked with primary masochism, then the primary masochism, like all the archaic motions, is also reactivated and encouraged by the redirection of aggressivity, itself reactivated, against the subject. If the tendency to death is the representative of the death instinct, it is easy to see that the reactivation of archaic motions and organizations associated with the loss of the unity of the ego encourages the disunion of the impulses, the disunion of the couple formed by the life instinct binding the death instinct. The direct expression of the death instinct is then facilitated, the most overt manifestation of which is suicide.

I must emphasize once again the interaction between disorders of identity and the adolescent's difficulty in making choices. He cannot make up his mind, for to do so merely accentuates his feeling of loss of identity. As a result of the increase of libidinal energy, all the genital and pre-genital impulses are reactivated. Every choice and every satisfaction is accompanied by the frustration of other wishes - a frustration that is all the more intolerable in that the typically pre-genital intolerance to frustration is being reactivated. This frustration is experienced as an obligation to renounce one's impulses, and therefore as a narcissistic loss of part of oneself, a loss of substance that may well alter one's identity. Each choice, and therefore each rununciation, is felt by the adolescent as partial death. In order to feel whole again, he wishes to satisfy his new demands without having to renounce pre-existing ones. But, at the same time, he is aware of the precariousness of a position which, in the last resort, would block the way to all demand and force him to deny himself *in toto*. There are also sudden mutations in his behaviour: at one time he may exert the most various, the most contradictory demands simultaneously, without renouncing any one of them, while at another he may avoid any situation involving choice, rejecting all demands *in toto,* and may fall into a depressive position, imbued with a feeling of his own inadequacy and powerlessness. Or, again, in accordance with one of the mechanisms already mentioned, he may try to reject some of his impulses. But this, as I have said, is always to deny a part of oneself and to give up being oneself. He may also, in an archaic projective process that is also being reactivated, shift responsibility for his impossibility on to whoever is soliciting his choice. He then feels this solicitation as an attack, causing a narcissistic wound that undermines the integrity of his ego - which he feels to be very fragile in any case.

B. The adolescent, his reality, and his morality

The movement, the ambivalence, and the paradox concern
not only his relation to himself and his Oedipal objects. They
also affect his relations with the external world, his perception
of that world, that is to say, what is; the rules that govern his
relations with it, that is to say, what must be; and how he
should situate himself in that world if he is to get the best out
of it, that is to say, what he must be. Subjective reality, the
superego and the ego ideal, gradually became organized in
childhood through parental upbringing. These formations have
close links, therefore, with the parental images; they are, like
them, deeply rooted in the ego, and, like them, form part of
the narcissistic inheritance.

These formations are rooted in the most archaic areas of
the personality and their development is directly linked with
the 'reality testing' and the castration fear of the Oedipal
situation. They represent to a remarkable degree the pregenital and genital bipolarity of the parental images and relations. Reactivated and called into question with the pubertal
awakening of the Oedipal situation, they achieve their
definitive organization only at adolescence, when they are the
cause of many of the deepest narcissistic wounds, and play a
particularly important role in the depressive and suicidal
process.

I do not intend to examine in detail the constitution of
these formations, or the various theories that have been propounded to explain their development. Nor could I provide
here a complete account of the complex question of the reshaping of these formations at adolescence. Instead, I shall
limit myself to mentioning those aspects most relevant to our
field of study.

The extent and depth of their reshapings are a result of the
importance of the parental contribution in the constitution
of these formations, and the fact that they represent major
elements in the dependence of the child on the parents, thus
sustaining the Oedipal relationship. Their reorganization is also
the *sine qua non* of the future adult's attainment of autonomy.
For a long time, the child has only a partial direct contact with

reality. Between the world and him are interposed the parents and their substitutes, and he perceives reality through the subjective reality of his educators.

Theoretically, education may be conceived as 'an incitement to the conquest of the pleasure principle, to its replacement by the reality principle'.[3] In fact, the parents and their substitutes use the path made by the transmission of reality to transmit in a projective form their own superego and their own ego ideal. There is in the child an at least partial fusion of his own subjective reality, that of his parents, their superego and their ego ideal. The adolescent has to disentangle them, therefore, and free them from parental dependence.

Subjective reality

'As the cares given to the baby are the prototypes of the cares given later to the child, the supremacy of the pleasure principle may, in fact, cease only with complete mental detachment from the parents,'[4] that is to say, during adolescence.

In the dual polarity of reality principle having to overcome the pleasure principle and knowledge of the world, subjective reality has become organized in childhood *pari passu* with the infantile impulses and the infantile perceptivo-motor equipment. At puberty this subjective reality is no longer adequate. Using his new instrumental and instinctual acquisitions, and new ways of adaptation, he must rethink the world anew. In a rather confused way, he feels that his childhood images are outworn and that he must now decide to renounce them. This involves yet another narcissistic loss. But he does not acquire a more satisfactory image of reality immediately. He must set about by trial and error to create his own subjective reality and to try to get a closer grasp of objective reality. Between the loss of the one and the integration of the other, he sometimes undergoes nothing less than eclipses of reality, while at other times he has a view of reality that is astonishing for its clarity and objectivity. The adolescent is like a blind man moving around in an environment whose dimensions have altered. The dimensions of childhood no longer suit him and he has not yet acquired those of the adult. Furthermore, the revival of his pre-genital type of projective activity provides him with a more or less opaque screen between himself and the world. He knows that he is being manipulated by instruments that he does not yet know how to use. So to the narcissistic loss of his subjective reality is added an unflattering image of himself - and yet another opportunity to undervalue himself.

The superego

The same, equally painful process occurs in relation to the superego. As the 'heir of the Oedipus complex', its constitution and organization are directly linked with the resolution of Oedipal guilt and anxiety. But, because of its pregenital roots, it is an important element in narcissism. In order to become an adult, the adolescent feels that he must work out a new morality for himself. He must 'renounce a fundamental part of the content of his superego . . . something which is an essential part of himself . . . free himself from part of his own person'.[5] He must renounce it because it is a mark of his dependence, because it is a morality that was imposed on him from the outside, because it is tied up with subjective reality and parental ideals. But then he is partially deprived of superego and the wholesale rejections, rationalizations, opposition are defences that reveal the gravity of the loss involved. This loss creates a void, a quite serious 'depression'. Proof of this is to be found in attitudes that seem to be intended purposely to provoke prohibitions and punishment; in fact, they are appeals to the parents to resume their archaic superego roles, in order both to fill the void caused by the rejection of the infantile superego and to bolster up the defences against the impulses.

But here, too, to narcissistic loss is added the moral incoherence that gives the adolescent a demeaning image of himself as an immoral or amoral being. He may reassure himself against this unsatisfying image of himself by acts of hypermoral scrupulosity of an archaic type, the superego persecuting. Such acts occur all the more readily in that they represent the emergence of parental demands that were precociously inter-

236 · Adolescent Suicide

nalized during the pre-Oedipal phase, with all their rigidity, intransigence, and lack of contact with reality; it is not unusual to see adolescents indulge in behaviour that seems self-punishing in character and heavily bound up with Oedipal guilt, but which is, in fact, due to a combination of regression, the resurgence of pre-superego archaic forms, and an attempt to heal narcissistic wounds.

In other cases, the adolescent may defend himself by rationalizing immorality or amorality as 'another kind of morality', which runs the risk of opening the way to the impulses, with all the guilt that they bring with them. He tries to escape either by going further along this line of behaviour, obeying a policy of 'evil' that is in fact profoundly masochistic, or by falling back on rigid, pre-superego prohibitions.

Thus, whichever course he adopts, the adolescent experiences a loss. If he wishes to work out a morality of his own, he renounces his infantile superego and undergoes a considerable narcissistic loss that leaves him temporarily with no scale of values, and with all the loss of self-esteem that this involves. If he maintains his infantile superego, he gives up the attempt to work out a morality for himself, and admits defeat in trying to establish a satisfactory relationship with the external world. This involves an equally considerable narcissistic loss.

The ego ideal

Of all the formations mentioned so far, it is undoubtedly the ego ideal that undergoes the most extensive and most painful reshaping in the course of adolescence. We know that the establishment of a realistic ego ideal plays a crucial role in the adolescent's ability to accede to an adult psychical life. The fact that this reshaping is so especially extensive and difficult can be explained by two facts.

First, the ego ideal not only has firm archaic roots, it is, unlike the superego, strongly organized from the pre-genital phase. It constitutes one of the most important representatives of narcissism - the Oedipal development having had the effect of reshaping a pre-existing organization on a more realistic basis.

The origin and type of organization of the ego ideal are such that damage to it constitutes the model of the narcissistic wound. To renounce the megalomaniacal forms of the ego ideal is to accept the greatest possible narcissistic loss.

The development of the ego ideal and its reshaping during adolescence constitute the most characteristic series of paradoxes to be found in this period. Throughout these chapters I have referred to the loss of self-esteem felt by the adolescent. But, at the same time, awareness of his increased capacities and strength, the enrichment of his ego, the appearance of new functions, the increase of existing ones, are all ways of increasing self-esteem and narcissistic gratification in so far as they satisfy the ego ideal.

By the same token, the reorganization of his subjective reality shows him that his childhood dreams are now outworn and that if he wishes to accede to a satisfactory adult life he must reduce his ambitions to more realistic proportions. But, at the same time, ideas of grandeur, desire for omnipotence, and megalomania are never so strong as at adolescence. And the ego ideal denigrates the ego, which fights back as best it can, a poor animal crouching at the foot of the statue of perfection. The reshaping of the ego ideal is a permanent confrontation between reality and megalomania. When reality wins, the adolescent undergoes a narcissistic loss at the level of his megalomaniacal ideal, and when this ideal wins, he undergoes a narcissistic loss by losing his subjective reality.

Furthermore, the ego ideal is the locus of reciprocal projection between parents and child. The child projects his own megalomania on to his parents. But the parents also project their own regressive ideal upon the child; they regard it as. quite normal that the child should realize their own megalomaniacal ambitions. The ego ideal is a permanent element in the parents/child relationship and a centre of extreme ambivalence. Both by regression before the Oedipal conflict and by reactivation of the archaic, megalomaniacal ego ideal and his projection of it on to his parents, the adolescent feels a revival in himself of the idealized images that he had made of his parents in the past, seeing them as all-powerful figures, capable of offering him the support, security and protection he needs, and of which, as we have seen, he still feels the need during adolescence. But, on the other hand, this all-powerful parental image makes him afraid, for it represents an obstacle to his maturation, a renunciation of his ability to become an adult, and also a dangerous submission to all-powerful figures who could destroy him if they so desired.

Furthermore, the increase in his perception of reality makes him feel that this idealized image of his parents has become outworn. The parents are excluded from the realm of the gods in which he had placed them. He is forced to perceive their imperfections, whereas, until recently, he had wanted to ignore them. He realizes that his parents' prohibitions and taboos, and their excessive ambitions, do not possess the sacred value that he had been led to believe. His parents seem to him to be like false gods, imposters who have tried to lure him into a trap. Paradoxically, perceiving reality idealized through the screen formed by the vestiges of his own archaic ideal, he reproaches his parents for their 'realism', accusing them of not having a correct view of reality, and regards them as being weaker than himself. This is one of the deepest losses that he has to undergo, and it explains his appeal to parental authority as a way of effacing this loss and re-establishing his parents in their omnipotence. But he then feels subjected to them once again, and he feels as great a loss as before.

Faced with the need to reconsider his parents on a human scale, in a realistic manner, which represents a loss both of the security that they provide and of the megalomaniacal ideal that he once projected on to them, he tries to save this ideal, or at least allow it to survive, by displacing it on to other individuals. As we saw in Chapter 15, the displacement is also motivated by the attempts at reorganization carried out with a view to renouncing the Oedipal situation. In this way he experiences sudden, violent attachments to friends of his own age, adults who exercise an educative role, or famous figures, either real or imaginary, whom he idealizes and endows with features of his own megalomaniacal dreams. But, against the test of reality, he is soon disappointed and has to undergo the loss both of the loved one and of his projection. We are brought back here to the process of massive projective identification, with its sudden investments and disinvestments. The adolescent is periodically left in a dangerous state of emptiness until, gradually, he is able to renounce the unrealistic aspects of his ideal.

Notes

1. Cf. in particular the works by P. Male, and E. Kestemberg's 'L'identité et l'identification chez l'adolescent', *Psychiatrie de l'enfant*, vol. V, fasc. 2, Paris, P.U.F., 1962.
2. Kestemberg, *ibid.*, 443.
3. S. Freud, *Formulations on the Two Principles of Mental Functioning*, stand. ed., vol. XII, 224.
4. *Ibid.*, 3.
5. J. Lampl de Groot, 'Adolescence', *The Psychoanalytic Study of the Child*, vol. XV, New York, Int. Univ. Press, 1960, 100.

17. Adolescence: depression or mourning? (Conclusion)

A. Depression?

The preceding chapters have confirmed the extent to which adolescence itself causes depression. What can be observed at the level of appearances is very like the traditional symptomatology of depression; I have shown how every reorganization attempted by the adolescent incurs a risk of depression, and how the subject is in the depressive zone. The analogy is a tempting one, and just as some authors regard the adolescent as psychotic, neurotic and psychopathic, perhaps I can add that he is also depressed. But by depressed, do I mean simply that he is in a state of depression or do I mean that he is truly depressive, that is to say, predisposed to depression?[1]

I think we should think hard before assimilating adolescence to pathological depression. To do so would be to cross the theoretical boundary between the normal and the pathological, if not to regard adolescence itself as a disease. This is, of course, a secondary argument; in the present state of our knowledge, the concepts of normal and pathological are sufficiently vague for this not to be a serious objection. But the evaluation of adolescent behaviour in terms of psychopathology is bound to create misunderstandings.

What we must find out, then, is whether the adolescent really is in a state of depression, and, if not, what it is that makes him look 'as if he were depressed'. Certainly the confusion in which we find ourselves is merely a reflection of the confusion in the adolescent's life, and of his own difficulty in distinguishing between what is normal and what is pathological.[2] But we cannot be satisfied with such a negative conclusion. The question is interesting not only from a theoretical point of view, it also has practical implications concerning the way in which we should behave towards adolescents, and towards suicidal adolescents in particular.

Apart from traditional clinical appearances, all the factors that make a subject liable to depression appear or reappear in an active form. Object losses are many and simultaneous: loss of the Oedipal object, loss of parental images with all the security and protection that they bring, loss of images of a known reality. Associated with these is the loss of self-esteem, so characteristic of a depression bound up with an impoverishment of the ego; with the general calling into question proper to adolescence, this loss of self-esteem may even go so far as to cause a feeling of loss of the ego itself, the most extreme form of narcissistic loss. And this impoverished ego is then subjected to the rule of the regressive and persecutive superego and the megalomaniacal, perpetually unsatisfied ego ideal, thus bringing about the split between the ego and the 'conscience' so typical of depressed subjects.[3]

At the same time, there is a revival of the pregenital motions, with all their archaic conflicts, frustrations and precocious object losses, and an exacerbation of intolerance to frustration, the introjection of the object, narcissistic identification. Similarly, there occurs the defusion of love and hate and 'the loss of love, a basic depressive situation, in which the subject is no longer, or feels that he is no longer, loved, and in which he can no longer, or feels that he can no longer, love'.[4] Now, this situation is to be found in the adolescent, who feels that he no longer deserves to be loved, or is able to love, because his love is bad and should be repressed. And to all this is added the destructive tendency that occupies a special position among the reactivated archaic motions.

Yes, this picture has a certain plausibility. And if it enables us to speak of adolescence as a depression, we must try and define the nature of this depression and situate it in the nosographical framework of depression. Certainly, the unity of depression must be preserved, but the form and outcome of depressive states are sufficiently varied to allow us to situate this so-called depression of adolescence.

It would be tempting to regard it as a melancholic, or, at

least, as a psychotic depression. This would be made all the
easier by the fact that the pubertal drive has often been compared to a psychotic drive. But this would imply that all
human beings underwent a psychotic depressive attack at
adolescence, and that the vast majority underwent only one
such crisis throughout their lives, while, for a small minority,
this crisis was repeated later in life. Similarly, confronted by
this incomplete clinical picture, one might conclude, as has
often been done in the case of melancholia, that this first
crisis is untypical and misleading.

But such a position would dilute the concept of melancholia to a dangerous degree, and, more important, reduce
the importance of the peculiarities of the basic personality.
Contrary to the traditional view, we now know that between
attacks of psychotic, especially melancholic, depression, the
personality is far from normal, that it appears to be psychotic
(or prepsychotic or parapsychotic, according to one's theoretical views) even during the intervals between attacks, and that
it is far from being improved after the first attack. So we
cannot endorse the hypothesis whereby psychotic depression
is expressed only in the temporary, and spontaneously curable,
depression of adolescence.

The same can be said of the hypothesis of neurotic or psychopathic depression. For what are we to make of a neurosis,
or a subjacent psychopathic personality, that disappeared for
the rest of the subject's life and lasted no longer than a
juvenile depression? If such were the case, we would have to
regard all adolescents as genuinely psychotic, neurotic, or
psychopathic, almost all of whom were cured spontaneously,
while a few remained fixated in the illness. I cannot, for my
part, subscribe to such a view.

So we are left with two possibilities. The first of these is
inferiority depression. What Pasche[5] says of this depression
certainly applies remarkably closely to our subject, and
P. Male has emphasized this fact.[6] One certainly finds in the
adolescent 'a painful self-deprecation . . . a feeling that one is
ugly, poor, physically, morally, or intellectually weak, incapable, half-finished'.[7] But Pasche himself says that it was
because of the dangers of too wide a clinical picture that he

chose a narrower point of view. By concentrating on one psychopathological peculiarity, he automatically excluded the normal phenomenon of adolescence.

The second hypothesis is that of reactional depression. The temptation to resort to this hypothesis is strengthened when one notes that the events likely to bring on such a depressive state are:[8]

1) loss of a loved one;

2) failure in an important interpersonal relationship;

3) difficulties of a professional or financial order, and, generally speaking, any event that damages the moral or social prestige of the subject;

4) failure of a collective ideal, religious, social, or political;

5) situations of unfamiliarity or loneliness.

Of these five causes, three are very common in adolescence; they are, one might say, its daily bread. The other two, the first and the fifth, though less frequent in reality, are very often experienced by the adolescent on a symbolic level. And when we remember that reactional depression (in the psychiatric sense) is particularly frequent between 16 and 30, we may well wonder whether every adolescent does not contain within himself the seeds of psychiatric depression and does not present a minor picture of reactional depression.

But reactional to what? Given the constancy of depressive reaction in the adolescent, one would have to suppose that for every adolescent there exist genuinely depressing circumstantial factors, and that if the conditions of the adolescent's life were altered one would thereby eliminate the possibility of depression. This is a very risky hypothesis and, as always when one invokes the questionable concept of reactional depression, one ignores the internal structures and movements of the subject. The adolescent becomes no more than a neutral body reacting indiscriminately to the environment. On the other hand, the view is becoming more and more widely held that reactional depression occurs in subjects whose personalities are such that they are predisposed to reactional depression. This view, however, is exposed to the contradiction between the notions of reactional disturbance and of predisposition.

Thus, in the end, it is not possible to assimilate what takes place at adolescence to any one of the syndromes of the psychopathological framework of depression. But the term 'depression' is used not only of pathological phenomena. The phrase 'depression as a fundamental state of the ego'[9] has been used by M. Klein, R. Spitz and other specialists in infancy of the 'depressive' phases of the first year of life. Without wishing to regard it as identical, one may wonder whether the so-called depressive phase of adolescence has similarities with these normal phases of infancy rather than with a psychiatric syndrome. But, if this is so, I share Nacht's misgivings[10] about using a pathological term like depression to describe normal phases of development.

B. Mourning?

In fact, isolating certain features of the adolescent and bringing them together to give them the appearance of a depressive syndrome is altogether too facile. But when confronted by the profound and complex signification of adolescent behaviour, such an approach is very tempting. Our desire 'to see the thing clearly' is frustrated; but this is one more reason to mistrust our tendency to excessive simplification - a tendency that leads all too easily to the sterotype of the depressed adolescent. It is easy enough to prove the inanity of our theoretical considerations on juvenile depression; one has only to take the elements that I have used to describe depression and see to what extent they show that one is not dealing with depression at all. I shall not go through them point by point, since this would involve us in pages of unnecessary refutation; instead, I shall concentrate on a few of these points by way of example.

Thus, there is the notion that adolescence leads above all to a 'rupture of the close, mutual bond of love that lies at the origin of any state of depression'[11] - the bond referred to being, of course, that with the mother. But the adolescent does not undergo this rupture. In his fundamental ambivalence, he fears the loss of the Oedipal object, but he desires and provokes the break with the mother, who would arrest the process of maturation if she maintained him in a state of dependence. Moreover, while there is certainly some instinctual defusion at work on the adolescent, it is by no means sure that the love impulses are relegated to a lesser position. Although the young adolescent may suppress his love for his mother, his love impulses are in no way diminished and certainly require an object to love. And he has no difficulty in finding this object. It is, of course, a substitute object, sought after in a compulsive fashion, but it alters the picture to a considerable degree. The adolescent does not have to do much to please, and thus have proof that he can be loved and love.

Another such notion is that his sense of identity is put to a severe test and is often damaged, but that it is just as often enhanced by what may seem to be hurting him. Adolescence is such that anything can be turned round in this way. What wounds also heals, what diminishes also increases, what gives pain also gives pleasure. The defences help to strengthen the ego. If, in the struggle against the impulses, prohibition wins, then the ego is enriched by a new capacity of control, it emerges stronger, more clearly defined. If the impulses win, then it is proof of the adolescent's growing strength, he feels confirmed in his new capacity as a man, equal to adults. Everything is true, and its opposite equally so. And, on the whole, there are too many differences between depression and adolescence to assimilate one to the other.

What most resembles depression, but is not depression, is mourning, and it could well be this that the adolescent is experiencing. A number of specialists in adolescence, notably Anna Freud[12] and Lampl de Groot,[13] have emphasized this work of mourning. Apart from the superficial resemblances, Freud himself showed that one of the chief differences between depression and mourning is that in mourning there is no diminution in the sense of self. 'It is really only because we know so well how to explain it that this attitude [mourning] does not seem to us pathological'.[14] Now, as we have seen, the adolescent does experience a diminution of the sense of self, and we certainly cannot explain adolescence easily. Perhaps this is why we tend to describe it as depression and to see it from a pathological point of view. But, in spite of this, the depressive aspect of the phenomenon of adolescence is more closely related to mourning. Unlike depression, they both share the notion of duration and, above all, the persistence of dynamic possibilities. With the adolescent, nothing is fixed, and we are not in the circle of endless repetition that we find in depression; on the contrary, each day is new, different from the day before. Indeed, do we not speak of the work of mourning in the same way as we speak of the work of adolescence, whereas we speak of a state of depression? The position of the adolescent towards object loss is closer to that of the bereaved than of the depressed subject.[15] Like the bereaved subject, he undertakes a work that will take him a long way from the painful situation, whereas the depressed subject is immobilized before the remnants of his lost happiness; the depressed subject cannot disinvest the lost object, he cannot undertake the work that would free his libidinal energy, which is what gives depression the appearance of a diminution of dynamism and loss of movement. On the other hand, it is this very movement and dynamism that enable the bereaved subject to mobilize his investments and recover available energy. Now, as we have seen repeatedly, adolescence is characterized above all by movement, by an increase of energy and dynamism, not by their diminution.

The essential difference between depression and adolescence is of a dynamic order. Nothing in adolescence is comprehensible if one is content simply to describe certain surface features. The fundamental reference is the exceptional dynamism of this period of life. Of course, the adolescent has to renounce his Oedipal and pre-Oedipal objects, the parental love-relationship and the lost paradise of satisfied and secure childhood. Of course, he has the feeling that he no longer has an ego, the ideal parental image has become tarnished, and he does not know where he is going. Of course, he experiences all these losses simultaneously, as so many narcissistic wounds. But for the adolescent, as for the bereaved subject, 'the verdict of reality [is] that the object no longer exists, and the ego . . . is persuaded by the sum of the narcissistic satisfactions it derives from being alive to sever its attachment to the object that has been abolished'.[15] And all his increased energy is invested in this work.

Like the bereaved subject, the adolescent remains at times sunk in the memory of his lost objects, and the idea of his own death crosses his mind. But as the dynamic of normal mourning allows the subject to undertake the necessary work, that of adolescence prevents anything becoming fixed. For apart from his losses, he discovers new objects and himself. His sexual feelings teach him that there are many pleasures awaiting him, and his ego is enriched by new functions that he discovers each day. And although, at times, he loses his self-esteem, there are others when he feels that his identity is considerably enhanced by the extraordinary adventure that he is experiencing.

C. Mourning, among others

The work of adolescence is, however, distinguished from mourning by a number of mutually contradictory aspects.

The object losses are many and simultaneous, associated with repeated narcissistic wounds, and one might say from this point of view that adolescence is a multiple bereavement. Furthermore, the adolescent's work of mourning takes place in much more difficult conditions than is usually the case in mourning. The adolescent's ego is less resilient than that of the bereaved adult. Undergoing radical reorganization as it is, and sometimes considerably weakened, it is more difficult for it to take on the work. Above all, reality testing takes place in unfavourable conditions, in so far as the image of reality acquired in childhood, when subjective reality is undergoing reorganization, figures among his losses.

If one adds the reactivation of pregenital conflicts, the revival of instinctual motions, the emergence of an archaic, persecuting super ego and a megalomaniacal ego ideal suscep-tible to wounds, the adolescent's mourning seems a very com-plicated kind of mourning. One might even conclude that it goes beyond the bounds of mourning, and that we must con-sider the possibility that at certain moments the adolescent is a potential depressive. This would bring us back to the hypothesis that adolescence is a predisposition to reactional depression.

From this point of view, it is certain that the association of this potential depression, the manipulation of the idea of suicide, and the tendency to act would constitute favourable conditions for the realization of the suicide act.

But, on the other hand, the adolescent has at his disposal far greater quantities of energy than the bereaved to carry out his work of mourning. Although he is sometimes prone to depression, these are passing moments, and, in accordance with the adolescent dynamic, a risk that exists at one moment has disappeared at the next. An adolescent may appear pessimistic at one moment and optimistic the next, lost in his dreams of greatness at one moment and displaying a realistic view of what he is and what will become of him the next.

For reasons of space I have had to isolate artificially those aspects of the work of adolescence that are of more direct concern to the subject of suicide. But these factors must be seen in their context. The work of adolescence is much richer, more complex, and more extensive than the work of mourning. As he undergoes losses, the adolescent makes gains on one front or another, or on both at once. It is perhaps from the confrontation between his objects and himself, from his ambivalence, accompanied by a disunion of the impulses and an intrication of the impulses and defences, that he derives the excess energy that drives him on to new investments and which, in the end, enables him to complete his work of adolescence.

Notes.
1. S. Nacht, 'Les états dépressifs', *Présence du Psychanalyste*, Paris, P.U.F., 1956, 97.
2. A. Freud, *op. cit.*, 267.
3. S. Freud, *Mourning and Melancholia*, stand. ed., vol. XIV, 247.
4. Nacht, *op. cit.*, 99.
5. F. Pasche, 'De la dépression', *Revue Française de Psychanalyse*, t. XXVII, 1963, no. 2-3, 191-208.
6. *Ibid.*, 209.
7. *Ibid.*, 192.

8. T. Lemperière, 'Les dépressions psychogènes réactionelles, d'épuisement, neurotiques', *Revue du Praticien,* 1 October 1963, 3022.
9. E. Zetzel, 'Contribution à la discussion, Congrès de Stockholm', *Revue Française de Psychanalyse,* t. XXX, 1966, 235.
10. Nacht, *op. cit.,* 97.
11. *Ibid.,* 99.
12. 'Adolescence', *The Psychoanalytic Study of the Child,* vol. XIII, New York, Int. Univ. Press, 1958, 262-3.
13. 'Adolescence', *The Psychoanalytic Study of the Child,* vol. XV, New York, Int. Univ. Press, 1960, 99.
14. S. Freud, *Mourning and Melancholia,* 244.
15. *Ibid.,* 255.

18·Factors and causes of adolescent suicide

In the preceding chapters I have examined a number of supposedly suicidogenic factors. The way in which they act has often remained obscure, but if we are to understand adolescent suicide we must have some knowledge of their mechanism of action. In fact, we must discover whether each of these factors may be regarded as a cause, or whether the concept of the cause of suicide must be approached from a different angle. But I have still not examined all the possible factors; before going any further, I would like to mention a few more.

A. A few additional factors

No study of this subject could claim to be complete. There is no end to the factors that could be attributed with a suicidogenic role. Anything in the collective or individual, biological or psychological life might be invoked. But this would merely confuse the issue rather than clarify it. So I shall examine only a few of the most frequently mentioned.

— *Intellectual level* is no longer seen as a suicidogenic factor. All authors (Duché, Fau, Gorceix, etc.) agree that it has no bearing on the matter, and that every level is represented. My own experience corroborates this view.

— *Seasonal variations*. This is the classic type of pseudo-precise notion that was once widely current. There is such a thing as a seasonal variation, but it is less important than is believed, of the order of 25%, and appears to be diminishing. On the other hand, we hardly know what factors intervene. Suicide is slightly more frequent in summer, but is this because of a climatic factor, a social factor (collective and public life being more developed at this time of the year), or because for adolescents it is the end of the school year and the time when examinations are held?

— *The notion of suicidal heredity* is also one of the notions more widespread than verified. It still finds support in certain quarters, but it is obvious that an act as complex as suicide cannot be explained by heredity. Observation of the facts tends to disprove this opinion: 'if one considers the facts in a statistically valid study, it does not seem, in the present state of our knowledge, that one can seriously sustain the notion of a suicidal heredity'.[1] At most, one might take into account the hereditary character of certain features such as impulsivity or difficulty in ideo-verbal elaborations, or even the depressive tendency - though this last hypothesis should be treated with caution, even in cases of manic-depressive psychosis.

— On the other hand, the possibility of *an organic factor,* particularly of a neurological nature, is worth consideration. But what investigations have been made are far from conclusive. Epileptic suicide is sufficiently rare as to be hardly mentioned in the statistics, and we are still ignorant of how the connection is made, or whether such suicides can be explained by epilepsy alone.

More interesting is the study of electroencephalographic disturbances, other than epileptic ones. According to Duché,[2] the E.E.G. is found to be normal in 75% of cases, while Fau[3] finds frequent anomalies. These are generally minor anomalies that may be correlated with the tendency to resort to action and with impulsivity. But what is the significance of this? It is difficult to distinguish between the strictly organic origin and the functional nature of these disturbances. Fau has developed this point in an interesting way, and, in any case, it would seem that these disturbances are similar to those found in the delinquents studied, in particular, by G. Verdaux.[4]

B. The suicide situation

Modern authors tend to insist on the unity of the suicidal group. This conception does raise certain difficulties, however, according to whether or not one regards the various suicidogenic factors as actual causes.

Are suicidogenic factors causes of suicide?

For a factor to be raised to the rank of a cause, it must be the necessary and sufficient condition to determine the suicide; that is to say, it must:

1) be found in all or at least in a majority of suicides;

2) cause suicide in a majority of cases in the general population in which this factor exists.

As we have seen, at least as far as adolescent suicides are concerned, no supposedly suicidogenic factor fulfils these conditions. On the one hand, none of those examined is to be found in all suicides. On the other hand, many of these factors are to be found with sufficient frequency, and sometimes in a constant fashion in the general population, while other factors are to be found more particularly in the population of adolescents with difficulties and disorders of various kinds, but none of them is specific to suicidal adolescents. The notion of a single cause of suicide based on the factors examined here cannot be endorsed as an explanation of adolescent suicide.

Faced with this obvious diversity of factors, it might be supposed that each of them is responsible for a certain number of young suicides. According to this view, each would be the single cause for a certain proportion of adolescent suicides, and the same act might have very different causes. Such a hypothesis is unacceptable; apart from the subsidiary argument that it runs counter to the notion of the unity of suicide, it is contradicted by the fact that each factor exists in the non-suicidal population and cannot therefore be regarded as a cause of suicide.

Since no single factor can be regarded as the cause of all suicides, it is very tempting to raise adolescence itself to the rank of a cause. The group of suicidal adolescents is often studied separately from other suicidal groups, which might lend credence to this notion. It is not unusual for people to speak quite overtly of a suicide being due to the crisis of adolescence. But this explanation is no more satisfactory than the others, since adolescence is the archetypal factor that exists constantly in the whole population. It cannot therefore be regarded as non-suicidogenic for the whole population and suicidogenic for a very small number of cases. However, the question of the relations between suicide and adolescent constitutes the very subject of this book and demands some consideration. The possibility that adolescence could become suicidogenic in certain circumstances is certainly a notion that is worth examination. But, to carry the argument to its absurd conclusion, if adolescence can be suicidogenic, one may well wonder, paradoxical and inadequate as it may seem:

Why do not all adolescents commit suicide?

As the resumption of the Oedipal development, adolescence is concerned above all with the resolution of the Oedipal situation, which involves renunciation of the Oedipal love object and the fear of castration. It involves object loss or narcissistic loss. It is perfectly conceivable that this loss is experienced in dramatic terms.

In my examination of the factors proper to adolescence, I drew attention several times to the emergence of ideas of death or of suicide, and of situations usually regarded as favouring suicide: object loss, narcissistic wounds, regression, disunion of the impulses, etc. And yet the overwhelming majority of adolescents do not commit suicide; this must mean that other factors come into play that have the effect of diverting the adolescent towards the pursuit of life. It seems to me that the principal anti-suicidal factor is one that I have returned to on innumerable occasions, and the one that best characterizes adolescence, namely, movement. Not only does it favour suicidogenic situations and the emergence of the suicidogenic tendency, but also, in the usual paradoxical way of adolescence, it prevents the realization of that tendency.

It is this tendency to movement that drives the adolescent to carry out, each time with as much conviction as the last, those sudden rapid revolutions in the psychological field in which all his wishes and all his constantly shifting preoccupations are involved. Combined with the extreme ambivalence of this period of life, it operates in such a way that the adolescent does not have time to realize his death wish, which turns out to be yet another 'passing whim'. And even if he does make an attempt to realize it, the realization is ill-prepared and often fails. As we have seen, the tendency to movement intervenes in the choice of less lethal methods and in the high frequency of attempts in relation to deaths.

At a deeper level, movement is the expression of the intense dynamism proper to adolescence. It derives from the considerable quantity of reserve energy that makes possible the work of adolescence and the development into adulthood. It is a manifestation of the particularly intense libidinal energy that enables the adolescent to face the resolution of the Oedipal situation. There is a direct relation between the anti-suicidal factors representing libidinal energy and the process of adolescence itself, whose aim is the establishment of the climate of genitality. Adolescence, the triumph of Eros, is also the triumph of life. The process of adolescence is not a suicidal factor. On the contrary, it is the various disturbances in that process that favour the suicide act. We must regard as suicidogenic whatever impedes the action of those factors that prevent all adolescents from committing suicide.

We may conclude from this that suicide is a modification in the normal process of adolescence. This links up with another obvious fact: suicide is not a state, but a process, which moves from life towards non-life, and of which the act of voluntary death is merely the culmination. Faced with the impossibility of explaining suicide by any one of the tradition-ally cited factors, one is forced to consider the role of their association in the 'convergent polydeterminism'[5] of suicide. A study of the causes of adolescent suicide confirms the findings of contemporary work, which tends to stress the association of suicidogenic factors. But the mere juxtaposed enumeration of the various factors is not enough in itself. The particular conjunction of the factors that come together to determine the suicide is determinant. This conjunction con-stitutes the suicide situation realized by the simultaneous existence of internal and external suicidogenic factors. But, on this basis, the crucial factor is the way in which they are associated and interact. We must embrace within a single dynamic conception what binds the different factors together,

and what binds them to the suicide act. The dynamic consequences of this conjunction constitute the suicidal process,
which is set in motion by the suicide situation. The suicidal
process is the true cause of suicide, and it is this that we must
now examine. The first question to ask ourselves, from the
standpoint of the adolescent, is:

*Can the suicide situation be realized as a result of the fact of
adolescence itself?*

One might suppose that the suicidal process develops out of
the normal process of adolescence, as a result of the chance
occurrence of so-called suicidogenic events. But as we have
seen, these events are common occurrences in the lives of all
adolescents. Their existence is not therefore a sufficient reason
to trigger off the suicidal process.

One might equally suppose that these so-called suicidogenic
events occur in circumstances that are both peculiar to and
potential in all adolescents. According to this view, the suicide
situation is realized by the coincidence of their occurrence
at certain particularly propitious phases of adolescence, phases
that correspond to the more marked emergence of the tendency
to suicide. There is, therefore, a chance conjunction of external
and internal factors that favours an arrest in the process of
adolescence, not to say a regression and a freeing of the impulses by disintrication. Such a suicide situation is theoretically
possible. I have met it in adolescents who have had temporary
ideas of suicide, without there being any real risk of realization.
But I have never observed it in genuine suicides. Whenever I
have been confronted by a realized suicide act or one that
might well have been realized, I have observed clinical elements
that indicated that we were not dealing with a hitherto normal
process of adolescence.

Who is the adolescent who finds himself in a suicide situation? Reference to clinical practice is indispensable if we are
to answer the question without falling into empty abstractions.

C. Clinical data

All the suicidal adolescents that I have examined presented clinical peculiarities that cannot be explained in terms of the suicide situation alone. Many authors share this opinion.

Apart from the clinical signs related to possible marked psychical disorders, which are, it must be remembered, a minority, a number of elements appear, if not constantly, at least with what seems to me to be a remarkable frequency. I wish to speak here not of clinical signs that are directly related to the tendency to suicide, but of psychological peculiarities of a permanent kind.

All such peculiarities are characterized both by their age and their fixity, which should tell us something of their origin. They ante-date not only the suicide situation, but also puberty. They may or may not have been noticed since childhood, but the retrospective investigation brings them easily to light, even if one's evidence is based on a secondary reconstruction by the individual concerned or by those around him.

Their fixity is particularly apparent in the case of adolescents. We know that all kinds of behaviour may be observed at adolescence, providing they are temporary. This fixity contrasts with the psychological movement natural to the adolescent.

There are a number of such psychological peculiarities, but a few of these must be examined in detail:

— *Peculiarities of mood* are extremely frequent. The usual background is not one of depression, but a sort of permanent moroseness and dissatisfaction, sometimes covered up by superficial hyperactivity or pseudo-syntonia. Reactions of resentment, disappointment and shame are more frequent than a feeling of guilt as such. Everything is related to a diffused anxiety of an archaic type, which, because of its overwhelming, undifferentiating character and its sheer force, is very different from the castration anxiety. Its brutal, all-or-nothing opposition may give the adolescent an appearance of moodiness and general moroseness.

— *Disorder in elaboration* is essentially a disorder due to inadequate conceptualization and verbalization of emotional and affective experience. Generally speaking, it is close to similar disturbances to be found in delinquency and in certain psychosomatic disorders, and constitutes a link between both types of behaviour; in fact, suicide is related to both, as an act and as self-destruction. I have often found instrumental disorders of the same type as those that I had previously observed in personalities of a delinquent type.[6]

Quite obviously, the existence of even a marked intellectualization does not exclude the existence of a disorder in elaboration. Usually, by its very defensive, maturative function, intellectualization is a phase of the development of elaboration. As we saw in Chapter 14, it is loaded with affects and acts as an emotional regulator. Here, on the other hand, intellectualization is built up in a void, the words do not carry an affective load. It is probably the disinsertion of language in relation to the libido - a consequence of the disorder in elaboration - that makes possible the construction of rationalizations about death and suicide, thus constituting one of the origins of the so-called philosophical justifications of suicide.

This disorder of elaboration, together with the tendency to act and temporary instrumental disorder, is found generally among adolescents. But in the state we are considering here, disorder in elaboration and its corollary, the tendency to resort to action, is characterized by its depth, its fixity, its long history.

— *The organization of the ego ideal* also has its peculiarities. One is dealing with an archaic, megalomaniacal ego ideal, with the usual features: demand for the absolute, absence or inadequacy of reshaping when put to the test of reality. We must also include in this picture inadequate integration of temporality - a factor on which Fau has quite rightly laid much stress.[7] These disorders are not necessarily of an overwhelming kind, and may remain unobserved in a superficial examination. But they are deeply embedded in the personality; they are on a par with intolerance to frustration; the intensity of the disappointment expresses the degree of pain felt on realizing that one cannot act omnipotently over reality in the satisfaction of one's wishes.

Sometimes, the disappointments may assume an appearance

of self-criticism of an apparently super-ego kind, but in fact they are pseudo-super-ego in origin and conceal the demands of the ego ideal. Of course, a taste for the absolute, with its demands on the self, exists in all adolescents. But, in this respect too, the suicidal adolescents are different, and for two reasons: the archaic ego ideal manifested itself before puberty and, in adolescence, it is remarkable for its fixity, its rigidity, its progressive inability to be affected by the test of reality. Each confrontation with reality becomes, not a factor for further development, but a wound and a reinforcement of archaic positions.

— *The inadequacy of the usual defence mechanisms* seems to me to be one of the most constant features in all suicidal adolescents. Faced with narcissistic wounds, damage to the ego ideal, and object losses, the adolescent usually has enough defence mechanisms at his disposal to perform his work of mourning. In the suicidal adolescent, two of these defence mechanisms are particularly inadequate.

The first of these is the mobility of investments - a corollary of movement. In all suicidal adolescents, there is an inability to disinvest the disappointing or lost object. Despite the pain that they give him, the adolescent maintains his investments, repeats his behaviour, broods on his disappointment, and shuts himself off from whatever is other, in a characteristic fixity of the kind mentioned earlier that constitutes a veritable aberration in the normal process of adolescence.

The other defence lies in the projective mechanism. Usually, when confronted by the gap that he feels between his wishes and ideal aspirations on the one hand, and the more modest possibilities of satisfactions offered by reality on the other, the adolescent reacts by making a projective defence. According to the level of his elaboration, he constructs projects and theoretical systems with the ultimate intention of bringing reality into line with his own ideal image of it, or he reacts by attempting at once to alter reality by resorts to action that may develop into delinquency. In the case of the suicidal adolescent, this mechanism is either disturbed, inadequate, or absent altogether. Either he turns his aggressivity directly back on himself, blaming himself for the gap between ideal and reality, which is reminiscent of the predominance of mechanisms of introjection. Or he tries at once to act on reality by resort to action, but, disappointed by the results thus achieved, he renounces action and turns the aggressive act back upon himself.

Even subjects that can be included in the traditional psychiatric framework are remarkable for the inadequacy or absence of the defence mechanisms characteristic of their psychopathological structure. The typical neuroses are exceptional. All authors are agreed that, generally speaking, psychotics do not present a typical picture of full development; as often as not, they are in a phase of beginning or remission, that is to say, periods when the psychotic defences are weak or unorganized. Delirium, in particular, is usually absent, and suicide tends to control it rather than accompany it. Even when delirium does exist, it seems to me to present peculiar characteristics. It takes the form of incipient delirium, either because it is only in its beginnings and is not yet deeply entrenched, or because it has not yet become organized. To take the classic example of schizophrenia, we know that the paranoid whose delirium is sufficiently developed resorts less to action and commits suicide less readily than the young hebephreno-catatonic whose delirium remains less marked. Or, in cases where overt delirium does exist - which, let me repeat, is much more unusual - it seemed to me to be imbued with self-accusatory and self-persecuting themes very close to melancholic themes, whatever psychosis was diagnosed, but without the delirious organization proper to melancholics.

Is the suicidal process specific?

This brief résumé of some of the clinical data confirms me in my belief that the suicidal process is not to be confused with the process of adolescence. On the contrary, it moves away from it, since it contains not only elements that belong to adolescence but also elements that are opposed to it. But although the clinical elements examined above are not to be found in the normal process of adolescence, they are not specific to the suicidal adolescent. In this respect, they resemble the suicidogenic factors to be found in many other cases. Most of these clinical data are to be found in many adolescents undergoing difficulties or disorders of various kinds. For example, the peculiarities of all juvenile psychopathology are marked by their fixity and their long history. Similarly, although the accentuation of the tendency to act may develop into dangerous action and disorder in elaboration, they are neither constant nor typical of the suicidal adolescent; they are to be found in other kinds of disorder, notably in delinquency.

To sum up, then, although the suicidal process seems to be the cause of the suicide act, and is certainly to be distinguished from the process of adolescence, its specificity is yet to be defined. But at this point we enter the sphere of hypothesis.

The notion that emerges with the greatest degree of probability is that of an inability to carry out the work of mourning involved in adolescence, combined with an inability to use either the usual defence mechanisms, or the pathological defence mechanisms characteristic of pathological mourning. The wound remains unhealed and unbearable in a way very different from the dynamic work involved in Oedipal renunciation.

Notes
1. D.J. Duché, 'Les tentatives de suicide chez l'enfant et l'adolescent', *Psychiatrie de l'enfant*, vol. VII, fasc, 1, Paris, P.U.F., 1964 55.
2. *Ibid.*, 7.
3. R. Fau *et al.*, 'Le suicide chez l'adolescent', *Annales Médico-psychologiques*, t. I, no. 1, January 1965, 7-8.
4. G. and J. Verdeaux, 'Électroencephalographie et délinquance. Etude comparative sur deux populations d'adolescents', *Revue de psychologie française*, t. VIII, no. 1, February 1963.
5. G. Deshaies, *Psychologie du suicide*, Paris, P.U.F., 1947, 184.
6. 'Déficits instrumentaux chez les psychopathes', *Annales Internationales de Criminologie*, 1963, 2, 438-45.
7. Fau *et al.*, *op. cit.*, 16.

Part Four
Hypotheses and conclusions

Introduction

19 The suicidal p

In the course of this book, we have touched on a wide variety
of points. And yet not only are we far from having exhausted
the question, we have not even succeeded in covering the
ground. Adolescent suicide touches on so many different
domains that it is practically impossible to deal with them all,
however summarily, within the limits of a single volume.
Every aspect of the human sciences would be involved.

But there are certain crucial points that we have not yet
examined. This is because they seemed to me to be too uncertain to be counted among the *données* of the problem.
Contemporary work has produced a number of fruitful and
probably justified ideas. But, in my opinion, they are still too
incomplete to be regarded as acquired notions.

I have stressed throughout this study that our knowledge
of adolescent suicide is small. We do not know the true
number of deaths or attempts. We do not know very much
about the causes of suicide, other than that a number of
factors come together to determine the suicidal process. But
what does this process consist of? We may safely presume
that it is to be distinguished from the normal process of adolescence, but we know very little more than that. From that
point on, we are in the domain of hypothesis. Yet it is only
when we understand what the suicidal process is that we can
understand its signification and function, its manifestation in
various kinds of behaviour, and its therapeutic treatment.

So it is around the notion of the suicidal process that the
most important questions revolve. But before going on to
examine these questions, let us try to clarify the hypotheses
that can be formulated about the suicidal process. It is this
process that gives the question its unity through all the diversity of the suicidogenic factors, the manifestations, and the
disciplines involved.

19·The suicidal process

We know little about the suicidal process other than that it gives suicide its individuality as an act committed by the subject upon himself, and unity to the association of heterogeneous factors, internal or external, individual or collective. But who is the suicidal adolescent? How does he see the environmental factors? How does the process develop within him? We shall now examine the various hypotheses that can be offered in answer to these questions.

Of course, behind these questions lies the problem of the origin of the suicidal tendency: does it lie with the death instinct or has it an acquired origin, that is to say, from primary masochism? The question of origin is certainly of fundamental concern, but it does not seem to me that a study of the suicidal process necessarily involves a prior study of origins. Provisionally, I propose to define as thanatogenic whatever 'drives a subject to suicide', without committing myself as to its origin. This intentionally vague term does not represent a theoretical position, but it is simply and solely a matter of linguistic convenience.

Similarly, we have seen that the thanatogenic tendency in the adolescent is opposed by the defences constituted by the work of adolescence itself, representing the libidinal energies. Again as a matter of linguistic convenience, I shall speak of a life tendency, without committing myself to the existence of a life instinct, or to the origin of the libido, and without giving the term tendency any other signification that that of 'something that drives towards . . .'

A. The potential suicide

We have already seen that the adolescent possesses peculiarities that make him more liable than others to suicide. It is obviously at this level that the effect of old suicidogenic factors is to be found.

The question arises as to when and how these old suicidogenic factors intervene, what is specific to them, and is there a pre-suicidal state or process?

These old, fixed peculiarities go back to childhood, in the course of which the various internal and environmental factors come together in the gradual building up of the ego. A proper study of them would involve the whole question of infantile development. Such a project is obviously impossible here, so I shall take three, apparently very different examples of the many suicidogenic factors.

— *Disorder in elaboration, and the corresponding tendency to resort to action* are characterized, in the first instance, by an inadequate phantasization and verbal communication of the emotions. The importance of the early mother/child relationship no longer requires demonstration. But I also spoke, in Chapter 13, of the possible role of verbal and psycho-motor instrumental deficit. The origin of this deficit is usually explained either as a disorder of the instrumental equipment, often of a constitutional kind, or as a disorder in affective development. Neither of these aetiologies can be denied, but such a dichotomy does not correspond to the complexity of the facts. This problem, which goes well beyond that of suicide, and which I cannot expand on here, has given rise to some important developments:[1] these show to what extent it is centred on the permanent confrontation of maturation and experience and conceived in terms of integration and organization. Similarly, we must note the early role, through the mother/child relationship, of the appearance of the father as a 'frustrating third party'[2] in the determination of the child's tolerance to frustration, which constitutes one of the factors in the resort to action.

Moreover, these functions intervene in turn in the process as a whole, as in the case, for example, of identification.

But can one go further and consider the role of the neuro-biological organization in the suicide act? Little work has been done on this subject. Courchet also considers motility from the point of view of organization, at the level of the earliest phases of the orality of 'the two primary stages, excitation and inhibition' thanks to 'the scansion . . . that avoids chaos, the return to primary reactions (raptus or inhibition) . . . the gesture of death'.[3]

It is also worth noting that Ajuriaguerra and his colleagues[4] attach great importance to relations between neurobiology and hypotheses concerning the death instinct and primary masochism, the organizing role of the libido, their relations with the early origin of anxiety, and the infant's catastrophic reactions.

To sum up, the problem of the origin of the resort to action, rather than a study of isolated factors, leads us to a consideration of the combined roles of constitutional *données* and neurological maturation, object relation and socio-cultural conditions, the processes of integration and organization, of their precocity and, possibly, of the extreme precocity of the motor organizations involved in the suicide act.

— *The frequency of the early absence of the father,* in itself an objective, statistical, and sociological piece of information, is also the reflexion of a complex process. Though not all fatherless children commit suicide much contemporary work stresses the frequency of broken homes, parental incompatibility, and a bad paternal image.

Sutter[5] insists, quite rightly, on this and introduces the concept of the 'inadequate authority syndrome'. But, in my opinion, this is the visible, partial effect of the subtle interplay of the identification process and the integration of childhood conflicts. It confirms the fact that a child usually feels the 'absence' of paternal authority early on, and poses the problem of the origin of the paternal image. Again, this vast, complex question goes well beyond that of suicide, and I can do no more than comment on it briefly.

The father/child relationship is imbued with the quality of

the mother/child relationship from the beginning of impulse organization, for at first the father is maternalized. He becomes differentiated and the father/child relationship is established, becoming progressively more complicated from the eighth month. Together with the frustrating father who deprives the child of the good mother there appears the father who protects him and frees him from the devouring, all-powerful bad mother. In either case, he is a third party, coming from outside and introducing himself into the binary mother/ child relationship. As the representative both of frustrating reality and gratifying reality, he is the basis of subjective reality. Just as one refers to the Imagos of the Good Mother and the Bad Mother, one can speak of a dual reference to the Imagos of the Good Father and Bad Father.[6] They play a crucial role in the mother/child defusion, and in the development of the ego and the ego ideal.

The integration and organization of the parental Imagos into a veritable quartet plays a determining role in the development of impulse organization. The quality of the double paternal image, its specificity and its differentiation from the maternal image marks the whole of subsequent development up to the Oedipus complex,[7] the transformation of the fear of fragmentation into the fear of castration and the setting up of defences against the risk of disorganization and a return to chaos.

The frequency of the early absence of the father leads us to the complexity of the first organizations of the ego and the multiplicity of factors involved: the personalities of the father and mother, the quality of their relationship, and the socio-cultural and economic factors that affect the father/mother/ child relationship. The break-up of the family and parental incompatibility may be regarded from the same point of view. But we must go beyond this, for conjugal compatibility may be maintained at the cost of a profound alteration in the paternal and maternal Imagos. The ways in which this understanding is reached are as important as the degree of understanding.

— *The absence of the adolescent's integration in a group,* that is to say, his social isolation, is an apparently very real factor, but one, nonetheless, that has a similarly complex origin. It always begins very early, dating from childhood, and it takes a great many different forms. The adolescent may feel weak, unable to accept competition. Or he may consider that groups and other people generally are uninteresting, that he has nothing to gain from them, or even that he may be hurt by them. Or, again, he feels that he has no right or desire to abandon his parents, fears that they will miss him, or only feels happy when he is with them.

All that was said above can be applied very easily to the origin of such feelings. The role of the persistence of the archaic mother/child relationship, the irruption of the father who is the first outsider in the mother/child relationship, the role of the father as representative of reality and social life, the impossibility of transcending the triangular situation by 'looking elsewhere', are all factors that explain the impossibility of socialization.

But social isolation, in turn, has consequences on the process of adolescence. The regression of the individual through his integration into the group, and the libidinal link that binds the individuals together and to the chief,[8] appear to play a positive role in adolescence, in particular:

— Through regression, the adolescent band or gang encourages the liberation of the thanatogenic tendency, but also its expression in collective hetero-aggressive behaviour, thus permitting the economy of auto-aggressive behaviour.

— The band strengthens the libidinal forces, that is, the defences against the thanatogenic tendency. Furthermore, it makes licit the libidinal link, especially the unconscious homosexual link, by avoiding guilt.

— The collective union of energies increases the feeling of protection against the feeling of external dangers coming from the adult world that is so strong in adolescence.

— The band facilitates the manipulation of the idea of death, whereas, individually, this might be prevented by prohibitions. By lowering the moral level, the band assists this manipulation, thus participating in the mastery of the thanatogenic tendency and avoiding its irruption by more archaic means.

Thus, social isolation, which is early in origin, is a sign of a disturbance in early development, and prevents the creation of effective defences against the thanatogenic tendency. Here, too, we find an intrication of factors, especially the early origin of the disturbances that it involves, and the secondary effect that aggravates the original disorder.

Is there a specific pre-suicidal process?

On the basis of the few examples examined above, it is obvious that any clinical sign or suicidogenic factor calls into question the development of the ego and all the factors involved in it: neurobiological maturation, the father/mother/child relationship, socio-economic and cultural factors. But this is so for all the processes, and is not specific to suicide.

Another obvious fact is the precocity of the process involved, situated as it probably is around the turning-point of Spitz's second organizer of the eighth month. The previous period sees the establishment of early impulse organization, the development of displeasure from 'undifferentiated, overall reaction'[9] to the appearance of anxiety, mechanisms of introjection and incorporation, and the formation of the maternal Imagos and mechanisms of projection.

After the eighth month, the paternal Imagos are integrated and anxiety becomes organized, especially in relation to object losses and the defences against anxiety - projection, identification, phantasization - which avoid the fear of fragmentation and disorganizing catastrophic reactions.[10]

The wrong integration of the thanatogenic tendency into the impulse organization gives it an autonomy that facilitates direct expression. From this point of view, one might posit the hypothesis of disturbances in the first organizations of the ego affecting subsequent organizations, and facilitating the simultaneous emergence of the thanatogenic tendency and the motor discharge of the resort to action. The quality and intensity of the libidinal and aggressive investments in a parents/child reciprocity are of crucial importance. The aggressive investment by the parents and the projection of their own thanatogenic tendency is set off, for example, against the libidinal investment. It is at this level that the frequency of pathological mourning, on the part of the parents, intervenes at the birth of the child. It is as if in the first months of life the first impulse organization was carried out to the detriment of the libidinal impulses, which, in favourable cases, constitute the first anti-thanatogenic defence.

Later, two modalities of the process may be considered. In the first, the libidinal investment is mainly narcissistic. But the alteration of the paternal Imagos and the persistence of the thanatogenic tendency make it not only badly defended by the projective activity, but inaccessible to the test of reality. It is a narcissism that is both massive and fragile.

In the second modality, the inadequacy of the libidinal investment prevents the satisfactory continuation of the organization of the ego and of the anti-thanatogenic defences, which culminates in a fragility of the organization that may eventually lead to a tendency to disorganization.

In both modalities, there is inadequacy or fragility in the organization of the ego. The only difference is that in the first there is an apparently strengthened narcissistic barrier, which is in fact liable to break down in a catastrophic reaction as a result of a narcissistic wound.

If a specific pre-suicidal process does exist in the potential suicide, it probably lies in the combination of a thanatogenic tendency that has been badly integrated and has remained more or less autonomous, and a fragile organization.

B. Present factors

Whether or not there is a pre-suicidal process, suicide is exceptional up to and including the beginning of adolescence. One can only conclude, therefore, that new facts intervene, either adolescence itself or events that accompany its progress. But since these facts, whether internal or external, are everyday occurrences in the life of every adolescent, it must be the way in which they are invested, and sometimes previously provoked by the pre-suicidal adolescent, that make them suicidogenic, and not their intrinsic quality. To understand how they operate, we must first disobjectify the question and refer to the fact that they are experienced by a subject with a peculiar organization that makes him a potential suicide. External facts are subjectified and collective facts individualized. I shall now deal wth a few of these facts.

— *The process of adolescence* is, on the one hand, the resolution of the Oedipal situation, and therefore loss of the love object and fear of castration, and, on the other, a reactivation of archaic motions, reorganization, and therefore temporary disorganization. The parental attitude facilitates to a greater or lesser degree the capacity to bear the Oedipal bereavement. But by reactivating pregenital motions, adolescence revives any pre-suicidal peculiarities that may be an obstacle to it. If fixated in an insufficiently integrated form, the thanatogenic tendency may be freed just as the defences are undergoing reorganization and are temporarily weakened. The disorganization peculiar to adolescence may therefore have a role to play if there already exists a tendency belonging to the pre-suicidal process. Moreover, if the fixation points that I have supposed to exist act as an obstacle to movement, the pre-suicidal process prevents the principal anti-suicidal defence that the adolescent has at his disposal from operating. The combination of pre-suicidal and adolescent processes may therefore have a negative character that is particularly liable to favour the suicidal process.

— *The death of the father during adolescence* is often to be found. The function of the father is important in adolescence in making possible the resolution of the Oedipal situation, the integration of autonomy, and the reorganization of subjective reality. Here, too, the two images of the good father and the bad father are indispensable, and the disorganization of the quartet of parental imagos at a time when the archaic impulses are being reactivated may have an influence on the development of an already excessive thanatogenic tendency. The death of the father incurs a risk of precipitating a latent process. But not all adolescents who lose their fathers commit suicide.

A careful analysis always reveals a peculiar quality in the father/child relationship. Often the paternal image is strongly maternalized, ill-defined and often too exclusively good. Sometimes, the father is loved and admired, but remains distant and inaccessible. Nevertheless, the child had hoped to bring about the necessary understanding with him, and his disappearance finally destroys that hope.

From behind this father/child relationship, there always emerge peculiarities in the mother/child relationship and in the relations between the parents. This may also be compared with the existence of an inadequate, effaced, and passive father, or the father who is 'too busy to bother', of whom many adolescents say: 'If only he'd pay more attention to my mother, she'd leave me alone and I'd be free to do as I like.' But the mother must also be willing to receive such attention.

Of the same order is the loss of someone close to the adolescent. The loss of a friend, 'the other self', is felt as a deep narcissistic loss, as a partial death, and can only be borne if there is enough movement, and if the thanatogenic tendency is not too strongly fixated. The death of an adult is felt as a parental loss to the extent that this adult is invested as a parental substitute or auxiliary, as compensation for an alteration in the parent/child relationship.

— *Educational failure,* one of the classic circumstantial factors put forward, is another example of the conjunction of factors. In young people who commit suicide after 'doing badly in an exam', the failure and the suicide are effects of the same peculiar process of investment. Yet the context is apparently very variable. Sometimes we are dealing with an excellent pupil who has what looks like a temporary lapse, but which in fact often marks the beginning of a process of pathological decompensation; and sometimes with a pupil whose failure is merely the culmination of a long series of failures. But in each case the failure is felt as a deep narcissistic wound and all educational activity is over-invested in an archaic mode, quite unrelated to reality. Almost invariably, this mode of investment is also that of the parents who, at one and the same time, project their own megalomaniacal ideal on to educational success, and use education as an instrument of repression. The whole situation has so imbued educational activity in the past that failure is inevitable.

The context of the general educational organization also has a part to play. This organization is still all too often a model of repressive and regressive pressure whose disorganizing and inhibitive effect on the structuring dynamism of adolescence is obvious enough. Although the egos of most adolescents can withstand these situations without damage and are able to find the necessary defence mechanisms, it is obvious that the ego of the pre-suicidal adolescent can undergo these disorganizing attacks only as reinforcements to tendencies that are already inside him.

Thus educational failure certainly constitutes the negatively privileged meeting-point of an event, of a particular mode of investment, and of repressive action on the part of both parents and society, that leaves no place for hetero-aggressivity.

We might re-examine all the suicidogenic factors that occur in adolescence. The suicidogenic value of an event depends basically on the way in which it is invested by the adolescent, his parents and the collectivity. The role of the suicidogenic event is to be understood by the way in which it is perceived subjectively by the pre-suicidal adolescent, and it is their conjunction, facilitated by the factors proper to adolescence, that constitutes the suicide situation.

C. Characteristics of the suicidal process

What I have said of pre-suicide as a tendency to disorganization will allow me to be brief on the subject of the suicidal process itself. But the question of the pathological character of suicide cannot be avoided.

The suicidal process as a process of disorganization

One can imagine all the possibilities, from the potential suicide ready to engage in the suicidal process in an almost spontaneous way to the potential suicide whose evolution towards the suicide act is subjected to the occurrence of a relatively important event, at least from the point of view of the archaic investment that it arouses or of the thanatogenic tendency that it reactivates. Similarly, one can refer to the modalities examined above according to the predominance of instability and inadequacy in the organization of the ego or to the predom-

inance of archaic narcissistic defences of a particularly
sensitive kind.

But, in any case, it is on the basis of the suicide situation
that the suicide process develops - a process of catastrophic
disorganization culminating in the disorganization of the
impulses, the freeing of the thanatogenic tendency, and motor
discharge. The purest suicidal process appears to be the
suicidal *raptus,* which Courchet[11] regards as the archetypal
suicide act. One might examine the hypothesis by which all
other suicide acts are attenuated forms of the suicidal *raptus*
brought about by the braking action of defensive formations
that are adequate to slow down the process but inadequate
to prevent suicide.

This approach would seem to confirm the differences
between the suicidal process and the process of adolescence,
which is reorganizing and structuring. The sudden increase in
the number of suicides at adolescence would seem to be due
not directly to the process of adolescence, but to disturbances
that impede the production of anti-thanatogenic defences.

The suicide act is therefore related to disturbances. Can
we deduce from them elements concerning the possibly pathological nature of suicide?

— *The suicide of mentally ill adolescents* cannot be explained
by the illness alone since the majority of the mentally ill do
not commit suicide. Is it triggered off by an event that may
provoke suicide if it happened to every patient, or by the pre-
existence in some of more specifically pre-suicidal elements?
Although one cannot be sure of the answer to this, a number
of facts may be noted.

Most suicides occur in an initial period or a period of
improvement in patients with few symptoms, that is to say, in
a period of reorganization; for example, during a transition
from pre-psychosis to psychosis, when there is a lack of symptoms expressing the formation of new defence mechanisms.

The majority of mentally ill suicidal adolescents is made up
of psychotics and psychopaths. The first have pregenital
structures and the second dysharmonic structures with a basic
instability or inadequacy of organization and the presence of
prevalent pregenital poles.

As for subjects regarded as neurotic, these are often subjects with 'neurotic features', rather than neurotic structures in the strict sense. They are perhaps regarded as such because the few detectable symptoms conceal an absence of organization or a more archaic organization. Similarly, not all hysterics have recourse to suicide, which occurs most often in those situated on the psychotic, rather than the neurotic side of hysteria.

Finally, it would appear that the suicidal mentally ill have a greater difficulty in elaboration than others: a difficulty in expressing themselves in words, in phantasy, and in delirium, which is similar to a difficulty in building up defences.

Broadly speaking, one finds archaic prevalent poles and inadequate defences - which corresponds to our earlier observations on the suicidal process. But this does not allow us to say why they commit suicide; a more detailed study of these cases would reveal either the role of circumstantial factors, or that of certain stages that are possibly more suicidogenic than others, as for example the rapidity of the disorganization involved in the so-called 'invasion' phase, which leaves no time for the psychotic defences to be built up.

Is the suicide act pathological in itself?

Although the justifications, apologias even, of normal suicide are hardly convincing, the opposite view is no more easy to accept, for it reintroduces the insoluble question of the boundary between the normal and the pathological. And yet, an act that expresses a particularly precocious disorder in the organization of the impulses, an inadequacy in the organization of the ego and of the defence mechanisms, must surely belong to the category of acute disorganizations just as much as any impulsive, dangerous resort to action, acute confusional delirium, or manic-depressive attack. It even represents the extreme degree of disorganization and, in that sense, constitutes a profoundly psychotic act.

But suicide cannot be regarded as a psychosis, since it is the inability to build up defensive barriers that makes it

possible. From this point of view, it may be regarded as a
failed psychosis. It might be compared with what is sometimes called delirium expressed in action, which represents an
inability to constitute a delirious defence. By using the hypothesis of an archaic fixation of the thanatogenic tendency
that remains autonomous, as in perversions, one may also
compare it with perverse behaviour.

Is suicide always an illness?

Even supposing that the suicide act is always pathological,
what are we to think of the 70 to 85% of suicidal adolescents
who do not come under the usual clinical classifications?
Several hypotheses may be posited:

I remarked earlier that I have never met any suicidal adolescents who present only the signs of the usual crisis of
adolescence. But some might have a sub-pathological structure
temporarily aggravated by adolescence, whereas it would have
had no serious effects either earlier or later. Though theoretically possible, this hypothesis has yet to be confirmed.

According to another hypothesis, one is dealing with
atypical forms or the beginnings of characterized pathological
states. Many authors have asked themselves whether suicide
is an illness, especially with regard to manic-depressive psychosis. Personally, I have met with relative frequency suicidal
adolescents who, while not presenting melancholic attacks as
such, present, even outside the suicide period, a structure
that is strongly reminiscent of those of manic-depressives in
the intercritical stage.

For other authors, the inadequacy of organization and the
dysharmonic persistence of archaic motions is reminiscent of
psychopathic disequilibrium. But this concept is so heterogeneous that recourse to it often seems more a matter of
convenience than anything else.

Lastly, there is the hypothesis that sees suicide as the result
of an inability on the part of the adolescent to carry out the
work of mourning: he feels an irreparable loss, the loss of an
object without which he cannot live, whether a real loss or a

delirious one. In fact, the loss is always narcissistic and is accompanied by a sensitivity to the narcissistic wound which is felt as a disorganizing, fragmenting action. These notions are similar to those of Grunberger on narcissism[12] and Pasche on inferiority depression.[13]

Object loss felt as a narcissistic lack that cannot be healed by the work of mourning is characteristic of depression. Indeed, depression might be regarded as the element common to the various structures, and the one that lends unity to the group of suicidal adolescents. But it is far from being the case that suicidal adolescents always present the usual clinical signs of overt depression, while, on the contrary, all adolescents may, at one time or another, present a temporary depressive movement. So we must distinguish between the depressive nucleus and clinical depression. The overt symptoms already indicate an attempt at defensive organization.[14] Some symptoms show that the subject hopes and knows that things could be otherwise. From this point of view, one might posit the hypothesis that suicide is a clinically failed depression.

Generally speaking, the suicidal adolescent seems to be unable to carry out the mourning involved in the process of adolescence, or to set up the defences characteristic of the various psychopathological structures, and it is certainly this inability to organize - a fundamental disturbance of the process of adolescence - that is pathological.

Notes
1. Cf. in particular J. de Ajuriaguerra, R. Diatkine and J. Garcia-Badaracco, 'Psychanalyse et Neurobiologie', in S. Nacht, *Le Psychanalyse d'aujourd'hui*, Paris, P.U.F., 1956, 437-98.
2. *Ibid.*, 481.
3. 'Le suicide', *L'Évolution Psychiatrique*, 1955, fasc. III, 474-6.
4. *Op. cit.*, 445-6 and 483-4.
5. J.M. Sutter and H. Luccioni, 'Le syndrome de carence d'autorite', *Revue de Neuro-psychiatrie infantile*, 7th year, no. 3-4, March-April 1959, 125.
6. Cf. Mendel, *La révolte contre le Pére*, Paris, Payot, 1968.
7. S. Lebovici, 'La relation objectale chez l'enfant', *Psychiatrie de l'enfant*, vol. III, fasc. 1, 1961, 166.
8. S. Freud, *Our Attitude Towards Death*, stand. ed., vol. XIV.

9.   Ajuriaguerra *et al., op. cit.*, 476.
10. Cf. Lebovici, *op. cit.*
11. Courchet, *op. cit.*, 469.
12. Cf. 'Préliminaires à une étude topique du narcissisme,' *Revue Française de Psychanalyse,* 1958, vol. III.
13. 'De la dépression', *Revue française de Psychanalyse,* vol. XXVII. no. 23, 1963.
14. Nacht, 'Les états dépressifs', *Présence du Psychanalyste,* Paris, P.U.F., 1956, 117-21.

20 · Functions, varieties, and boundaries of the suicide act

The functions, varieties, and boundaries of suicide are closely related, and are often used to interpret one another. They are not specific to adolescent suicide, but they are of particular relevance to it on account of the complexity of its factors, its boundaries in relation to other adolescent behaviour, and the high proportion of attempts and the controversial question of their ratio to suicide deaths.

Recent work in the field has introduced new data and opened up new possibilities. But however well founded these data may be, it seems to me that they should still be regarded as hypotheses, not as to their existence, which seems to be beyond dispute, but as to their signification and mechanism. Only when we know more about the suicidal process will we be in a position to accept them completely.

Behind all these data and hypotheses lies the question of the unity of the suicide act. In my view - and it is one that I have expressed on a number of occasions - in the present state of our knowledge the suicidal group should be regarded as unitary. The central axis of suicide is the suicidal process, on the basis of which certain modalities due to variations in the factors involved may vary and give to the act a slightly different form and function

A. Functions of suicide

The notion of the function of suicide has been enriched in a particularly interesting way by the work of Stengel,[1] which has been taken up in France by teams of specialists in Lyon,[2] Toulouse,[3] and Grenoble.[4] This work is particularly concerned with attempted suicide, but I believe that the study of functions may, indeed must, be applied to the suicide act as a whole.

However, if we are to avoid certain ambiguities and a distortion of the very concept of function, we must first make a few points clear. Thus, it seems to me to be wrong to see these functions in terms of the 'intention' expressed by the suicidal subject before or after the act.

We must distinguish between what occurs at the moment of the act, that is to say, at the moment of extreme disorganization, when everything happens in terms not of intention but of impulses, and what the subject thinks before or after the act, that is to say, when the disorganization is not adequate.

Furthermore, the declarations made by the suicidal subject are often rationalizations that have only a greater or lesser relation to the functions of the suicide. These functions can only be understood at an unconscious, psychical level of which the subject is usually unaware. However, certain suicidal subjects seem to have a remarkable awareness of the signification and motivations of their act; it sometimes happens that deeply buried data rise to the level of consciousness as a result of certain upheavals, especially after the occurrence of the suicide act itself. But are they expressed in the same way after the post-suicide reorganization as at the moment of suicidal disorganization? In any case, such declarations must be treated with the utmost caution. Confronted with a subject who seems to elaborate and verbalize his conflicts and motivations especially well, one may be surprised at first sight that he has any need at all to have recourse to the suicide act. But if one listens attentively one can often discover, behind statements that are comprehensible because they are rationalized and also because we interpret them in the light of our own views on suicide, a much more archaic signification, lacking in a hypothetical symbolism.

Another important point is that 'the suicide practically always makes his gesture in relation to others'.[5] Obviously, this is basically true. But who is this other? If we are to answer this question, we must leave behind any objective conception of the Other. In my opinion, an alteration of reality always occurs in the suicidal subject, even if at first it is hardly perceptible, as in the case of manic-depressives in an intercritical period. The suicide always projects particularly archaic *données* on to the real Other. Although the suicidal adolescent directs his reproaches at his parents as they are in the present, and even though these reproaches may seem to be justified, his act is also partly directed at the parents of his early childhood.

A third point, generally accepted as obvious, is that suicide is a matter of functions and not of types. The various functions co-exist, and certain of these may be dominant in the same suicide. Their intrication reflects the intrication of the suicido-genic factors that determine the suicidal process and affect its development. The unity of the suicidal process and of its functions is constituted by the fundamental notion that suicide is primarily, above all, and always self-murder, that is to say, an act intended to realize the thanatogenic tendency. The modalities of the suicidal process and the functions of suicide are in direct ratio to the hazards of the union and disunion of the thanatogenic tendency and the life tendency. If one fails to understand the central position of the thanato-genic tendency, one forecloses the question.

It is around the thanatogenic tendency that the functions, as an expression of that tendency or as a defence against it, are ordered. To see no more than a desire to live or a desire to die is to see only one of the terms of the suicidal process, and therefore to deny that process. It is to this bi-polarity, or rather to this characteristic duality of the suicidal process, that Stengel refers. 'It seems to be . . . a "twin-faced Janus" with one face directed towards destruction and death, and the other towards human contact and life'.[6] It is a conception that is very close to Freud's duality of the instincts, and, following the Lyon team, we can group the functions of suicide according to whether they represent the face turned towards life or the face turned towards destruction.

The functions representing the thanatogenic tendency

I shall not dwell at length on these, since they are the most obvious ones, and since the function of destruction constitutes the suicide act. Of course, there is still the question of the primary or secondary character of auto- or hetero-aggressivity. But once this question has been asked, one is bound to emphasize, as do all the authors, the presence of the auto-aggressive and hetero-aggressive functions in all human conduct. Furthermore, the hetero-aggressive function poses the problem of the Other that I mentioned earlier. One should treat with caution the notion that some of the suicide's aggressivity is intended for the real Other. This aggressivity seems to appear only when this Other is clothed in archaic projections, and assumes the value of an introjected object. He is then integrated into the ego and challenges the role of heredity-aggressivity.

The catastrophic function is, in my view, a constant and fundamental one. It is bound up with the more or less sudden disorganization characteristic of the suicidal process, and is an inevitable accompaniment of it. But the very notion of catastrophic function seems unsuitable; it is the representation of the suicidal process itself that constitutes a catastrophic disorganization.

The functions representing the life tendency

The ordeal aspect is one of the more frequently emphasized functions in adolescent suicide. This 'bet',[7] this 'ancient ordeal . . . the outcome of which is regarded as a divine judgment',[8] is a way of questioning fate, and, if need be, of forcing its hand, that often colours the motivations of the suicidal adolescent. But it is not specific to the suicide act; it determines or affects all adolescent behaviour, and is even one of its fundamental characteristics. It may be compared with initiation rites, ancient or modern. The need to put oneself to the test, to run risks, is part of the adolescent process. It enables the adolescent to see more clearly what he is and what he is becoming - and this need is expressed in a variety of situations, including school examinations, sports activities, and behaviour involving an element of danger.

But it is sometimes very difficult to draw the line between such behaviour and suicide. The testing of the adolescent by some kind of ordeal or trial represents the emergence of over-activated magic rites. But the ordeal of the suicidal adolescent is characterized perhaps by the strongest and most unreal megalomaniacal colouring. It expresses the desire to maintain or re-establish omnipotence over the world. In its most extreme form, it is present in a type that I have met on several occasions: the desire for suicide appears at a time when the adolescent becomes convinced, beyond all possible doubt, that he is not immortal. The only possible reparation is to revenge oneself upon fate by imposing upon it the decision as to the place, the date, and the method, that is to say, to kill oneself voluntarily. And often, there is also involved a secret desire to survive the act, which allows the subject to retrieve some hope of omnipotent immortality 'since death did not want me'. This was the case with one suicidal adolescent with whom I dealt: having survived, in an incredible way, two very serious attempts, he had acquired a feeling of immortality, that nothing could kill him. The fact that this feeling may protect him from further attempts does not make his prognosis any more favourable.

I agree with C. Vauterin that the function of the appeal, the cry for help, is undoubtedly the best representative of the life tendency. But the true appeal presupposes an adequate integration of reality for it to be addressed to a real Other. It is frequent before and after suicide, and this is borne out by the frequency of telephone calls.[9] But does it exist at the moment of suicide itself? If it does, it would seem to be an appeal to an unreal, introjected Other, and ultimately, therefore, a vain, empty one. That is why I believe that this function of the appeal is less common than it seems if one takes the moment of the act itself. It may even be the case that the act results from the failure of earlier true appeals and represents the abandonment of appeals.

— *The functions of flight and blackmail* seem to me to be rather obscure and dubious. Flight is the need to end a state that is so painful as to be unbearable. But do not all living beings try to end the tension and displeasure that spring from unsatisfied needs? In which case, all satisfaction, all search for pleasure must be regarded as a flight; and it is, indeed, a flight from painful feelings. Is suicide more of a flight than any other form of human behaviour? What is specific to it is perhaps the nature of the need and the quality of the pain. This need, as I have said, is a need to discover or rediscover an object (or a function made possible by the existence of the object) without which life is not possible. It is also the peculiarly archaic character of pain subjected to the law of all or nothing. Is suicide a means of retrieving this object, or of suppressing the seat of need and pain, that is to say, the ego?

The function of blackmail is often put forward in the case of adolescents, but my own experience leads me to distrust this notion. First, one has to set aside all the cases in which blackmail is cited by those around the adolescent, or by the adolescent himself after the event, with a view to minimizing the situation and reassuring oneself by turning tragedy into comedy. It is true that some suicidal adolescents do seek to put pressure on other people. But the concept of blackmail, which always has pejorative implications however much one may try to avoid them, is an obstacle to the understanding of such adolescents. A better knowledge of the suicidal process of adolescence should enable us to re-examine them from a fresh point of view. For who is this Other, what is this demand, and why have recourse so easily to the act of self-destruction? It might well mean that the demand is overwhelming, even vital, and that very archaic forms of behaviour relationship persist; in which case, suicide-blackmail would be one of the most pathological forms of behaviour.

The apparent harmlessness of the method used, the proximity of another person, and the conscious hope that one will survive are not enough to dismiss the question. But they might represent a life tendency sufficiently strong to win the struggle at the moment of the act itself. In any case, as far as the use of the term blackmail is concerned, I place myself unhesitatingly among those authors who condemn it, for it always implies a reproach, whether conscious or unconscious.

Is suicide a language?

It is often said, but seldom written, that suicide is a language. The hypothesis of such a function would affect the signification of the other functions, but it seems to me to reveal a major misunderstanding. For on the contrary, suicide is a non-language, an act made possible by a disturbance in the function of elaboration. It expresses an inability to communicate, and an archaic position at the level of pre-language in object relationship. To suppose that suicide is a language is to place it at the wrong level: it is an act, not a symbolic gesture. And so, if we are to speak of the functions of suicide, we can hardly consider them as a means of communication. But one can say that they are the result of a failure in communication that leads the subject to exteriorize his emotional experience and the life and death tendencies at an archaic, pre-language level.

Are the functions of suicide specific to suicide?

Apart from the function of blackmail, which seems to have been rejected, and the functions of catastrophe and flight, which seem to be no more than the visible signs of the suicidal process, the other functions do not seem to be specific to suicide, at least in the adolescent. The functions of destruction, like the functions of ordeal and appeal, operate in all human conduct. Perhaps they are specific to suicide in their modalities or in the dominance of certain of these functions, especially the functions of destruction, which remain covert in other human behaviour. It may also be that the dominance of each function varies in time according to the different phases of the suicidal process, and the degrees of the union and disunion of the impulses.

The problem of the functions has been particularly discussed in relation to adolescent suicide. This is understandable, in so far as these functions represent the life tendency and the thanatogenic tendency. It is in adolescence that one can observe most clearly the various ways in which these tendencies combine, from the virtually pure death act to behaviour that is almost entirely life orientated, in which the thanatogenic tendency plays no more than a subsidiary, temporary role. The apparently most contradictory functions may therefore be attributed, quite correctly, to the adolescent suicide act.

B. Types of suicide and the boundaries of suicide

I shall not describe the many different clinical types of
suicidal adolescent: this has already been done in great detail
in various recent works. It would certainly be interesting to
attempt a comparative study between the symptomatic
varieties and the role of the various suicidogenic factors,
especially those peculiar to adolescence, but our knowledge
is still too limited for such an undertaking. On the other hand,
the notion of the suicidal process leads us to re-examine the
question of the unity of the group of suicidal adolescents in
relation to the gravity of the act.

The suicide attempt and suicide death ratios

The question is of particular interest in relation to adolescents,
since the total number of suicide acts is as high among the
young as among adults, death being proportionately lower
among adolescents.

Having considered the various hypotheses put forward, can
we still support the notion of the unity of the suicide act,
deaths and attempts, that we advanced at the outset? It seems
to me, at least as far as adolescents are concerned, to be neither
possible nor desirable to make a separation. There is a danger
that behind this separation there will emerge the traditional
distinction between good suicides, whether fatal or very nearly
so, and bad suicides, which prove to be harmless or even
simulated.[10] There is all too strong a tendency to reject
suicidal adolescents, accusing them of pretence and denying
their desire to die, and this serves as an obstacle to further
research.

Furthermore, many attempts that are really 'accidental'
survivals would be difficult to classify: there are suicides that
have been saved thanks to modern techniques, and attempts
that have proved harmless as a result of a mistake in the choice
of method. We know that a number of suicidal adolescents
have survived purely by chance.

But can we say that the other attempts are not really
suicide at all? It seems to me that some of the arguments put

forward by those who advocate a distinction are quite inadequate. For example, if one can say that a subject has carried out his act at one time rather than another because he did not really want to die, one can equally well say that he is not dead because he carried out his act at one time rather than another, for reasons that may have nothing to do with his 'intention' of dying, such as material circumstances or ease of execution, or the time at which the event that 'triggered off' the suicide act occurred - an event that may temporarily reinforce the desire to live, or combine with others to influence the subject in the direction of suicide.

Nevertheless, quite apart from any chance factor, not all suicide acts are equally serious. But the distinction into two categories is lacking in flexibility. It would be better to think in terms of different degrees, taking as one's basis both the unity of the suicidal process and the duality of its elements. Since the suicidal process is a process of disorganization moving in the direction of the simultaneous freeing of the tendency to resort to action and the thanatogenic tendency, suicide occurs when there is a direct act of self-destruction. The suicide attempt belongs to the group of suicide acts situated between the two extremes, that is to say:

Between the manipulation of the idea of death and the suicide death

In most adolescents, the thanatogenic tendency is integrated in the course of development in such a way that it remains constantly in an inferior position within the organization of the ego. As a result of the process of adolescence, it is only slightly freed, and it is mastered without much difficulty thanks to defence mechanisms like intellectualization. It seldom appears in a free state as a passing idea of suicide, but more often as a generalization of the idea of death. Thus, the mastered thanatogenic tendency has a part to play in the progressive process of adolescence. Sometimes, its freeing may be more overt and the idea of suicide makes its appearance, but this idea remains manipulable and, above all, is not

accompanied by a sufficient freeing of the tendency to act
to produce the suicide act.

At the other extreme, in a minority of suicide cases, the
thanatogenic tendency is freed completely, or almost so, in
a total disorganization that also eliminates all mastery over
motor discharge. The life tendency is inadequate or ineffective,
and an overwhelming, inevitable act of self-destruction results.

The majority of suicide acts are situated between these two
extremes, according to the modalities of the suicidal process,
which in turn depend on possible qualitative and quantitative
differences in the relations between the life tendency and the
thanatogenic tendency. These relations affect the rapidity
and depth of the disorganization, and the persistence of anti-
suicidal defences. On them depend the many degrees of
seriousness to be found, and the many types of attempts.
Some suicide acts are the result of a fairly pure thanatogenic
tendency, others of a thanatogenic tendency that has been
sufficiently mastered to be totally integrated into the process
of adolescence. Presumably, these intermediate suicide acts
represent partial disorganizations. The representatives of the
life tendency remain sufficiently strong and structured to be
able to combine with the thanatogenic tendency during the
suicide act, and so deflect it from its aim. It is these that give
the suicide act the appearance of not being 'serious', and
lead, paradoxically, to the adolescent being reproached, either
explicitly or implicitly, with not wanting sufficiently to die.

— *The boundaries between suicide and other more or less
similar behaviour* are difficult to draw, particularly in adolescence. The death impulses emerge with great frequency on
account of the disintrication of the impulses during the work
of adolescence. But although all adolescent experience and
behaviour bear traces of death, can one call them suicidal?
We must exercise caution when dealing with this subject, for
we incur the risk of diluting the notion of suicide in general-
izations that will rob it of any specificity. In fact, we would
need a better knowledge of the suicidal process and of its
possible specificity if we were to lay down boundaries.

If we define suicide as an act aimed primarily at self-murder,
the question of boundaries might be discussed in relation to

the two criteria of the act and its self-destructive aim.

From what we know of the suicidal process, it is obvious that the criterion of the conscious intention of suicide is contingent. Awareness of a desire for suicide is only one modality of the suicidal process that is probably related to the defences opposing disorganization, and we can posit the hypothesis, as yet unverified, that the idea of suicide is an attempted defence against suicide. The unconscious suicide is therefore just as authentic as the conscious suicide. Since Freud's work,[11] a number of studies[12] have stressed this, especially with regard to failed acts as a result of impulsive behaviour, which is often close to the suicidal *raptus*. These unconscious suicides are often disguised as road accidents or accidents incurred during sporting activities.[13] This question is of the utmost importance with regard to adolescence, when accidental deaths are more frequent than at any other period of life, and it has often been said that some of these deaths were in fact suicides. While having no figures at my disposal to prove it, I can unhesitatingly assert that unconscious suicide is relatively frequent at adolescence.

However, it is not always easy to assert that a fatal act was unconscious suicide. There is the question of the boundaries between suicide and various forms of dangerous behaviour. Behaviour involving risk is part of the adolescent process: the need to master danger, to measure one's physical and mental strength, belongs to the various initiation trials, and also lends to an increased self-awareness. The manipulation of risk is the counterpart on the level of action of the manipulation of the idea of death: both are factors involved in progress. The question of suicide is posed in terms of risk, whether it is reasonable or otherwise. Unreasonable risk, involving notoriously dangerous behaviour, is suicidal in so far as the excessive need to have recourse to action is a sign of difficulty in elaboration, of a tendency to motor discharge, and the beginnings of the suicidal process. We have two criteria to guide us: the degree of risk, and the temporary character of behaviour that serves a progressive, ordalic function, or its repetitive character, which is symptomatic of a change in the adolescent process and the fixation of archaic forms.

The criterion of the act raises the problem of the boundaries between suicide and the various processes which are concerned with death without fitting the definition of the resort to action, particularly other destructive processes, principally the psychosomatic disorders and mental anorexia. Psychosomatic disorders do have certain similarities with suicide: the frequent absence of phantasization and anxiety, a tendency to express emotion through the body rather than in verbal communication. But in the first the appeal is to the visceral apparatus, and in the second to the motor apparatus. Attempts have sometimes been made to assimilate psychosomatic disorders and suicide. But, again, our degree of knowledge requires us to tread warily, and anyway, this question does not concern adolescence in particular. The only disorders that are of especial relevance are those concerning the genital apparatus, these being indicative of a difficulty in integrating the pubertal drive, an increase of the libidinal impulses, and a fear of castration, combined with the persistence of archaic positions.

Mental anorexia is a widespread problem in adolescence. It is self-destructive and may lead to death. Like suicide, it is indicative of the persistence of archaic positions at the level of orality, of unintegrated ambivalence in an excessively close relationship with the mother - the good mother whose care and attention one demands, and the bad mother whom one distrusts as a poisoner. But though the refusal to eat is fatal, there is no act, and the risk of death is distant and gradual.

Suicide may be compared with the prostration of the melancholic and the catatonia of the schizophrenic. Both involve an inability to take the necessary steps for the maintenance of life and, quite apart from any suicide act, culminate in death if one allows the spontaneous development to continue without taking those steps. How can they be situated in relation to suicide? They may be regarded as a disappearance of the life tendency, thus leaving the thanatogenic tendency to spread more and more. They may also be regarded as a kind of negative suicide, the death act being replaced by a non-life act.

Toxicomania, another major problem in modern youth,

occupies an intermediate position. It is not directed towards death, not at least to an immediate death, but in so far as it consists of the absorption of poison it is a death act. It expresses a disturbance in the organization of the impulses, brought about by provoking death in the future and an immediate pleasure - but it is an archaic pleasure, that of being able to hallucinate like the infant at the beginning of the objectal stage.

It would seem that there are degrees in the relations between these various forms of behaviour and suicide. For example, suicide is relatively frequent among toxicomanic adolescents, while it does not appear to have any correlation with the psychosomatic disorders or with anorexia. Several hypotheses are possible. All these forms of behaviour may be regarded as suicidal in the proper sense of the term, and be placed, together with attempted suicide, among the intermediate forms of suicidal behaviour mentioned above. Or only some of them, such as the toxicomania, may be regarded as such, while others, such as anorexia, which have certain similarities with suicide without being identical, may be regarded as suicidal equivalents or para-suicides. Or, again, this latter category may be categorically excluded from the field of suicide.

To sum up, then, there are, between the mastered thanatogenic tendency of the normal adolescent and the overwhelming, inevitably fatal suicidal act, various forms of behaviour whose suicidal significance is open to question. In one group are to be found suicide acts that can be differentiated according to the degree and the modality of disorganization that frees simultaneously motor discharge and the thanatogenic tendency. In another group are the disturbances to the life tendency that culminate in a death similar to that of seriously frustrated infants. The first kill themselves and the second cease to live, their passivity giving full rein to the thanatogenic tendency. But at what point does the boundary line of suicide end?

There remains the question of partial mutilations. At the time when the adolescent must take on the fear of castration, the fact that he cannot elaborate his fear but must act it out expresses, to say the least, a state of serious disharmony and the presence of archaic fixations. But often, too, self-mutilation, it seems to me, must be included among those 'deliriums in action' that express an inadequate attempt at defensive organization. In which case it belongs to the disorganizing suicidal process, and is seldom followed by suicide as such. Self-mutilation probably has a number of various significations, some of which, but not all, are suicidal, and this, too, raises the question of boundaries.

The functions and boundaries of adolescent suicide raise, therefore, the question of its definition. It seems obvious enough to me that it excludes the criterion of consciousness and intention, but includes the notion of act. Whether or not the act leads directly or indirectly to death, whether or not the risk involved is slight or serious, seems to me to be of secondary importance. Among all the acts of the adolescent that include the thanatogenic tendency, the boundary of suicide is situated according to the prevalence of the thanatogenic tendency.

It seems to me that we do not as yet know enough about the suicidal process to be able to fix this boundary with any greater precision.

Notes

1. Cf. in particular E. Stengel and N.G. Cook, *Attempted Suicide. Its Social Significance and Affects,* London, Oxford University Press, 1961.
2. M. Colin, C. Vauterin and J.L. Michaud, 'La tentative de suicide', *Lyon Médical,* 1962, no. 11-15, 365-75.
3. L.M. Raymondis, Y. Schektan, P. Moron and L. Gayral, 'Une enquête psycho-sociale sur les tentatives de suicide et leur exploitation statistique', *Annales Médico-psychologiques,* vol. I, no. 4, 1965, 563-607.
4. Fau *et al.,* 'Le suicide chez l'adolescent', *Annales Médico-psychologiques,* vol. I, no. 1, January 1965.
5. J. Vedrinne, *L'intoxication aiguë volontaire,* Paris, Masson, 1965, 80.
6. *Ibid.,* 81.
7. Fau *et al., op. cit.,* 14.
8. Vedrinne, *op. cit.,* 82.

9.   We should stress here the important role played by such organizations as S.O.S. Amitié, the Samaritans, etc.
10.   Cf. Vedrinne, *op. cit.*, 38.
11.   S. Freud, *Psychopathology of Everyday Life*, stand. ed., vol. VI, 191.
12.   Cf. in particular the works of R. Held.
13.   Cf. G. Mendel, 'Fatigue, dépression nerveuse et suicides incon-scients', *Revue de Médecin Psychosomatique et de Psychologie médicale*, no. 2, 1967, 155-62.

21·Treatment and research

Treatment and theoretical research are more indissolubly linked in the case of adolescent suicide than in that of other subjects. Of course, as always, the treatment is dependent on the degree of knowledge, and research, if it is to be of any value, must operate in close contact with clinical experience. But they are dependent above all on the resistances that we tend to erect *vis-à-vis* the suicidal adolescent. They also require adequate equipment, and are both involved in an unending struggle with the political authorities for recognition of their needs. They differ on one point: whereas research requires a certain degree of systematization, it would be neither possible, nor desirable, to codify treatment.

Both questions should really be dealt with at greater length than is possible here. All I can do, then, is to offer a few reflexions on the way in which our observations and hypotheses may affect the therapist and the researcher.

A. Treatment

It would be quite impossible in a few pages to go over all the various kinds of treatment required by suicidal adolescents, involving as it does the treatment of psychosis, neurosis, etc. I would simply like to consider how the existence of the suicide risk and the elements of the personality that make the adolescent suicidal affect the progress of treatment. I have no wish to systematize the problem or to arrive at a 'recipe' as to how to behave towards the suicidal adolescent. Such an approach would be reassuring, but it would run counter to the requirements of treatment; it could even become a suicidogenic factor, for it would replace the personal confrontation with the subject and the individual quality of the treatment, which are indispensable conditions for any progress.

But before continuing, there is an embarrassing question that must first be dealt with:

Have we the right to prevent someone from committing suicide?

This question is hardly ever examined in books and articles, except as a problem in philosophy, but it often crops up in conversation in medico-psychological circles. Of course, the question seems less crucial in the case of adolescents because they are minors and we have a moral and legal responsibility for them. But this is simply to avoid the question. It certainly raises the unavoidable problem of man's freedom to dispose of his life as he wishes. The argument in favour of non-intervention is not very convincing. On the one hand, the individual who kills himself does so not in order to exert his freedom to die, but because he is no longer free to live. To help him to be free is above all to help him acquire the means (in every sense of the term) to live. On the other hand, the argument ignores the fact that the life tendency is always present in the suicide and that the suicide act often takes place because the representatives of the act of life are not recognized, the appeals not heard. In fact, to refuse systematically to intervene is to have no wish to feel concerned by the death of the Other in order to protect oneself, it is to misunderstand his appeal, which is a representation of the life tendency and, possibly, to increase the risk of suicide, thus intervening directly.

But to 'take steps' in a systematic way is just as dangerous, since it is also an expression of one's own fear, and amounts to a rejection of the suicide. To help may sometimes involve taking steps, at others it may require us to take the risk of not doing so, for this may be a way of reinforcing the life tendency and not fixating a temporary, and relatively superficial tendency to suicide. It is a question, therefore, of calculating the risk involved, which is not always easy when one is dealing with changeable adolescents. One must offer the adolescent the possibility of expressing his tendency to suicide without dramatizing it, but must not drive him towards the suicide act by an attitude of indifference. So, without concentrating overmuch on the immediate risk, one cannot ignore the importance of:

The calculation of the suicide risk and its prevention

This involves, first, the evaluation of the elements of the pre-suicidal process and of the process of adolescence. The conjunction of these elements can certainly make such an evaluation a very delicate task. But the problem is not specific to suicide. It is typical of the diagnostic and prognostic uncertainty that affects adolescence as a whole. However, the following elements must be taken into account: an excessive tendency to act, difficulty in elaboration, verbalization, and phantasization, a loss of adolescent movement combined with an excessively strong and fixated emergence of the thanatogenic tendency.

The second stage involves the evaluation of present factors capable of precipitating the process towards suicide. The alert must be given by a conjunction of certain phases of the suicidal process, certain phases of the process of adolescence, and certain events - sometimes in rapid succession - that may be felt as a wound or as an irreparable loss. It may be important to avoid, or at least postpone, an event that the adolescent would be unable to withstand at that moment. By gaining time, it may be possible to allow the moment of danger to pass, thus averting suicide. If families and educators could be made to act in this way, it would have an appreciable preventative effect. It would be particularly beneficial if certain decisions concerned with schooling could be made less wounding, or could be postponed. A better preparation of the pupil and of his family might avoid a good many accidents.

Similarly, it is useful to find out whether the adolescent has anyone to tell that he feels wounded or distressed - family, friend, teacher, etc. When the adolescent is being treated, it is obviously in this context that this factor must be evaluated. This leads us back once more to the preventative role of treatment.

Another aspect that has to be evaluated is that of risky behaviour proper to adolescence. Such behaviour is often, quite rightly, a cause of concern to adults, and there may be a great temptation to prevent it. But this may have detrimental effects. By preventing the process of adolescence, one might fixate the thanatogenic tendency and orientate its expression towards other, possibly more dangerous means. In so far as such behaviour is essentially an attempt to master the thanatogenic tendency, and is a calculated risk, it may be better to allow such behaviour to take its course.

The situation is more delicate when there is an additional risk of unconscious suicide, which is not always easy to evaluate. But what attitude should one adopt? Simply to prevent such behaviour incurs a risk of even increasing the suicidal tendency. Even more than other forms of behaviour, it poses the problem of the urgency of a treatment in depth of the suicidal tendency.

The prevention of the suicide act confirms the need for individualized attitudes, consisting sometimes of intervention and sometimes of abstention. In fact, the problem is a general one and arises in relation to all the:

Therapeutic indications

They range from an acceptance of the suicide risk, without any other therapeutic decision, to urgent hospitalization and the treatment of acute cases.

Quite obviously, there is no such thing as treatment for suicide as such, apart from its prevention at the moment the act is taking place. There is also treatment of a medico-surgical kind for the consequences of a suicide attempt - but that is another question. What, then, of the prevention of suicide through the treatment of the suicidal tendency? But this is still too limited a point of view; the suicidal adolescent is both an adolescent and, possibly, a psychotic, a depressive, a psychopath, etc. There is therefore no treatment of the suicidal tendency, but various different treatments whose progress is influenced by the existence of a suicidal tendency.

Although the decisions to be taken are relatively clear in

acute cases and the risk overt and immediate, there still remains the problem of the later, post-critical treatment. But in such cases it is often carried out in the context of obvious psychical disorders and it is the treatment of these that is a matter of dispute.

The problem arises at once where other cases are concerned, and very often comes into play during the first interview. When the adolescent simply displays a tendency to suicide, without any obviously immediate risk, this first interview, it seems to me, is similar to that which takes place with numerous adolescents, but the characteristics are much more accentuated: the overwhelming nature of the demand, extreme ambivalence, and sudden, total changes of mood and attitude.

Generally speaking, the suicidal adolescent will commit himself more readily and more rapidly than other adolescents to the therapeutic relationship because he feels that what he is demanding is indispensable to him if he is to go on living. This poses the reciprocal problem of the therapist's commitment to the adolescent. A reticent attitude, an attempt to impede the establishment of the relationship, may be seen by the suicidal adolescent as a rejection, a justification for his pessimism and despair that may make him refuse any new consultation for a long time, and may even aggravate the tendency to suicide. To allow and even to encourage the immediate establishment of a positive relationship may be urgently required as compensation for an unbearable wound. But this presupposes that the doctor is willing and able to commit himself for what may be a long period of time, whatever the technical or practical conditions may be (shortage of time, for example).

But there are suicidal adolescents who refuse all treatment (apart from those who refuse to attend even the first consultation, which is often an indication of the seriousness of the case). Such cases are extremely susceptible to narcissistic wounds; the megalomaniacal Ideal is so demanding that they feel all help as a sign of their own inadequacy, of their non-value and as additional proof of the need to punish themselves by death. They pose the most delicate problems, and sometimes the least dangerous course is to do nothing. It is not always easy to resign oneself to doing nothing, and still less to persuade family and friends, who often want the subject to be hospitalized in order to reassure themselves, of the wisdom of this course. Even when hospitalization makes effective therapy possible it is not without danger, but if it consists merely of supervision it may aggravate the wound and open the way to a later suicide attempt.

In less serious cases, one can maintain contact, and avoid too painful a wound, by proposing a few interviews to talk things over, and by promising to respect the adolescent's freedom to decide at any time whether or not to go on with them. Or one can propose a number of very occasional interviews, even at the subject's own request, so as to leave him entirely free.

The need for narcissistic protection, which is very marked in these cases, impregnates all relations with suicidal adolescents and one must always give them proof of their freedom. Certain interruptions in treatment are a way of testing our good faith in this regard, and treatment can be resumed only if we display a non-authoritarian attitude during these interruptions.

These cases illustrate a point of fundamental importance; it is vital that one should not suddenly break down the defences, and in particular the symptoms, of the suicidal adolescent, if one wishes to avoid the risk of precipitating the suicidal process. This can only be attempted if one is in a position to respond to the underlying demand, and, of course, if the suicidal adolescent himself is capable of withstanding this demand.

The importance of the relationship that is established in the first consultation shows that the therapeutics of adolescent suicide can only be conceived in a context of psychotherapy, whether in the form of occasional interviews or of regular sessions of a psychoanalytic type. But we must take into account the considerable contribution made in recent years by:

Drug treatment
Apart from the chemical treatment for particular mental disorders, such as neuroleptics in psychoses or certain

tranquillizers, there are the thymoanaleptics that have played an important role since their appearance. In so far as one presupposes a link between suicide and depression, the anti-depressants ought to be useful. It is true - and this notion is now widely accepted - that they are most effective when the depressive syndrome is overt. But I have also observed that they sometimes have an appreciable effect on certain adolescents with a sub-depressive state that is concealed by pseudo-characteral disorders, who are all the more likely to give way to a sudden suicidal impulse. I have found that a moderate dose, taken over a relatively long period, has often been highly useful. But the effect is usually temporary, and it is necessary to use this period of improvement to facilitate the beginning of psychotherapy. I have no wish to go into greater detail concerning the pharmacological action of these drugs, but would refer the reader to the work of J. Delay and P. Deniker.[1] As these authors point out, the drug intervenes in the relationship with the therapist and affects the psychotherapeutic outcome. The notion that drug treatment should be followed by psychotherapy is now well established. But the drug/psychotherapy relation affects the adolescent in particular, in three ways:

In addition to those who refuse all treatment, certain adolescents refuse all drugs. This may, of course, be due to a phobia about ingesting a product possessing a mysterious effect, which is relatively frequent in the adolescent who is afraid of introducing 'impurities' into his body. But more often, the prescription of drugs at the first consultation is seen as a rejection, as an attempt to avoid responding to his demand on the rational level: 'That's not what I came for' is a frequent, sometimes implicit, often explicit, response. Thus it is important to establish a relationship before proposing a prescription; the drug is then accepted as an additional aid.

Other adolescents are more willing to accept a prescription and consultations intended solely to monitor the drug treatment than regular sessions of psychotherapy. They often have too strong a narcissistic defence to allow them to accept a relationship involving commitment, but are conscious nevertheless of the need for treatment. For them, it is often a means of maintaining a limited contact. Very often the combined action of the beneficial effect of drug treatment and repeated interviews gradually increases confidence and participation, in a way that may lead to psychotherapy.

— *The development of the psychotherapy* is deeply affected by the subject's dual aspect as adolescent and as suicidal, each emphasizing the other, often in one direction only.

The psychotherapy of the suicidal adolescent presents the same modalities as any form of adolescent psychotherapy, such as those described by P. Male.[2] But it is particularly affected by the more or less fusional, archaic character of the demand, which is often associated with mistrust, narcissistic defence, the variability of the tonality and the difficulty of verbalizing the emotions, which enhances the importance of the non-verbal elements. The vital importance of the demand creates the risk either of gratifying too much, which tends to fixate the subject in regressive positions, or of refusing all gratification, which would cause the subject to abandon all hope.

It is therefore of the utmost importance that one's technique should extend from bold interpretation at certain moments to, at others, a mere presence, in which verbalization intervenes very little. There is also the problem of facilitating a rapid transference, without forcing it and thus creating a narcissistic wound. Without describing the modalities of psychotherapy in further detail, one might emphasize the need for flexibility, which poses, in particular, the delicate question of the tolerance to the resort to action. To refuse it completely is not without its dangers, since action is sometimes the only means of expression, or at least of discharging emotions. But too easy acceptance in this respect may encourage and fixate it. A certain tolerance is necessary, but the degree of tolerance still has to be determined. The integration of the act into the psychotherapeutic situation is often the first stage towards a resumption of the process of elaboration. Similarly, it is useful at certain moments to provide the adolescent with the word that will help him to say what he feels, to enrich his vocabulary with an emotional charge, and, at the same time, to show him that one can say certain things. But, again, it is important not to substitute oneself for him, not to say things for him.

Tolerance to action is of particular importance at moments of greatest suicide risk. This risk may require additional, un-expected sessions, or at least the possibility of being reached by telephone. This does not have to be a permanent arrangement, and patients are quite capable of waiting several hours, when the obstacle is a temporary, unavoidable one (the therapist not being at home, for example) and not a refusal. In fact, they seldom abuse this right, and in any case it is better that they should bother us at home than commit suicide. But there is always the risk of going too far, of the desire for and fear of the fusional relationship, and it is always between these two risks that one has to find one's way.

— *The quality of the counter-transference* dominates the therapeutic enterprise, here more than elsewhere. Everything that I have just said illustrates this fact. This problem is much more important than that of the technical modalities from the first interview to the end of treatment. It is interesting that Male, in relation to the psychotherapy of the adolescent,[3] and Nacht, in relation to the treatment of depressives,[4] both insist on 'the quality of the presence of the psychoanalyst . . . who acts not so much by what he says as by what he is'. It is quite obvious that this has particular relevance in the treatment of the suicidal adolescent.

A real and not a pretended availability is an absolute con-dition, and the suicidal adolescent must not be disappointed. But the therapist is often put severely to the test. He has to face up to death quite openly, and cannot evade his own attitudes to it. He is also subject to extreme ambivalence, and to the impossibility, in the end a beneficial one, of being able to refer to a reassuring system. For it is no easy thing to commit oneself to a relationship, to manipulate gratification and frustration, when what is at stake at every moment is not a neurotic symptom or a character trait, but the adolescent's life.

The importance of availability poses the problem of the number of suicidal adolescents that the therapist can be responsible for. It must obviously be a limited number, and

for reasons that are as personal as practical. But there is then
the very difficult problem of those who are seen by the
therapist and who, after the first interview, feel rejected if
treatment is not offered.

— *The prevention of suicide,* like treatment, goes beyond
that of the act. True prevention lies with the pre-suicidal
process. At that level, it is not a matter of specific prevention;
one is dealing with every aspect of health, of mental health, of
upbringing between birth and adolescence, not forgetting the
effect of social and economic factors. These are of too general
and too varied a character to be dealt with here; I can do no
more than emphasize once again the importance of the
mother/child relationship, then the father/mother/child
relationship in the first few months of life, a stable and diver-
sified family organization, socialization, the integration of
reality, etc. These aspects are now sufficiently well known.
However, I should like to say something about two points
concerning the prevention of suicide.

The first concerns the now recognised importance of the
paternal image for children living with a parental couple, and
also for those living with a mother alone or in a purely
feminine constellation. One must then analyse the contribution
of real social circumstances and of the mother's unconscious
refusal to allow her child to establish a relationship with a
stranger, either to protect the image of the absent father, or
to remain within the intimacy of a relationship *à deux.* In such
a case it is of the utmost importance, from the point of view
of the prevention of suicide and many other disorders, to help
the mother to resolve this conflict. But it sometimes happens,
in childhood and above all in adolescence, that the boy does
not really meet a man with whom he can establish positive
relations. Educators, and particularly teachers, can play a
positive role in this domain if they are prepared to establish
a correctly mastered positive relationship. Many adolescents
in this situation complain of having met teachers with whom
they had a good relationship, but that it was kept at too great
a distance or became too imprisoning.

The other point concerns the prevention of disorders of
elaboration. Again, prevention must take place between birth

and adolescence. The mother/child relationship forms the basis of communication. But we must not ignore everything that later contributes to the development of language, and I agree unreservedly with Courchet[5] as to the preventative value of teaching in verbal acquisition. I would add everything concerned with physical education. Speech and psychomotor re-education may also serve as prevention. Quite obviously, it would be simplistic to believe that the problem can be solved solely with the help of educational and re-educational techniques, but their contribution should not be ignored. The main problem, however, concerns above all the elaboration of the emotions and of the affects, and of their integration into a positive relationship. But in so far as the psycho-motor and verbal equipment participates in their communication, it has a preventative role to play.

The problem of the preventative role of elaboration and communication is posed in a crucial way during adolescence. The suicide risk may vary according to whether the difficulties of verbalization and communication inherent in adolescence are accentuated by a prohibitive and repressive environment or attenuated by an environment that accepts expression and responds. It is vital that the adolescent should be allowed to express himself, be encouraged to enrich his communication, and above all be allowed to integrate his sexuality, to overcome the Oedipal situation and the castration anxiety. It is obvious that the attitudes of the family and of the school intervene in all this. And this brings us of course to the problems of educational reform and dialogue, which, in various ways, preoccupy so many people at present.

To sum up, prevention concerns all supposedly suicidogenic factors, that is to say, all the various factors involved in the development of the individual, organic, affective, cognitive, educational, social, cultural, and economic.

But, in the last resort, the primary factor of prevention is the degree and quality of the interest that we bring to adolescent suicide, the desire to understand, free from the resistances and fears that it arouses in us, and we are thus brought back to our own attitudes to it. If there is to be any hope of real prevention, we must be capable of approaching the question of adolescent suicide without fear and without resistance. Then only will we reach an understanding of it.

B. Research

All research into adolescent suicide, by improving our knowledge and by altering our attitudes, is directly involved with its prevention and treatment. I have already pointed out to what extent the paucity of research until quite recently was evidence of certain resistances.

So far, I have been mainly concerned with established notions. But although a radical reappraisal is necessary to all research, this is merely a preliminary measure; the proper study of adolescent suicide is yet to be done. Everything has to be re-examined; the traditional notions, so long regarded almost as facts, have yet to be confirmed, and the hypotheses that I have myself posited will have to be verified in minutest detail. The statistics will have to be re-examined *in toto,* the role of suicidogenic factors will have to be demonstrated, and the existence, nature and development of the suicidal process will have to be looked at afresh. In fact, this book ends not with statements, but with questions.

The need for research into adolescent suicide is obvious. But before ending, I should like to point out how much a knowledge of adolescent suicide would help us in other fields.

The study of adolescent suicide can help us to gain a better understanding of adolescence as a whole. Firstly, it would confirm or weaken the possible suicidogenic role of adolescence itself. Secondly, by following the course of the thanatogenic tendency and its visible peculiarities in the suicidal adolescent, we should gain a better understanding of the dynamics and complexity of the adolescent process. Research into the boundaries of suicide, the fact that all adolescents have preoccupations with death and suicide but that only a few commit it, gives us an opportunity of trying to solve the paradox by which the adolescent who most resembles the sick adolescent is the normal adolescent, whereas their futures are quite different. Suicide also enables us to compare the tendency to act proper to the adolescent, the resort to hetero-aggressive action, and the resort to auto-aggressive action, and a study in depth would probably deal with the nature of the act itself.

Furthermore, the suicide of adolescents may make a useful contribution to the understanding of suicide in general. The phenomena of intrication and disintrication, of the reactivation of archaic motions, allow us to observe the development of the tendency to suicide better in the adolescent than in the adult.

Similarly, the question is often asked: is adolescent suicide different in nature from adult suicide? Does adolescence play a specific role or does it affect only the modalities of the suicide?

One fact is certain: the number of suicide acts, which is virtually nil in childhood, suddenly increases at adolescence and probably does not vary from then on; all that changes is the death/attempt ratio. It may be that it is at adolescence that the tendency to suicide becomes definitively fixed, and that adult suicide originates in adolescence, at a time when the thanatogenic tendency secures its grip. It would be useful, in the case of suicidal adults, to have information as to the frequency of attempted suicide and of the tendency to suicide from their adolescent period. But our information is too inadequate on this point and opinions diverge. For some specialists, the adolescent suicide act is rarely repeated in adulthood, for others, previous attempts can often be found in cases of suicidal adults.

Opinion is also divided about the frequency of repeated attempts during adolescence itself. Some consider such repetitions to be rare and attach a great deal of importance to the ordalic function of a suicide attempt. Others consider them to be frequent, often followed by fatal suicide, and stress the auto-aggressive function. But earlier attempts are often not known - which brings us back to the problem of our ignorance of the number of attempted suicides among adolescents.

The fundamental question, the question that dominates all the others, is still that of the origin of the suicidal tendency. For convenience, I have used the terms life tendency and thanatogenic tendency. But what do these terms imply? A duality of the instincts; a life instinct and a death instinct; or primary masochism? Although certain facts may plead in favour of the death instinct and of an instinctual duality, none can prove the existence of such an instinct or such a duality, and these concepts remain controversial. Knowledge of adolescence might help us to make progress here. The reactivation and modifications of the organization of the impulses certainly facilitate an approach to the question.

But would a possible answer be enough? It does not seem that the death instinct, if it exists, could of itself explain suicide. There is a great difference between the process of mortualization that operates in every living being, the 'let death do its work' of the catatonic, and the self-destructive act. And there is still the question of what it is that makes one commit the suicide act. This something may reside in a certain modality of the organization of the impulses, in the co-existence of a tendency to resort to action, or in some other domain still to be explained.

To sum up, research into adolescent suicide involves the participation of various different disciplines. But on the basis of such research, interesting facts might be collected in quite different fields, so numerous and varied are the factors that intervene in the suicidal process. Confronted by so many questions, one can only express astonishment once more that research has been so scanty and, above all, that the State has not been more concerned with a question that has always caused more damage than poliomyelitis.

But the problem is not primarily of a statistical or economic order. To ask why and how certain young men wish to die touches on the very bases of the life of the human mind. The question is of fundamental human importance, even if it remains unanswered and even if the number of suicidal adolescents is not great.

Notes
1. *Méthodes chimiothérapiques en psychiatrie*, Paris, Masson, 1961.
2. *Psychothérapie de l'adolescent*, Paris, Masson, 1961.
3. *Ibid.*, 61.
4. *La Présence du Psychanalyste*, Paris, P.U.F., 1956, 127.
5. 'Le suicide . . .,' *L'Évolution Psychiatrique*, 1955, no. III, 482.

Index